JavaFX™
Developing Rich Internet Applications

Jim Clarke
Jim Connors
Eric Bruno

Addison-Wesley

Upper Saddle River, NJ • Boston • Indianapolis • San Francisco

New York • Toronto • Montreal • London • Munich • Paris • Madrid

Capetown • Sydney • Tokyo • Singapore • Mexico City

Library of Congress Cataloging-in-Publication Data:

Clarke, Jim.
  JavaFX : developing rich internet applications / Jim Clarke, Jim Connors, Eric Bruno.
      p.   cm.
  Includes index.
  ISBN 978-0-13-701287-9 (pbk. : alk. paper)
  1. Java (Computer program language) 2. JavaFX (Electronic resource)
3. Graphical user interfaces (Computer systems) 4. Application
software Development. 5. Internet programming. I. Connors, Jim, 1962–
II. Bruno, Eric J., 1969– III. Title.
  QA76.73.J38C525 2009
  006.7'6—dc22

                                        2009014387

ISBN-13:   978-0-13-701287-9
ISBN-10:   0-13-701287-X
Text printed in the United States on recycled paper at R.R. Donnelley in Crawfordsville, Indiana.
First printing, May 2009

For Debbie, Mike, Tim, and Chris for supporting me in this endeavor.
To my parents who sacrificed so much to allow me this opportunity.

—Jim Clarke

To mom and dad for their unwavering commitment to family.
To Cynthia, Terrence, Nicholas, and Gina without whom I am nothing.

—Jim Connors

To my children, Brandon and Ashley.

—Eric Bruno

Contents

Foreword

It is not often that you get the chance to witness (let alone participate in!) the birth of a truly disruptive technology. We are now at a juncture where information is pervasive—there is a convergence that will allow us to seamlessly move from one information source to another as we conduct our daily lives. Whether we are operating our smart phones, watching television, using our laptops, or interacting with screen-based devices that are yet to be invented, we are constantly connected to the world.

The key to making this vision a reality is the implementation of a common platform that works across all these screens. The Java platform set the bar for "write once, run anywhere"; JavaFX raises that bar by allowing us to write rich, immersive applications that run not only on every platform, but look good on every screen.

JavaFX is more than that, of course. It's about

- Employing visual effects to make the graphics stand out and appear real
- Adding animation to bring the screen to life
- Engaging the auditory and visual senses to more effectively convey information
- Combining all of these qualities to create compelling applications that are also fun to use

Of course, these capabilities are useless if applications cannot be crafted easily and quickly. Another goal of JavaFX is to make development simpler, easier, more productive—and more fun. The JavaFX script language was built from the ground up to support the scene-graph-based programming model, allowing the code to have a structure similar to the data structures it creates. Instead of looking for an esoteric "main" routine, the primary entry point is a "stage." The stage has a "scene," and "nodes" make up the elements in the scene. The analogy to the real world should be clear to all.

Second, the language supports, as a first class concept, the notion of *binding* between data elements. What used to take many lines of repetitive (and error-prone) listener code is now represented using a simple bind declaration. As a result, the display and your data model are automatically kept in sync, without having to write the many lines of code that would otherwise be required to connect them.

Lastly, the JavaFX platform provides a robust set of framework classes that allow you to quickly and simply exploit the most advanced features, such as animations, visual effects, and sophisticated visual transitions. All this adds up to a highly productive environment that allows you to quickly deploy the most advanced applications to both desktops and mobile devices in a fraction of the time.

Programmer productivity is only part of the story—rich applications also require participation from graphic designers and UI designers. JavaFX provides tools to integrate the graphic design process with the development process. For instance, the creative folks typically design the application's look and feel, produce graphical assets, and then hand all of this over to the development team to create the program logic. The JavaFX Production Suite facilitates this handoff in an efficient way that allows developers and designers to collaborate easily.

When I joined the JavaFX project, I knew that I had embarked on a journey to create the best Rich Internet Application platform on the planet—a journey that has only just begun. I invite you to join this journey, with this book as your starting point. It begins with the basics and builds up to deploying a full-fledged application in JavaFX, covering all the features and capabilities that JavaFX provides along the way. Once you learn JavaFX, I'm sure you will be just as enthusiastic about this technology as I am. I welcome you aboard.

John Burkey
Chief JavaFX architect

Preface

Welcome to Rich Internet Application development with JavaFX.

This book is about creating more engaging user applications using special effects and animation. In this book, we will focus on using JavaFX for creating Rich Internet Applications.

Building upon the widely adopted and popular Java Platform, JavaFX provides a new level of abstraction that greatly simplifies graphical user interface development while at the same time bringing all the flexibility that Java technologies provide. This creates an elegant, yet powerful, platform for building full feature and compelling applications.

What Is JavaFX?

JavaFX is actually a family of products developed at Sun Microsystems. There are initiatives for mobile phones, consumer, television, and desktop devices. The cornerstone to these projects is JavaFX. JavaFX is a platform that includes a high performance declarative scripting language for delivering and building a new generation of Rich Internet Applications.

The primary focus of JavaFX is to make graphical user interface development easy while embracing more compelling features like visual effects, sound, and animation. JavaFX includes a ready-made framework to support graphic components and to easily include multimedia features like pictures, video, audio, and animation. Using the Java platform at its core, JavaFX works seamlessly with the Java platform and can easily leverage existing Java code. This also allows JavaFX to leverage the "write once, run anywhere" capability provided with the Java platform.

Why JavaFX?

Anyone who has ever written a graphical user interface application can appreciate the complexity of creating such an application. Though the resulting user interface can produce a powerful user experience, developing a cool application can be a daunting task. It takes a skilled developer who knows the graphical language and framework inside-out to pull off a well-written UI. JavaFX addresses this complexity.

Furthermore, graphic design and programming are two distinct skills. Graphic designers focus on the human interaction with the application, and are more interested in keeping the human's interest and making the system intuitive. On the other side, the program developers are typically concerned with implementing business logic and interacting with back-end servers. It is a rare breed that masters both of these skills. JavaFX's goal is to bridge these two crafts by allowing the graphic designer to dabble in an easily understood programming language, while at the same time allowing the developer the flexibility to implement the business rules behind the user interface.

JavaFX does this by

- Simplifying the programming language
- Providing ready-built user interface components and frameworks to support UI creations
- Making it easy to update existing UI applications
- Providing a cross-platform environment that delivers on "Write Once, Run Anywhere"

Rich Internet Applications

For many years, the programming paradigm has been centered on a client-server architecture employing a "thin" client. In this architecture, most of the processing was in the server with the client merely displaying the content. In a thin client system, data must be transmitted to the server for processing and a response sent back. This is very true of the HTML screens introduced with the original Internet browsers. However, by leveraging compute power on the client side, it is now possible to perform actions on the client, thereby reducing the round-trip latency to the server.

A Rich Internet Application is an application that allows a good portion of the application to execute on the user's local system. Primarily, the client application is designed to perform those functions that enhance the user's experience. Furthermore, communications with the server do not have to be initiated from a user action, like clicking on a button. Instead, a server itself can update the client with fresh content asynchronously as needed and without waiting for the end user to perform some action or by employing other tricks in the client like periodically polling the server.

So what is old is new again. In a sense this is true, but this really represents an evolution of the client server paradigm rather than a retrenchment back to the old days of the monolithic program that did everything. The key to a Rich Internet Application is striking the proper balance between behavior that should stay on the client with the behavior that rightfully belongs on the server. JavaFX is a framework that embraces the Rich Internet Application model.

Why This Book?

JavaFX is a new technology and we set out to help you get started quickly by exploring key features of JavaFX and how it should be used. We purposely did not want to do a language reference document as the language itself is fairly simple. Our main goal is to help you to quickly and productively create cool user interfaces.

This book's primary audience is comprised of developers (of all levels) and graphic designers who need to build Rich Internet Applications. There are different types of developers and designers that this book targets:

- Java developers who are currently building Rich Internet Applications with Java Swing
- Java developers who are interested in learning JavaFX for future projects
- Non-Java application developers who wish to use JavaFX for Rich Internet Application development
- Graphic designers, animators, or motion-graphic designers who wish to use JavaFX to add special effects, animation, and sound to their creations

How to Use This Book

This book has thirteen chapters. The first four chapters cover the basics of JavaFX, how to get started, what the graphic designer's role is, and the basic language. The next five chapters cover the advanced features you expect in a Rich Internet

Application. These include basic UI design, special effects, animation, multimedia, and browser display. Chapter 10 covers using JavaFX in a Web Services architecture. Chapter 11 describes JavaFX's interaction with the Java platform and assumes you are knowledgeable about Java. The last two chapters cover JavaFX code recipes and a complete Sudoku application.

Beyond the Written Page

With the expressive platform that JavaFX provides, it is hard to fully demonstrate all its capabilities on the written page. To fully appreciate all the features and capabilities that JavaFX brings, we suggest visiting the book's Web site http://jfxbook.com. There, you can see the full color versions of the figures used throughout the book. Also at the Web site, you can run the demos in full color and experience firsthand the richness of the animations and multimedia.

We have used a building block approach with basic concepts covered first and more complex features addressed later in the book, so we suggest you read each chapter in sequential order. If you are a graphic designer, you may be more interested in Chapter 2. You can safely start there, then jump back to Chapter 1 to dig deeper into JavaFX. If you are an "über"-coder, you can safely skip Chapter 2, but we still suggest you eventually read it just to know what the "dark" side is doing. Chapter 11 assumes you have a good understanding of the Java platform and APIs. If you do not plan to comingle your Java classes with JavaFX source in your application, you can safely skip this chapter. The last two chapters show some code examples based on the foundations laid down in the earlier chapters.

Here's the book in a nutshell:

- **Chapter 1: Getting Started.** This chapter gets you set up and shows the basics of creating and running a JavaFX program.
- **Chapter 2: JavaFX for the Graphic Designer.** This chapter explains how a graphic designer would use JavaFX to create JavaFX Graphical Assets.
- **Chapter 3: JavaFX Primer.** This chapter covers the basic JavaFX Script syntax.
- **Chapter 4: Synchronize Data Models—Binding and Triggers**. JavaFX Script introduces a data binding feature that greatly simplifies the model-view-controller design pattern. This chapter explains the concepts of data binding in the JavaFX Script language.
- **Chapter 5: Create User Interfaces**. The primary focus of JavaFX is to create rich user interfaces. This chapter explores the visual components

available to create user interfaces and demonstrates how the features of JavaFX work together to produce a rich user experience.

- **Chapter 6: Apply Special Effects**. A key to Rich Internet Applications is applying cool special effects to bring user interfaces alive and make them appealing to use. This chapter explores the special effects that JavaFX provides, including lighting, visual, and reflection effects.

- **Chapter 7: Add Motion with JavaFX Animation**. Animation makes the user interface vibrant and interesting. This chapter explains the concepts behind the JavaFX animation framework and provides examples of fade in/out, color animation, and motion. It also demonstrates an animation using Graphical Assets generated by the graphic designer.

- **Chapter 8: Include Multimedia**. This chapter explores how to include pictures, sound, and videos in your application.

- **Chapter 9: Add JavaFX to Web Pages with Applets.** (*Applets are back and these are not your father's applets.*) This chapter explores embedding JavaFX applications within Web pages and shows how to undock the applet from the Web page and demonstrate interaction with JavaScript.

- **Chapter 10: Create RESTful Applications**. JavaFX provides frameworks for working easily with JavaScript Object Notation (JSON) and Extensible Markup Language (XML). This chapter explores both options.

- **Chapter 11: JavaFX and Java Technology.** This chapter explores how JavaFX interacts with the Java platform.

- **Chapter 12: JavaFX Code Recipes**. Code recipes are general reusable solutions to common situations in programming. This chapter provides an overview of some code recipes applicable to programming JavaFX applications.

- **Chapter 13: Sudoku Application**. This chapter explores creating a Sudoku game application in JavaFX.

As we introduce topics, we have tried to inject our own experiences to help you avoid trial and error kinds of mistakes and "gotchas." Throughout the chapters, we have sprinkled Developer Notes, Warnings, and Tips to point out things that might not be obvious. We have also tried to include as many examples and figures as possible to illustrate JavaFX features and concepts.

This book is intended to cover the general deployment of JavaFX, whether it be on the desktop, mobile, or eventually the TV profiles. However, there is a bias toward the desktop version and specific features for JavaFX mobile are not covered. Still, the basic concepts and features covered in this book will also apply to these other profiles and to future releases of JavaFX.

Staying Up-to-Date

This book is written to the JavaFX 1.1 Software Development Kit (SDK). As this book goes to press, JavaFX 1.2 is being finalized. We have tried to include as many JavaFX 1.2 features as possible; however, not all features were fully defined in time. Please check out the book's Web site, http://jfxbook.com, for updates for the JavaFX 1.2 release.

This book is jam packed with demo and example code. To illustrate some features in print, we have abbreviated some of the examples. The complete code used in this book is available on the book's Web site at http://jfxbook.com. You can also check this site for updates, errata, and extra content. There is also a forum for sharing information about the book and JavaFX.

Acknowledgments

The authors would first like to thank the staff at Sun Microsystems and Addison-Wesley for making sure this book saw the light of day. We are particularly appreciative to Vineet Gupta, Craig Ellis, and Scott Stillabower for humoring us while we still tried to do our day jobs.

It was almost three years ago when Craig Ellis called and asked if we would create a demo for JavaONE using a new technology called JavaFX. He instructed us to contact Chris Oliver to get started. Within a week of looking at Chris's early work, we were sold. We would like to thank Chris for his early support and for putting up with our stupid questions to learn the first incarnations of JavaFX script. Also, we would like to thank Chris for being the inspiration for the entire JavaFX platform. It has come a long way since his first single-handed early prototypes to a full-fledged platform.

Writing a book for a new technology is challenging as there is very little existing documentation. The process required many hours of trial and error testing, email trails, and source code deciphering to determine how things really work. This process also required bouncing ideas, concepts, and assumptions off various people on the JavaFX team to make sure we were on the right track. We would especially like to thank Brian Goetz, who kept steering us in the right direction. We would also like to thank members of the JavaFX engineering team including Joshua Marinacci, Chris Campbell, Per Bothner, and Martin Brehovsky for doing technical reviews and keeping us honest.

We also wanted to get the perspective of those who had never seen JavaFX before so we enlisted and persuaded many of our associates to do reviews. We are most grateful to Geertjan Wielenga, who spent numerous hours reviewing every chapter and providing us with indispensable feedback. We are also thankful for the valuable insights provided by Andy Gilbert, Manuel Tijerino, Gamini Bulumulle, and Dr. Rainer Eschrich.

Besides writing, there are numerous activities that go on behind the scenes to bring a book together. Huge thanks go to Greg Doench for keeping us in line from day one and holding our feet to the fire to meet an ambitious production schedule. We could not have pulled this off without him. Of course there are many people behind the scenes, but we want to personally thank our production editor, Anna Popick, and our copyeditor, Kelli Brooks. We would also like to thank Myrna Rivera for handling the business side of this project.

On a personal note, Jim Clarke would like to add the following: "Foremost, I would like to thank the other Jim and Eric for joining me on this mission. It has been a long time in the making from our original, 'Hey let's do a book' to now. I also want to personally thank Geertjan Wielenga, who went over and above the call of duty in reviewing all of the chapters. Above all, I am appreciative to Brian Goetz for being my sounding board on ideas and complaints. The entire JavaFX engineering team is applauded for putting out such a fantastic platform. I want to particularly thank Robert Field, Richard Bair, and Shannon Hickey for answering my numerous questions."

Jim Connors would like to add the following: "If they say you can judge a person by the company he keeps, then I am truly fortunate having Jim Clarke and Eric Bruno as friends. It has been a privilege to work with Jim and Eric these last few years; their positive influence has impacted me profoundly and made me a better person. I would also like to thank my wife, Cynthia, and children, Terrence, Nicholas, and Gina, for having the patience to put up with me and the strange hours that writing a book entails. Finally, despite these last few tumultuous years, Sun Microsystems remains one of the finest companies in the world. I thank the corporation for instilling a culture that allows individuals to challenge conventional thought and be the best they can be."

Eric would like to share the following: "For the past few years, I've worked very closely with Jim Clarke and Jim Connors on a number of projects, and have benefited tremendously as a result. Because of them, I've grown as a technologist, a writer, and as a professional. Therefore, first and foremost, I need to thank them for moving this project along even as I dragged my feet while I had other commitments. Thanks for your patience and dedication. I also need to thank Craig Ellis, for getting us started working together with JavaFX, and Greg Doench, for helping to move the project along from its beginnings almost two years ago."

About the Authors

Jim Clarke is a principal technologist with Sun Microsystems and has spent the last twelve years developing with the Java Platform. Prior to that time, Jim specialized in distributed object technologies. For the past two years, Jim has been working directly with JavaFX and participated on the JavaFX compiler team. Jim is a graduate of the University of Notre Dame and has been in the computer science field for thirty years. You can catch his blog at http://blogs.sun.com/clarkeman/.

Jim Connors, a longtime member of Sun's System Engineering community, has spent the last decade helping customers further utilize Java technology ranging from Java Card and Java Micro Edition through to Java Enterprise Edition. His current focus involves providing software solutions to Sun's embedded market, including real-time Java, Solaris, and most recently JavaFX. Jim has twenty-five years' experience in systems software development including stints as a compiler developer for both the C and ADA programming languages. Along with Jim Clarke and Eric Bruno, Jim developed and demonstrated one of the first applications utilizing JavaFX Script back at JavaONE 2007. A regular blogger, you can read his occasional rantings at http://blogs.sun.com/jtc.

Eric Bruno is a systems engineer at Sun, with a focus on Java RTS in the financial community. He is the author of the books *Java Messaging* and *Real-Time Java™ Programming* and has dozens of technology articles to his name. He is currently a contributing editor for *Dr. Dobb's Journal* and writes their online Java blog. Prior to Sun, Eric worked at Reuters where he developed real-time trading systems, order-entry and routing systems, as well as real-time news and quotes feeds, in both Java and C++.

1

Getting Started

"The way to get started is to quit talking and begin doing."

—Walt Disney

Installing the JavaFX Platform

In this chapter, you will learn how to install the JavaFX Script Software Development Kit (SDK) either in a command-line environment or with an Integrated Development Environment (IDE). You will also develop your first JavaFX Script application, compile it, and run it.

The JavaFX Script programming language comes in a Software Development Kit (SDK), based on Java Platform, Standard Edition (Java SE) 1.6. So you will need the following:

- The latest Java SE Development KIT (JDK) for your operating system (Java SE 6 Update 10 or later; for Mac, latest Java for Mac OS X 10.5).
- The NetBeans IDE for JavaFX 1.2, Eclipse Plugin for JavaFX, or the JavaFX Software Development Kit (1.2) for your environment. The NetBeans IDE for JavaFX 1.2 is available for Microsoft Windows XP, Microsoft Vista, Apple Mac OS X Leopard, Linux, and OpenSolaris x86 (available late 2009).
- Optionally, the JavaFX Production Suite graphical toolkit for exporting JavaFX files from Adobe Illustrator CS3, Adobe Photoshop CS3 and converting Scalable Vector Graphics.

For starters, you need to make sure you have the latest Java SE Development Kit (JDK) installed. If you want to take advantage of the new Applet features that JavaFX facilitates, you will need Java SE 6 Update 10 or later. If you are running Windows, Linux, or Solaris, you can download the latest Java Development Kit from http://java.sun.com./javase/downloads/index.jsp. If you use Mac OS X, download the latest Apple release for the Java Platform from http://developer.apple.com/java. As of writing this chapter, Java for Mac OS X 10.5 Update 3 now supports Java 6 Update 7. This release from Apple still does not support the Applet drag feature described in Chapter 9, Add JavaFX to Web Pages with Applets.

To create your first JavaFX Script application, you have several options. First, you can download the NetBeans IDE for JavaFX 1.2 based on NetBeans IDE 6.5 from http://javafx.com. Or, from the same site, you can download the JavaFX SDK and use your favorite editor, compile and run the JavaFX application from the command line. If you choose to use Eclipse, download the JavaFX Plugin for Eclipse from http://kenai.com/projects/eplugin after downloading the JavaFX SDK.

There is also a set of tools and plug-ins for designers to export graphical assets into JavaFX applications, the JavaFX Production Suite. These will be discussed in more detail in Chapter 2, JavaFX for the Graphic Designer, from http://www.javafx.com.

Setting Up NetBeans IDE for JavaFX 1.2

You can install the NetBeans IDE for JavaFX 1.2 directly from javafx.com. There are installers for Microsoft Windows XP, Microsoft Vista, Macintosh, Linux, and Solaris x86. After NetBeans IDE is installed, launch the NetBeans IDE. There should have been a desktop launcher created during the install process. To create your first project, do the following:

1. Launch NetBeans IDE for JavaFX.
2. Start the New Project wizard by choosing **File | New Project** from the main menu.
3. In the **New Project** wizard, select **JavaFX** Category and **JavaFX Script Application** project type.

   Figure 1.1 shows what the NetBeans IDE looks like when creating a new JavaFX Project.
4. In the **Name and Location** window, type in the Project Name, MyFirstJavaFXApplication. Change the location for the project files, if you want, then press Finish.

   Figure 1.2 shows the Name and Location window.

NetBeans IDE then creates the project directory in the specified project folder and gives it the same name as your project, MyFirstJavaFXApplication. In Figure 1.3, notice the `Main.fx` class file below the `myfirstjavafxapplication` package in the Source Packages node. This file was created because you left the

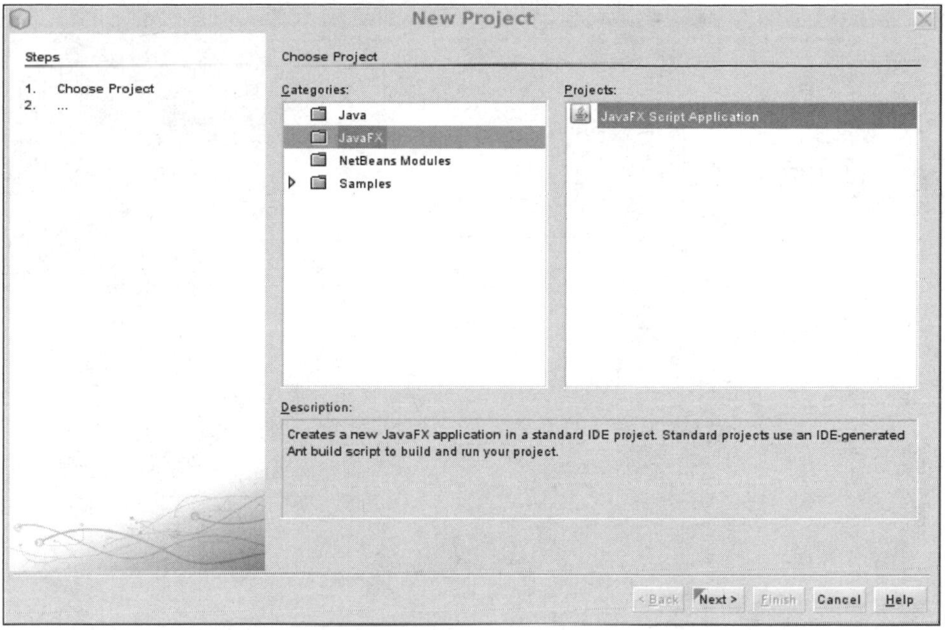

Figure 1.1　New JavaFX Project

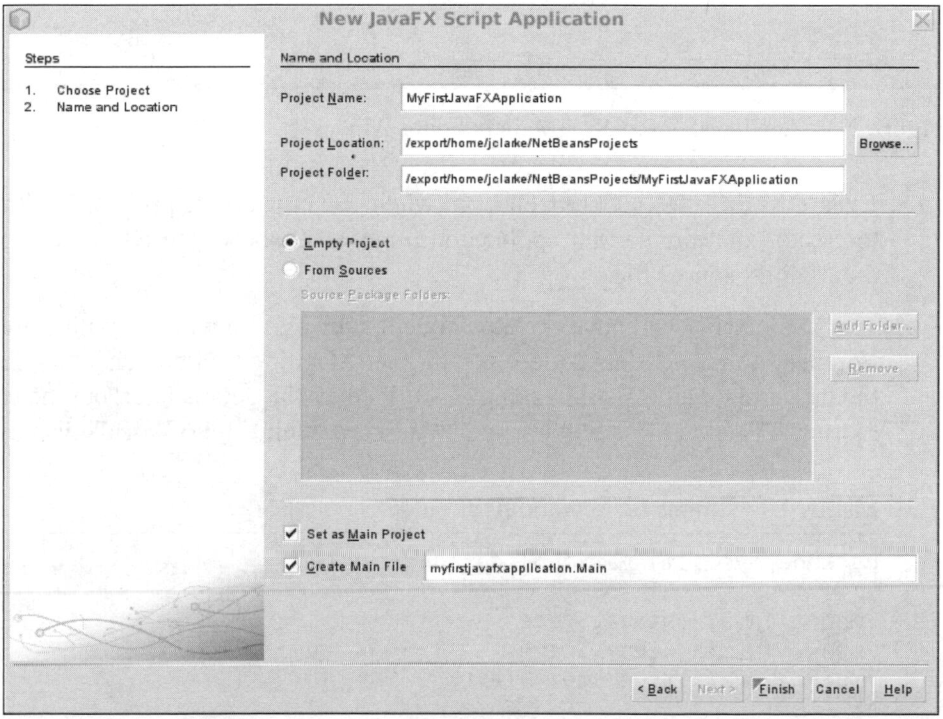

Figure 1.2　New JavaFX Project – Name and Location

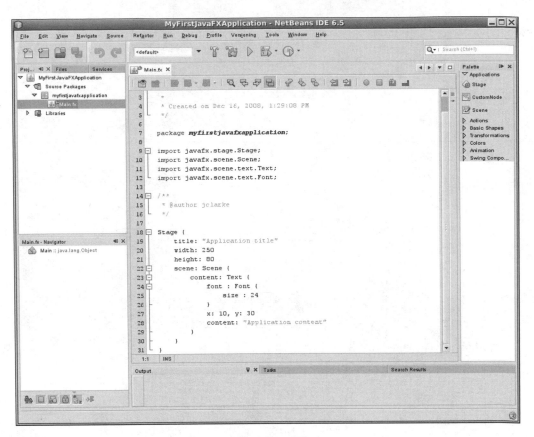

Figure 1.3   New JavaFX Project – Main.fx Editor Window

Create Main File checkbox checked when you created the project. Use this file to create your simple first application. Figure 1.3 shows the editor window for the Main.fx source file.

The Main.fx file will have skeleton code that displays a window with some text. You need to modify this code. Like all good "Getting Started" chapters, let's do the proverbial Hello World example. We'll cover the details later, but the code in Listing 1.1 will show a window on the desktop, with "Hello World" displayed.

Listing 1.1   Simple Hello World Application

```
package myfirstjavafxapplication;

import javafx.stage.Stage;
import javafx.scene.Scene;
import javafx.scene.text.Text;
```

```
import javafx.scene.text.Font;


Stage {
    title: "My first JavaFX Application"
    width: 400
    height: 80
    scene: Scene {
        content: Text {
            font : Font {
                size : 24
            }
            x: 10, y: 30
            content: "Hello World"
        }
    }
}
```

To view the resulting screen while editing the file, use the **JavaFX Preview** mode. To enter the preview mode, click on the Preview icon at the top left of the Main.fx editor (see Figure 1.4). This opens a new window on top of the Main.fx editor window and lets you see what the screen will look like as you type in your changes. Figure 1.4 shows the preview window.

For example, let's change your application to scale Hello World by a factor of 4. This is done by using the scaleX and scaleY attributes for the Text element. These attributes will cause the Text to scale 4 times anchored from its center point. Figure 1.5 shows the changes instantly in the preview window.

By using Preview mode, you can quickly see the impact of your changes. It allows you to test new effects out without having to cycle through the edit, compile, run loop for each iteration of changes. As soon as you type the change, the screen updates with the latest view.

Hello World is kind of boring, so let's have some fun and spice it up. We'll add a gradient background, make the font bigger, and add a reflection effect. Using the original example for Hello World, you add the code to get your desired effect. You will learn what each part of this new code does in later chapters, but for now we want to show you what is possible. Figure 1.6 shows this far more interesting Hello World example.

Listing 1.2 shows how this was done. It is actually quite simple and concise. That is the beauty of the JavaFX Platform.

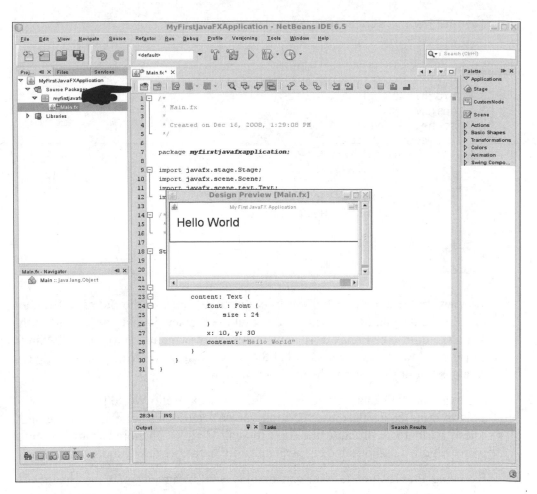

Figure 1.4   JavaFX Preview Mode

Figure 1.5   JavaFX Preview Mode – with Modification

Figure 1.6   Hello World

Listing 1.2   Cool Hello World Application

```
package myfirstjavafxapplication;

import javafx.stage.Stage;
import javafx.scene.Scene;
import javafx.scene.text.Text;
import javafx.scene.text.Font;
import javafx.scene.shape.Rectangle;
import javafx.scene.paint.Color;
import javafx.scene.paint.LinearGradient;
import javafx.scene.paint.Stop;
import javafx.scene.effect.Reflection;


var stage:Stage = Stage {
    title: "My first JavaFX Application"
    visible: true
    width: 400
    height: 200
    scene: Scene {
        var text:Text;
        content: [
            Rectangle {
                width: bind stage.width
                height: bind stage.height
                fill: LinearGradient {
                    endY: 1, endX: 0
                    stops: [
                        Stop {offset: 0.0
                            color: Color.rgb(153, 153, 153);
                        },
                        Stop {offset: 0.5
                            color: Color.WHITE;
                        },
                        Stop { offset: 1.0
                            color: Color.rgb(153, 153, 153);
```

continues

```
                },
            ]
        }
    },
    text = Text {
        translateX:
                bind (stage.width-
                        text.boundsInLocal.width)/2
        translateY: bind stage.height /2
        content: "Hello World"
        effect: Reflection { fraction: 0.7}
        font: Font {name:"ArialBold", size: 64}
    }
]
}
}
```

Distributing the Application

To compile the entire project, click on the Project *MyFirstJavaFXApplication* in
the Projects tab on the left of the NetBeans IDE screen. When the project is highlighted, click with the right mouse button to bring up a menu of options, select
Build Project. This automatically saves all updated source files for the project,
compiles the JavaFX Script and any Java source files, and then places the class
files into a Java Archive (JAR) file underneath the *dist* directory. Besides generating the JAR file to run the application locally either from a desktop launcher or
command line, it also generates support files for using the application as a Java
Applet in a browser and for using it with the Java Web Start launcher either within
a browser or from the desktop. These two options will be explained in detail in
Chapter 9. Figure 1.7 shows the project menu with the Build Project item selected.

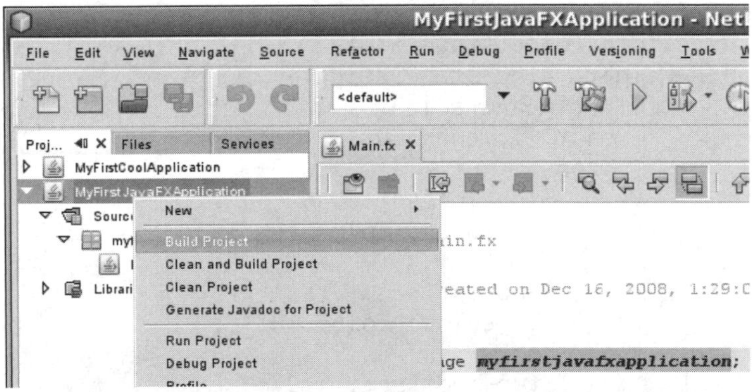

Figure 1.7   Build JavaFX Project

After your application is completed, built, and ready to be deployed, you can build an archive file using the entire contents of the *dist* directory. Common tools for this are *zip* and *tar*. Another option is to include these files in an install tool.

Distribution Files

MyFirstJavaFXApplication.jar

MyFirstJavaFXApplication.html

MyFirstJavaFXApplication.jnlp

MyFirstJavaFXApplication_browser.jnlp

lib/

To run the application, make sure the JavaFX SDK is installed, then install the distribution, and run the following command:

```
javafx -cp dist/MyFirstJavaFXApplication.jar
myfirstjavafxapplication.Main
```

Using this command, you can easily create desktop launchers to run your application. Or you can use the Java Web Start by launching the dist/MyFirstJavaFX-Application.jnlp file.

Developer Warning: The -jar option to execute directly from the JAR file does not currently work with JavaFX; however, this is a known bug and will be addressed in a future release.

There is also a means for deploying JavaFX applications via the World Wide Web using Java Applets or the Java Web Start protocol that we will discuss in Chapter 9. The MyFirstJavaFXApplication.html, MyFirstJavaFXApplication.jnlp, and MyFirstJavaFXApplication_browser.jnlp provide example files that may be used for this.

Command Line

If you want to develop without the NetBeans IDE for JavaFX 1.2 development kit, download the JavaFX SDK from www.javafx.com. There are installers for

Table 1.1   JavaFX SDK Installation

Operating System	Default Install Directory	Compile Command	Run Command	JavaDoc Style
Windows	`C:\Program Files\JavaFX\ javafx-sdk1.2`	javafxc.exe	javafx.exe	javafxdoc.exe
Mac OS	`/System/Library/ Frameworks/ JavaFX.framework/ Versions/1.2`	javafxc	javafx	javafxdoc
Linux/ Solaris	Current directory	javafxc	javafx	javafxdoc

Microsoft Windows XP with Service Pack 2 and Vista, Apple Mac OS X 10.5.2, Linux, and OpenSolaris.

Install the packages, and there will be executable programs for compiling the JavaFX Script source, running the JavaFX Script application, and for generating JavaDoc style documentation (see Table 1.1).

To run your first application, these are the basic steps:

1. Use your favorite editor and save the source for your program to a file.
2. Run the JavaFX compiler, *javafxc*, using this source file to create Java class files.
3. Run the application using the `javafx` command.
4. Optionally, create a JavaDoc style documentation for your program.

Duplicating the Hello World example discussed in the NetBeans IDE for JavaFX 1.2 section, create a file using your favorite editor with the following content as shown in Listing 1.3.

Listing 1.3   Hello World Application – Editor Version

```
import javafx.stage.Stage;
import javafx.scene.Scene;
import javafx.scene.text.Text;

var stage:Stage;
stage = Stage {
    title: "My first JavaFX Application"
    visible: true
```

```
        width: 400
        height: 100
        scene: Scene {
            content: Text {
                x: 10
                y: 20
                content: "Hello World"
            }
        }
}
```

Save this to MyFirstApp.fx, then compile using the `javafxc` command. (Make sure the SDK bin directory is in your command path.)

```
$ javafxc MyFirstApp.fx
$
```

This produces one or more class files in the current directory. Next, run the first program by using the `javafx` command:

```
$ javafx MyFirstApp
```

If all goes well, you should see something similar to Figure 1.8.

There you have it: your first JavaFX Script application. You are now ready to move on to more interesting content.

The `javafxc` compiler command is very similar to the `javac` compiler command. Accordingly, the `javafxc` command uses the same format and options as the Java compiler command. The basic format of the `javafxc` command is

```
$ javafxc <options> <source files>
```

Figure 1.8 JavaFX SDK Hello World

The `javafx` runtime command is actually a wrapper that invokes the standard java command that includes the JavaFX Script jar files. Because the JavaFX compiler produces standard Java class files, you can include these class files, along with any other JavaFX or Java class files, in a Java Archive (JAR) file. To include these JAR files when running your JavaFX application, you just add these jar file locations to your classpath when invoking the `javafx` command.

```
$ javafx -cp directory/MyJarFile.jar MyFirstApp
```

Now you have the basics for getting your JavaFX Script application up and running from the command line. This will suffice for small applications, but as your application grows in size and complexity, you will quickly find that using the command-line option becomes more cumbersome and complex. When your project becomes this large, you may want to consider the NetBeans IDE for JavaFX 1.2, Eclipse IDE with the JavaFX Plugin, or a build tool such as Apache Ant.

JavaFXC Ant Task

Apache Ant is a Java-based build tool written with the key advantage of being cross-platform and OS independent. Ant makes it easy to develop on one platform and deploy to another; as a result, it has become one of the more popular build tools today. You can download the latest ant binaries from http://ant.apache.org/. If you are using the NetBeans IDE for JavaFX 1.2, Ant is already included in the Net-Beans IDE package.

The JavaFX Software Development Kit provides an Ant task for compiling JavaFX Script source files. To declare this in an Ant build.xml file, use the `taskdef` Ant task.

For a simple first application, the build.xml file in Listing 1.4 compiles any .fx files in the current directory. Ant is smart enough to know when files need to be compiled, so after a JavaFX Script file is compiled, it will not be compiled again until the JavaFX Script source file is updated.

Listing 1.4   Sample Ant Build.xml File

```xml
<?xml version="1.0" encoding="UTF-8"?>

<project name="My First JavaFX Application"
         default="compile" basedir="." >
    <property name="javafx.dir"
        value="${user.home}/javafx-sdk" />
    <property name="javafx.lib" value="${javafx.dir}/lib" />
    <property name="javafx.bin" value="${javafx.dir}/bin" />
```

```
<taskdef name="javafxc"
    classname="com.sun.tools.javafx.ant.JavaFxAntTask"
    classpath="${javafx.lib}/javafxc.jar" />

<target name="compile" >
    <javafxc srcdir="." destdir="."
        includes="*.fx" classpath="."
        executable="${javafx.bin}/javafxc"/>
</target>

</project>
```

To build the first application, change the directory to the directory where you saved the MyFirstApp.fx file, copy or save the build.xml file to this directory, and then execute the ant command:

```
bash-3.2$ ant
Buildfile: build.xml
compile:
   [javafxc] Compiling 1 source file to /export/home/jclarke/
Documents/Book/FX/code/Chapter1
BUILD SUCCESSFUL
Total time: 1 second
bash-3.2$
```

Eclipse

If you prefer to use the Eclipse IDE, you need to first download and install the JavaFX SDK for your environment from http://javafx.com. Next, you need Eclipse 3.4 or later; Eclipse IDE for Java EE Developers is recommended. Lastly, you need to download and install the Eclipse plug-in for JavaFX from http://kenai.com/projects/eplugin. To install the Eclipse plug-in for JavaFX, just unzip it in the directory where Eclipse is installed. For example, if Eclipse is installed in C:\Program Files\eclipse, unzip the Eclipse plug-in for JavaFX from the directory, C:\Program Files.

To create your first JavaFX project, launch Eclipse. From the workbench space under Project Explorer, right-click and select **New | Project.** Figure 1.9 shows the New Project menu selection.

Next, create a Java Project by selecting **Java | Java Project** from the New Project wizard. Figure 1.10 shows this window with the selections.

Name the project—for example, MyFirstJavaFXProject. Figure 1.11 shows the Create a Java Project window with the project name entered.

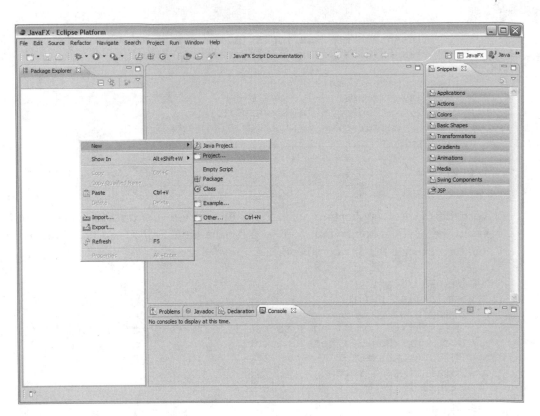

Figure 1.9   New Eclipse Project

Figure 1.10   New Project Wizard

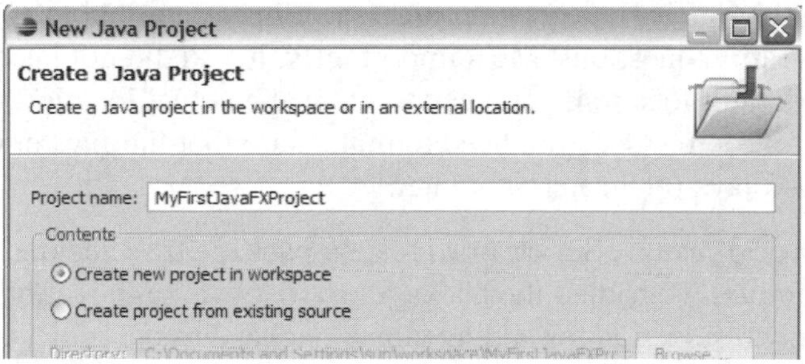

Figure 1.11 Create a Java Project Window

This creates a project with a Java Perspective; next, we have to add a JavaFX Nature. To do this, right-click on **MyFirstJavaFXProject** and select **JavaFX | Add JavaFX Nature**. Figure 1.12 shows the menu for adding a JavaFX Nature to the project.

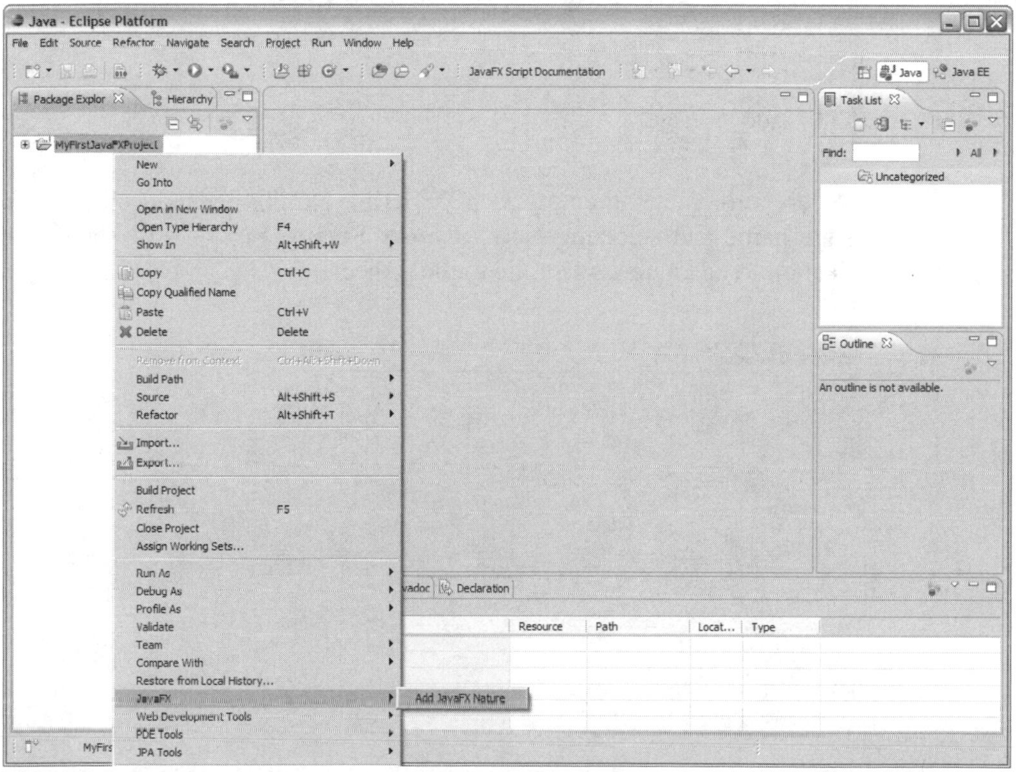

Figure 1.12 Add JavaFX Nature

The first time you add JavaFX Nature to a project, you may be asked to confirm or set several configuration questions. Most importantly, if you did not install the JavaFX SDK in the default location, you need to enter the actual location where it is installed on your system. Also, you need to make sure that the Java environment is pointing to use Java 6 Update 10 or later.

To create the Hello World JavaFX Script, first create a package by selecting **New | Package**. In this example, we named the package myfirstjavafxapplication. Figure 1.13 shows the menu selection for adding a new package to the project.

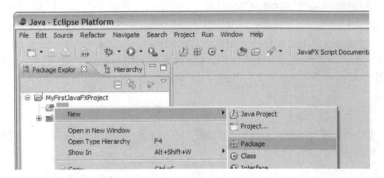

Figure 1.13   Add Package

The next step is to create an empty JavaFX Script. Do this by right-clicking on the package name and selecting **New | Empty Script**. Figure 1.14 shows the menu selection to add a new script file to the project.

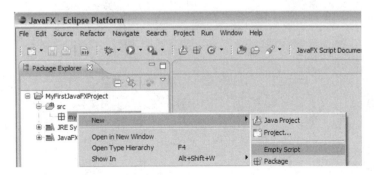

Figure 1.14   Create Empty JavaFX Script

Figure 1.15 shows the new Script wizard for the new script file with the script name Main entered.

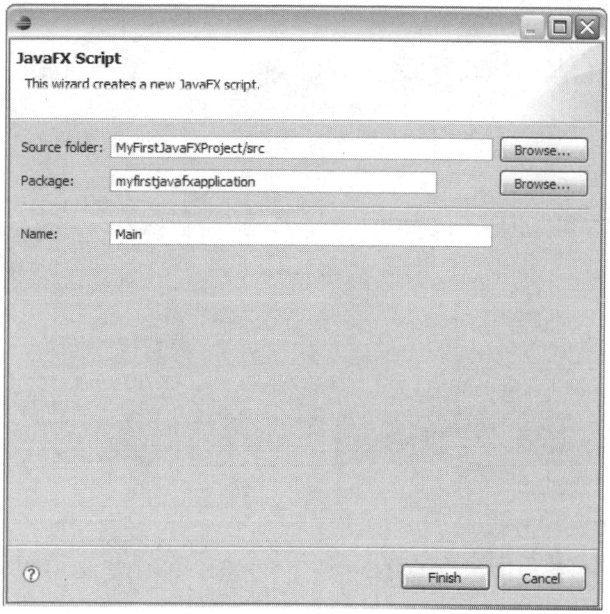

Figure 1.15   Create JavaFX Script Dialog

Give the script a name, Main, and click Finish. This creates an empty script file called Main.fx. Edit the script file with the Hello World example and save it. To run it, select the Run icon and the application window should appear. Figure 1.16 points out the Run icon from the tool bar, with the running application displayed.

One main difference between NetBeans IDE for JavaFX 1.2 and the JavaFX plug-in for Eclipse is there is no Preview mode for JavaFX in Eclipse. However, it is easy to run the application to see what the screens look like while developing.

This section concludes the basics for getting started with Eclipse. For more detailed information and configuration options, check the documentation that is available with the Eclipse plug-in for JavaFX. The documents contain detailed instructions for installing the JavaFX plug-in and configuring Eclipse for the first time to recognize JavaFX files. After Eclipse is configured for JavaFX, development is similar to the NetBeans IDE for JavaFX 1.2.

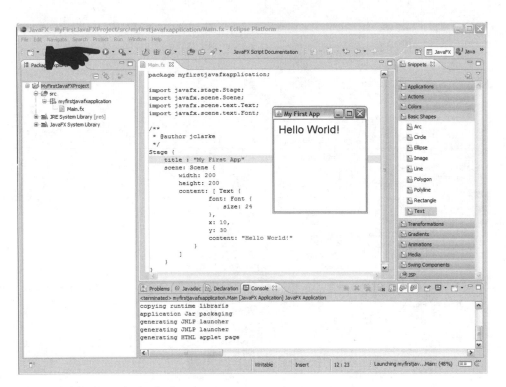

Figure 1.16   Running a Script

Chapter Summary

This chapter has shown you how to get started writing your first JavaFX application. It has detailed how to download and install the NetBeans IDE for JavaFX 1.2, the Eclipse plug-in for JavaFX and the JavaFX SDK, how to write and compile a simple JavaFX program, both from the command line and using the NetBeans IDE for JavaFX 1.2, and how to distribute that program to an end user. It has also provided a small glimpse of what is possible with the JavaFX Platform.

From here, we will explore the JavaFX Platform in greater detail and describe the major capabilities that you can leverage in your applications. Throughout the next few chapters, we will cover concepts required to build a straightforward animation, a total solar eclipse. This allows us to explore animation, graphics, and special effects. We will also explore a Sudoku application written in JavaFX Script. This application demonstrates some of the key features of JavaFX Script including data binding and triggers. The next chapter starts us off by looking at JavaFX from a graphic designer's eyes.

2

JavaFX for the Graphic Designer

"Creativity is allowing yourself to make mistakes.
Art is knowing which ones to keep."

—Scott Adams

Graphic Design and JavaFX

In a JavaFX environment, the goal for the graphic designer is to use his or her creativity to forge graphical assets and then export them for JavaFX in the form of JavaFX Objects. First, the graphic designer helps to design the visual presentation and then often generates his or her designs using various symbols, drawings, texts, images, colors, and special effects. After the graphic designer generates the graphical assets in the form of JavaFX Objects, it is up to the application developer to use those graphical objects in a Rich Internet Application.

Typically, graphic designers use specialized design tools to develop graphical assets. Of these, Adobe Illustrator CS3 and Adobe Photoshop CS3 are the most popular. Another common graphical format is Scalable Vector Graphics, or SVG, and most graphic design programs provide SVG export capabilities.

This chapter discusses the process that the graphic designer will need to follow to export his artwork to a form that can be used in JavaFX. Specifically, we describe the procedure to export graphical assets from Adobe Illustrator CS3 and Adobe Photoshop CS3. In addition, we discuss the SVG to JavaFX Convertor utility to convert Scalable Vector Graphic files to JavaFX.

The graphical assets described in this chapter will later be used in Chapter 7, Add Motion with JavaFX Animation. This chapter focuses on the graphic designer, and what he or she needs to do to generate graphical objects. Chapter 7 focuses on the JavaFX programmer and what he or she needs to do to use those objects in an application.

JavaFX Production Suite

The JavaFX Production Suite is a set of tools for converting graphics to a format that can be used for JavaFX applications. You can download the JavaFX Production Suite from the JavaFX Web site (http://www.javafx.com) and it supports Microsoft Windows XP, Service Pack 2, Microsoft Vista, and Macintosh OS X 10.4+ on Intel. If you already have Adobe Illustrator CS3 or Adobe Photoshop CS3 installed, simply execute the binary installer for JavaFX Production Suite and the appropriate Adobe plug-ins will be installed on your system. These plug-ins allow you to export from the respective Adobe products to a format that can be processed by JavaFX. Let's see how this works.

In our example, we want to create an animation of a solar eclipse. In this animation, there is, of course, the Moon in its orbit; but, also, the Sun goes through several phase changes as the eclipse approaches totality and subsequently returns to normal. We will use this example in Chapter 7 when we explain how to implement animations in JavaFX. However, let's first look at the graphical assets required for this.

Adobe Illustrator CS3

Using Adobe Illustrator CS3, we need two backgrounds: one is the blue sky as normally seen in daylight and the second is a dark sky with stars. As the eclipse progresses to totality, the blue daylight sky will fade out while the dark sky will fade in, peaking at totality, before the process reverses itself. To accomplish this, you need to create a separate layer for each background: one called jfx:bluesky and the other jfx:darksky. The naming convention jfx:*layerName* will help later when we export the layers to JavaFX.

Graphical layers are discreet graphical assets that can be layered on top of each other to provide a combined visual effect. This is analogous to using a clear film representing each layer. Each film will contain its graphical components so that when you lay one film over another you get a combined visual. For animations, you can take a foreground layer on top of a background layer and then, over time, move the foreground layer across the background layer.

The jfx:bluesky and jfx:darksky layers are illustrated in Figures 2.1 and 2.2. These figures are available in full color at our Web site, http://jfxbook.com.

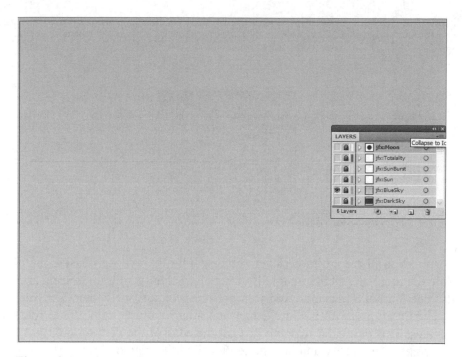

Figure 2.1 BlueSky Layer

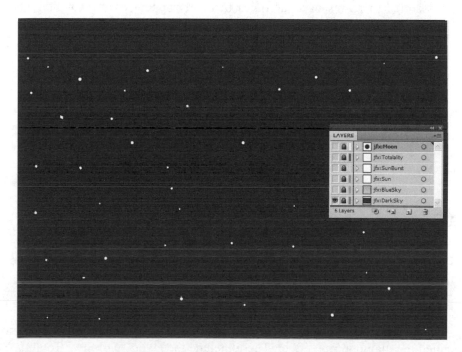

Figure 2.2 DarkSky Layer

Now that the background layers are complete, we then create a layer that merely holds the darkened moon. This is basically a blurred black circle. Figure 2.3 shows this layer.

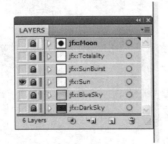

Figure 2.3   Dark Side of the Moon Layer

For the Sun, there are three layers representing the eclipse phases: the normal Sun, the moment just before totality where a final burst of light is seen, and totality. The normal Sun is a blurred yellow circle with a white center. The Sun Burst is a basic ellipse with a white center and a surrounding halo effect, rotated 45 degrees. This particular image will be at the edge of the dark moon, right before and right after totality and is commonly called the diamond ring effect. Totality view will be a center white circle with a halo effect. There are some yellow curve lines added to represent solar flares that only appear during totality. The sun layer is illustrated in Figure 2.4 and can be seen in color at http://jfxbook.com.

Figure 2.4   Sun

Figure 2.5 shows the Sun Burst layer. This is the layer that is shown in the diamond ring effect immediately before and after totality.

Figure 2.6 shows the Totality layer.

Figure 2.7 shows the combined layers for the moment before totality, commonly called the diamond ring effect. These include the layers DarkSky, Totality, Sun-

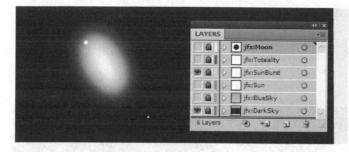

Figure 2.5   Sun Burst

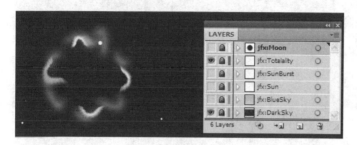

Figure 2.6   Sun Totality

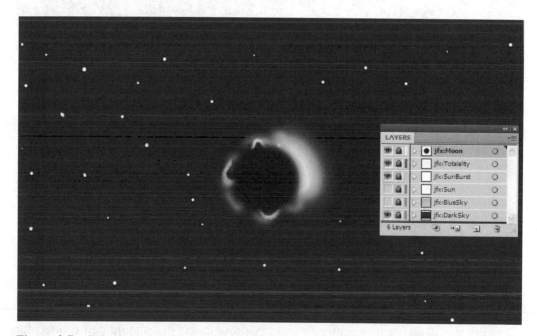

Figure 2.7   Solar Eclipse Diamond Ring Effect

Burst, and Moon, respectively. When combined on top of each other, these look like Figure 2.7.

Figure 2.8 shows the view at totality. This includes the layers DarkSky, Sun, Totality, and Moon.

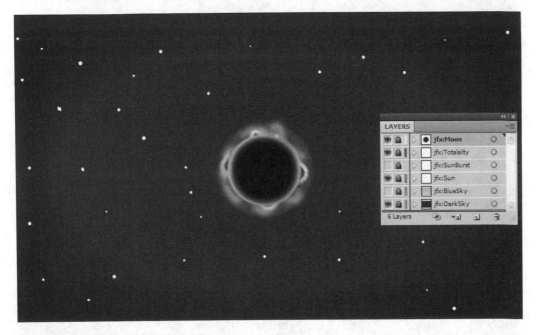

Figure 2.8   Total Solar Eclipse View

For this entire solar eclipse animation, there are six exported layers: jfx:Moon, jfx:Totality, jfx:SunBurst, jfx:Sun, jfx:BlueSky, and jfx:DarkSky. To implement the animation, the backgrounds will be jfx:BlueSky and jfx:DarkSky. As the Moon starts to cover the Sun, the BlueSky layer fades out of and the DarkSky layer fades into view. As the Moon nears total coverage over the Sun, the Sun Burst layer becomes visible, and then the Totality View replaces the Sun Burst view. This whole process reverses itself as the Moon moves out of the Sun Disc. The primary objects are the Moon and the Sun, with the Sun going through three phases. In Adobe Illustrator CS3, the combined screen with all layers visible is shown in Figure 2.9. The full color view of all these layers can be seen at http://jfxbook.com.

To use these layers in JavaFX, you need to export them. By default, only layers with the prefix jfx: (case does not matter) will be exported. This allows the graphic designer to specifically identify those layers that should be exported for use in JavaFX, while allowing the designer the ability to name other layers for his/her own purposes. This default behavior can be overridden by unchecking the Preserve "JFX:" IDs Only option when exporting.

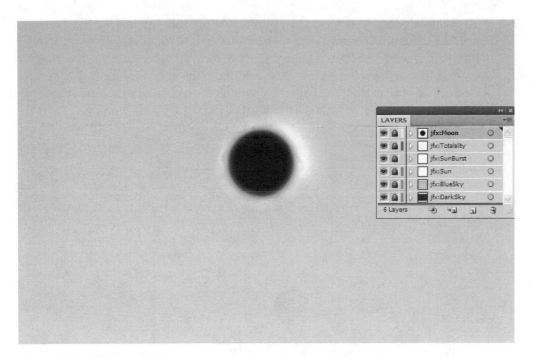

Figure 2.9   All Layers View

To export the layers, from Adobe Illustrator, choose **File | Save for JavaFX**; this brings up the JavaFX Export Options window. Figure 2.10 shows the menu for this.

Figure 2.10   Save for JavaFX

From this window, you have the option to show the preview of the exported JavaFX file, choose to only export 'JFX:' layer IDs (the default) or all IDs, or choose to embed the fonts in the exported file. To actually save the JavaFX exported file, depress the **Save** button, and the plug-in creates a JavaFX archive files with an .fxz extension. This file contains the exported graphics in an optimized format. Figure 2.11 shows the JavaFX Export Options window.

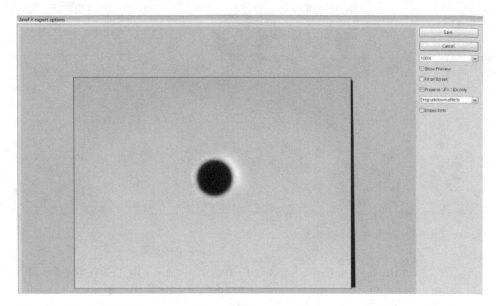

Figure 2.11   JavaFX Export Options Window

Figure 2.12 shows the Save for JavaFX dialog.

We will explore this generated code in detail in Chapter 7, but for now simply know that there is a direct correlation from the Adobe Illustrator layers and objects created in the JavaFX exported code. For our solar eclipse example, there will be JavaFX Objects for the Moon, Sun, SunBurst, Totality, BlueSky, and DarkSky. These objects were exported, because we named them all with a jfx: prefix when we created the layers in Adobe Illustrator.

Adobe Photoshop CS3

Exporting to JavaFX in Adobe Photoshop is similar to how it is done in Adobe Illustrator. First, create the images for each layer, then export to JavaFX archive format. Figure 2.13 shows the layers we created with Adobe Illustrator in the

Figure 2.12 Save for JavaFX Dialog

previous section, but now they are loaded in Adobe Photoshop. To do this, save the Adobe Illustrator graphics to Photoshop format, then load into Photoshop. You will notice that the same layers for DarkSky, BlueSky, and so on are shown. Figure 2.13 shows these layers as presented in Photoshop. A full color view is available at http://jfxbook.com.

To export to JavaFX, select **File | Automate | Save for JavaFX,** as shown in Figure 2.14.

This brings up a JavaFX Export Options window as shown in Figure 2.15.

Just like we did for Adobe Illustrator, from this window, you have the option to show the preview of the exported JavaFX file, choose to only export JFX: layer

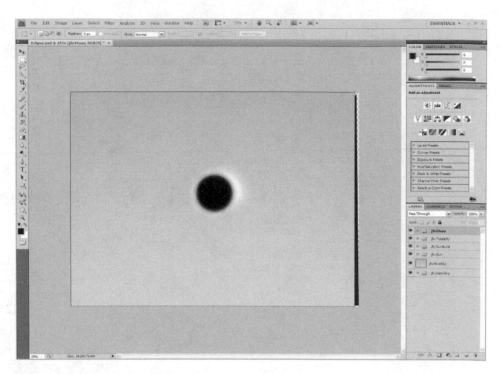

Figure 2.13   Photoshop Eclipse Layers

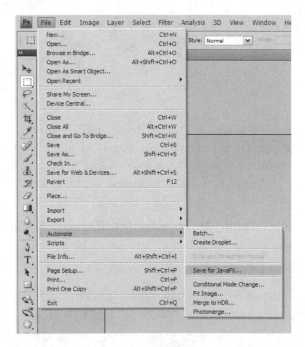

Figure 2.14   Save for JavaFX

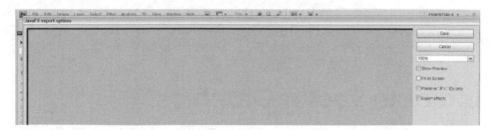

Figure 2.15 JavaFX Export Options Window

IDs (the default) or all IDs, or choose to embed the fonts in the exported file. To actually save the JavaFX exported file, depress the **Save** button, and the plug-in creates a JavaFX archive file with an .fxz extension. This file contains the exported graphics in an optimized format. One major difference from the JavaFX export produced from Adobe Illustrator is that the graphical objects that the Photo-Shop JavaFX plug-in produces are rasterized, so PhotoShop generates a larger JavaFX Archive file. Figure 2.16 shows the dialog for exporting the PhotoShop layers for JavaFX.

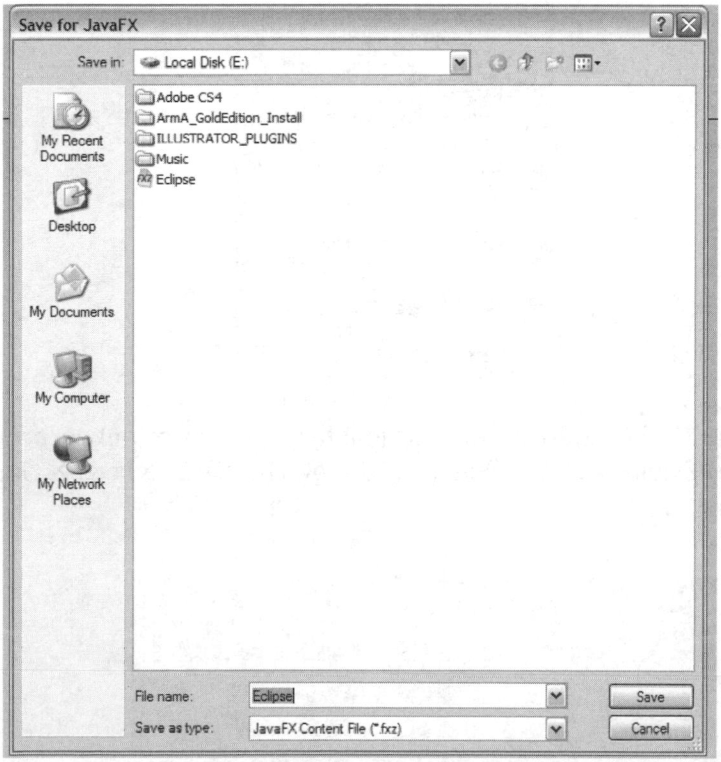

Figure 2.16 Save for JavaFX Dialog

In the File Name field, enter the exported filename. In the Save as Type field, select JavaFX Content File (.fxz), and click **Save** to save the file. Later in Chapter 7, the developer will use this file to create an animation for the solar eclipse.

Scalable Vector Graphics

Scalable Vector Graphics (SVG) is an open and free standard language for describing two-dimensional graphics using The Extensible Markup Language (XML) developed under the World Wide Web Consortium (W3C) process (http://www.w3.org/Graphics/SVG/). SVG provides for vector graphic shapes using paths of either lines or curves, images, and text.

JavaFX Production Suite includes an SVG conversion utility that converts SVG graphic files to JavaFX Archive File format. To demonstrate, we saved the solar eclipse images we created previously in the Adobe Illustrator section to an SVG file, Eclipse.svg. To run the conversion utility in Windows, select **Start | All Programs | JavaFX Production Suite | SVG to JavaFX Converter** as shown in Figure 2.17.

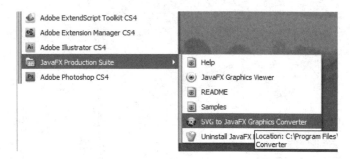

Figure 2.17   SVG to JavaFX Converter

This opens the SVG Converter tool. This tool has an option to only export JFX: layer IDs (the default) or all IDs. Figure 2.18 shows the SVG to JavaFX Graphics Converter window.

Figure 2.18   SVG to JavaFX Graphics Converter Window

Select the SVG source file, Eclipse.svg, and then enter the output file, Eclipse.fxz. This creates a similar JavaFX archive file as when we exported to JavaFX directly from Adobe Illustrator.

Chapter Summary

In this chapter, we learned how to create graphical assets. The JavaFX Production Suite is a set of tools to assist in creating JavaFX graphical objects created in Adobe Illustrator, Adobe Photoshop, and Scalable Vector Graphics. Besides the example demonstrated here, there are many samples available with JavaFX Production Suite. These are located under the install directory, in the sub-directory named Samples (Windows: C:\Program Files\sun\JavaFX Production Suite\Samples).

In the next chapter, Chapter 3, JavaFX Primer, we explore the domain of the JavaFX programmer. This starts with a detailed description of JavaFX language syntax and some basic features.

3

JavaFX Primer

"I'm still at the beginning of my career. It's all a little new,
and I'm still learning as I go."

—Orlando Bloom

JavaFX Script Basics

JavaFX is partially a declarative language. Using a declarative language, a developer describes what needs to be done, then lets the system get it done. Olof Torgersson, Program Director for the Chalmers University of Technology Master's program in Interaction Design and Associate Professor at Göteborg University, has been researching declarative programming for over 10 years. From his analysis of declarative programming approaches, we find this definition:

> *"From a programmer's point of view, the basic property is that programming is lifted to a higher level of abstraction. At this higher level of abstraction the programmer can concentrate on stating what is to be computed, not necessarily how it is to be computed"*[1]

JavaFX Script blends declarative programming concepts with object orientation. This provides a highly productive, yet flexible and robust, foundation for applications. However, with this flexibility comes responsibility from the developer. JavaFX Script is a forgiving language and being declarative, it assumes inherent rules that may obscure a programming fault. The most obvious of these is that null objects are handled by the runtime engine and seldom cause a Java Null Pointer exception. As a result, the program will continue when a null is encountered

---

1. Torgersson, Olof. "A Note on Declarative Programming Paradigms and the Future of Definitional Programming," Chalmers University of Technology and Göteborg University, Göteborg, Sweden. http://www.cs.chalmers.se/~olof/Papers/wm96/wm96.html.

within an expression, and will produce a valid result. However, the result may not have been what you expected. Therefore, the developer needs to be extra vigilant when writing code and more thorough when testing it. At first, this may seem alarming; however, this is offset by the ease of use and greater productivity of JavaFX and by the fact that JavaFX tries to mitigate the user from experiencing a crash.

One of the benefits of JavaFX being a declarative language is that much of the "plumbing" to make objects interact is already provided within the language. This allows the developer to be able to concentrate more on what needs to display, and less on how to do it. The next sections provide an overview of the JavaFX Script language including syntax, operators, and other features.

JavaFX Script Language

As we already mentioned, JavaFX Script is a declarative scripting language with object-oriented support. If you are already acquainted with other languages such as Java, JavaScript, Groovy, Adobe ActionScript, or JRuby, JavaFX Script will look familiar, but there are significant differences. While supporting traditional pure scripting, it also supports the encapsulation and reuse capabilities afforded by object orientation. This allows the developer to use JavaFX to produce and maintain small- to large-scale applications. Another key feature is that JavaFX Script seamlessly integrates with Java.

Conceptually, JavaFX Script is broken down into two main levels, script and class. At the script level, variables and functions may be defined. These may be shared with other classes defined within the script, or if they have wider access rights, they may be shared with other scripts and classes. In addition, expressions called *loose* expressions may be created. These are all expressions declared outside of a class definition. When the script is evaluated, all loose expressions are evaluated.

A very simple script to display Hello World to the console is

```
println("Hello World");
```

Another example, showing how to do a factorial of 3, is shown in Listing 3.1.

Listing 3.1   Factorial of 3

```
def START = 3;
var result = START;
```

```
var a = result - 1;
while(a > 0) {
    result *= a;
    a--;
}
println("result = {result}");
```

Developer Note: If your script has exported members—that is, any external accessible members such as public, protected, and package, functions or variables—then all *loose expressions* must be contained in a run function. For example, if we change the result variable in the previous example to add public visibility, we need to create the run function.

```
public var result:Number;

function run(args : String[]) : java.lang.Object {

    var num = if(sizeof args > 0) {
            java.lang.Integer.valueOf(args[0]);
        } else {
            10;
        };

    result = num;
    var a = result - 1;
    while(a > 0) {
        result *= a;
        a--;
    }
    println("{num}! = {result}");
}
```

The run method contains an optional String[] parameter, which is a sequence of the command-line arguments passed to the script when it runs.

If you do not have exported members, you can still include a run method. However, the run method, itself, is considered exported, even if you do not include an access modifier with it. So, once you add a run method, all loose exported expressions must now be contained within it.

Apart from the script level, a class defines instance variables and functions and must first be instantiated into an object before being used. Class functions or variables may access script level functions or variables within the same script file, or from other script files if the appropriate access rights are assigned. On the other hand, script level functions can only access class variables and functions if the class is created into an object and then only if the class provides the appropriate access rights. Access rights are defined in more detail later in this chapter.

Class Declaration

To declare a class in JavaFX, use the *class* keyword.

```
public class Title {
}
```

Developer Note: By convention, the first letter of class names is capitalized.

The `public` keyword is called an access modifier and means that this class can be used by any other class or script, even if that class is declared in another script file. If the class does not have a modifier, it is only accessible within the script file where it is declared. For example, the class `Point` in Listing 3.2 does not have a visibility modifier, so it is *only has script visibility* and can only be used within the `ArtWork` script.

Listing 3.2   Artwork.fx

```
class Point {// private class only
            //visible to the ArtWork class
    var x:Number;
    var y:Number;
}

public class ArtWork {
    var location: Point;
}
```

Developer Note: For each JavaFX script file, there is a class generated using that script filename, even if one is not explicitly defined. For example, in the previous example for `ArtWork.fx`, there is a class `ArtWork`. This is true even if we had not included the `public class ArtWork` declaration.

Also, all other classes defined within the script file have their name prepended with the script file's name. For example, in the previous example, class `Point` is fully qualified as `ArtWork.Point`. Of course, if `ArtWork` belongs to a package, the package name would also be used to qualify the name. For example, `com.acme.ArtWork.Point`.

To extend a class, use the `extends` keyword followed by the more generalized class name. JavaFX classes can extend at most one Java or JavaFX class. If you extend a Java class, that class must have a default (no-args) constructor.

```
public class Porsche911 extends Porsche {
}
```

JavaFX may extend multiple JavaFX `mixin` classes or Java interfaces. `Mixin` classes are discussed in the next section.

An application may contain many classes, so it is helpful to organize them in a coherent way called *packages*. To declare that your class or script should belong to a package, include a package declaration at the beginning of the script file. The following example means that the `Title` class belongs to the `com.mycompany.components` package. The full name of the `Title` class is now `com.mycompany.components.Title`. Whenever the `Title` class is referenced, it must be resolved to this full name.

```
package com.mycompany.components;
public class Title {
}
```

To make this resolution easier, you can include an import statement at the top of your source file. For example:

```
import com.mycompany.components.Title;

var productTitle = Title{};
```

Now, wherever `Title` is referenced within that script file, it will resolve to `com.mycompany.components.Title`. You can also use a wildcard import declaration:

```
import com.mycompany.components.*;
```

With the wildcard form of import, whenever you refer to any class in the `com.mycompany.components` package, it will resolve to its full name. The following code example shows how the class names are resolved, showing the fully qualified class name in comments.

```
package com.mycompany.myapplication;
import com.mycompany.components.Title;

// com.mycompany.myapplication.MyClass
public class MyClass {
    // com.mycompany.components.Title
    public var title: Title;
}
```

A class can have package visibility by using the `package` keyword instead of `public`. This means the class can only be accessed from classes within the same package.

```
package class MyPackageClass {
}
```

A class may also be declared abstract, meaning that this class cannot be instantiated directly, but can only be instantiated using one of its subclasses. Abstract classes are not intended to stand on their own, but encapsulate a portion of shared state and functions that several classes may use. Only a subclass of an abstract class can be instantiated, and typically the subclass has to fill in those unique states or behavior not addressed in the abstract class.

```
public abstract class MyAbstractClass {
}
```

If a class declares an abstract function, it must be declared abstract.

```
public abstract class AnotherAbstractClass {
    public abstract function
                setXY(x:Number, y:Number) : Void;
}
```

Mixin Classes

JavaFX supports a form of inheritance called mixin inheritance. To support this, JavaFX includes a special type of class called a mixin. A mixin class is a class that provides certain functionality to be inherited by subclasses. They cannot be instantiated on their own. A mixin class is different from a Java interface in that the mixin may provide default implementations for its functions and also may declare and initialize its own variables.

To declare a mixin class in JavaFX, you need to include the mixin keyword in the class declaration. The following code shows this.

```
public mixin class Positioner {
```

A mixin class may contain any number of function declarations. If the function declaration has a function body, then this is the default implementation for the function. For example, the following listing shows a mixin class declaration for a class that positions one node within another.

```
public mixin class Positioner {
    protected bound function centerX(
                node: Node, within: Node) : Number {
```

```
                (within.layoutBounds.width -
                                node.layoutBounds.width)/2.0 -
                                    node.layoutBounds.minX;
        }
        protected bound function centerY(node: Node,
                                    within: Node) : Number {
            (within.layoutBounds.height -
                        node.layoutBounds.height)/2.0 -
                                    node.layoutBounds.minY;
        }
    }
```

Subclasses that want to implement their own version of the mixin function must use the override keyword when declaring the function. For instance, the following code shows a subclass that implements its own version of the centerX() function from the Positioner mixin class.

```
    public class My Positioner extends Positioner {
        public override bound function centerX(node: Node,
            within: Node) : Number {
        (within.boundsInParent.width -
                        node.boundsInParent.width )/2.0;
        }
    }
```

If the mixin function does not have a default implementation, it must be declared abstract and the subclass must override this function to provide an implementation. For instance, the following code shows an abstract function added to the Positioner mixin class.

```
    public abstract function bottomY(node: Node,
                within: Node, padding: Number) : Number;
```

The subclass must implement this function using the override keyword, as shown in the following listing.

```
    public class My Positioner extends Positioner {
        public override function bottomY(node: Node,
                within: Node, padding: Number) : Number {
            within.layoutBounds.height - padding -
                                node.layoutBounds.height;
        }
    }
```

If two mixins have the same function signature or variable name, the system resolves to the function or variable based on which mixin is declared first in the extends clause. To specify a specific function or variable, use the `mixin` class name with the function or variable name. This is shown in the following code.

```
public class My Positioner extends Positioner,
                        AnotherPositioner {
    var offset = 10.0;
    public override bound function
            centerX(node: Node, within: Node) : Number {
        Positioner.centerX(node, within) + offset;
    }
}
```

Mixins may also define variables, with or without default values and triggers. The subclass either inherits these variables or must override the variable declaration. The following listing demonstrates this.

```
public mixin class Positioner {
    public var offset: Number = 10.0;
}

public class My Positioner extends Positioner {
    public override var offset = 5.0 on replace {
        println("{offset}");
    }
}
```

If a class extends a JavaFX class and one or more `mixins`, the JavaFX class takes precedence over the `mixin` classes for variable initialization. If the variable is declared in a superclass, the default value specified in the superclass is used; if no default value is specified in the superclass, the "default value" for the type of that variable is used. For the `mixin` classes, precedence is based on the order they are defined in the `extends` clause. If a variable declared in a `mixin` has a default value, and the variable is overridden without a default value in the main class, the initial value specified in the `mixin` is used.

Mixins may also have `init` and `postinit` blocks. Mixin `init` and `postinit` blocks are run after the super class's `init` and `postinit` blocks and before the subclass's `init` and `postinit` blocks. Init and `postinit` blocks from the `mixin` classes are run in the order they are declared in the `extends` clause for the subclass.

Object Literals

In JavaFX, objects are instantiated using *object literals*. This is a declarative syntax using the name of the class that you want to create, followed by a list of initializers and definitions for this specific instance. In Listing 3.3, an object of class `Title` is created with the text "JavaFX is cool" at the screen position 10, 50. When the mouse is clicked, the provided function will be called.

Listing 3.3   Object Literal

```
var title = Title {
    text: "JavaFX is cool"
    x: 10
    y: 50
    onMouseClicked: function(e:MouseEvent):Void {
       // do something
    }
};
```

When declaring an object literal, the instance variables may be separated by commas or whitespace, as well as the semi-colon.

You can also override abstract functions within the object literal declaration. The following object literal, shown in Listing 3.4, creates an object for the `java.awt` `.event.ActionListener` interface and overrides the abstract java method `void actionPerformed(ActionEvent e)` method.

Listing 3.4   Object Literal – Override Abstract Function

```
import java.awt.event.ActionListener;
import java.awt.event.ActionEvent;

var listener = ActionListener {
    override function
            actionPerformed(e: ActionEvent) : Void {
        println("Action Performed!");
    }
}
```

Variables

JavaFX supports two kinds of variables: *instance* and *script*. Script variables hold state for the entire script, whereas instance variables hold state for specific instantiations of a class declared within the script file.

There are basically two flavors of variables: *unassignable* and *changeable*. Unassignable variables are declared using the def keyword and must be assigned a default value that never changes.

```
public def PI = 3.14;
```

These variables cannot be assigned to, overridden, or initialized in object literals. In a sense, these can be viewed as constants; however, they are not "pure" constants and can participate in binding. (For more information on binding, see Chapter 4, Synchronize Data Models—Binding and Triggers.)

Consider the following example of defining an *unassignable* variable that contains an object. The object instance cannot change, but that does not mean the state of that instance will not.

```
def centerPoint = Point{x: 100, y:100};
centerPoint.x = 500;
```

The actual Point object assigned to centerPoint remains unchanged, but the state of that object instance, the actual x and y values, may change. When used in binding though, centerPoint is constant; if the state of centerPoint changes, the bound context will be notified of the change.

Changeable instance variables are declared using the var keyword with an optional default value. If the default value is omitted, a reasonable default is used; basically, Numbers default to zero, Boolean defaults to false, Strings default to the empty string, Sequences default to the Empty Sequence, and everything else defaults to null.

Script variables are declared outside of any class declaration, whereas instance variables are declared within a class declaration. If a script variable is declared with one of the access modifiers—public, protected, or package—it may be used from outside of the script file, by referring to its fully qualified name. This fully qualified name is the combination of package name, script name, and the variable name. The following is the fully qualified name to a public script variable from the javafx.scene.Cursor class for the crosshair cursor.

```
javafx.scene.Cursor.CROSSHAIR;
```

Instance variables are declared within a class declaration and come into being when the object is created. Listing 3.5 illustrates several examples of script and instance variables.

Listing 3.5   Script and Instance Variables

```
import javafx.scene.Cursor;
import javafx.scene.paint.Color;

// import of script variable from javafx.scene.Cursor
import javafx.scene.Cursor.CROSSHAIR;

// Unchangeable script variable
def defaultText = "Replace ME"; // Script accessible only

// Changeable script variable
public var instanceCount: Integer; // Public accessible

public class Title  {
    // Unchangeable instance variables
    def defStroke = Color.NAVY; // class only access,
            //resolves to javafx.scene.paint.Color.NAVY

    // Changeable instance variables

    // defaults to the empty String ""
    public var text:String;
    public var width:  Number; // defaults to zero (0.0)
    public var height = 100; // Infers Integer type
    public var stroke: Color = defaultStroke;
    public var strokeWidth = 1.0; // Infers Number type
    public var cursor = CROSSHAIR;
            //resolves to javafx.scene.Cursor.CROSSHAIR


    ...
}
```

You may have noticed that some of the declarations contain a type and some don't. When a type is not declared, the type is inferred from the first assigned value. `String`, `Number`, `Integer`, and `Boolean` are built-in types, everything else is either a JavaFX or a Java class. (There is a special syntax for easily declaring `Duration` and `KeyFrame` class instances that will be discussed in Chapter 7, Add Motion with JavaFX Animation.)

Table 3.1 lists the access modifiers for variables and their meaning and restrictions. You will notice reference to initialization, which refers to object literal declarations. Also, you will notice variables being bound. This is a key feature of JavaFX and is discussed in depth in Chapter 4.

Table 3.1 Access Modifiers

Access Modifier	Meaning
`var`	The **default** access permission is script access, so without access modifiers, a variable can be initialized, overridden, read, assigned, or bound from within the script only.
`def`	The **default** access permission is script access; a definition can be read from or bound to within the script only.
public `var`	Read and writable by anyone. Also, it can be initialized, overridden, read, assigned, or bound from anywhere.
public `def`	This definition can be read anywhere. A definition cannot be assigned, initialized (in an object literal), or overridden no matter what the access permissions. It may be bound from anywhere.
public-read `var`	Readable by anyone, but only writable within the script.
public-init `var`	Can be initialized in object literals, but can only be updated by the owning script. Only allowed for instance variables.
package `var`	A variable accessible from the package. This variable can be initialized, overridden, read, assigned, or bound only from a class within the same package.
package `def`	Define a variable that is readable or bound only from classes within the same package.
protected `var`	A variable accessible from the package or subclasses. This variable can be initialized, overridden, read, assigned, or bound from only a subclass or a class within the same package.
protected `def`	Define a variable that is readable or bound only from classes within the same package or subclasses.
public-read protected `var`	Readable and bound by anyone, but this variable can only be initialized, overridden, or assigned from only a subclass or a class within the same package.
public-init protected `var`	Can be initialized in object literals, read and bound by anyone, but can only be overridden or assigned, from only a subclass or a class within the same package. Only allowed for instance variables.

You can also declare change triggers on a variable. Change triggers are blocks of JavaFX script that are called whenever the value of a variable changes. To declare a change trigger, use the on replace syntax:

```
public var x:Number = 100 on replace {
    println("New value is {x}");
};
public var width: Number on replace (old) {
    println("Old value is {old}, New value is {x}");
}
```

Change triggers are discussed in more depth in Chapter 4.

Sequences

Sequences are ordered lists of objects. Because ordered lists are used so often in programming, JavaFX supports sequence as a first class feature. There is built-in support in the language for declaring sequences, inserting, deleting, and modifying items in the sequence. There is also powerful support for retrieving items from the sequence.

Declaring Sequences

To declare a sequence, use square brackets with each item separated by a comma. For example:

```
public def monthNames = ["January", "February", "March",
                "April", "May", "June",
                "July", August", "September",
                "October", "November", "December"];
```

This sequence is a sequence of Strings, because the elements within the brackets are Strings. This could have also been declared as

```
public def monthNames: String[] = [ "January", .....];
```

To assign an empty sequence, just use square brackets, []. This is also the default value for a sequence. For example, the following two statements both equal the empty sequence.

```
public var nodes:Node[] = [];
```

```
public var nodes:Node[];
```

When the sequence changes, you can assign a trigger function to process the change. This is discussed in depth in the next chapter.

A shorthand for declaring a sequence of `Integers` and `Numbers` uses a range, a start integer or number with an end. So, `[1..9]` is the sequence of the integers from 1 thru 9, inclusive; the exclusive form is `[1..<9]`—that is, 1 through 8. You can also use a step function, so if, for example, you want even positive integers, use `[2..100 step 2]`. For numbers, you can use decimal fractions, `[0.1..1.0 step 0.1]`. Without the step, a step of 1 or 1.0 is implicit.

Ranges may also go in decreasing order. To do this, the first number must be higher than the second. However, without a negative step function, you always end up with an empty sequence. This is because the default step is always positive 1.

```
var negativeNumbers = [0..-10]; // Empty sequence
var negativeNumbers = [0..-10 step -1]; // 0,-1,-2,...-10
var negativeNumbers = [0..<-10 step -1]; // 0,-1,-2,...,-9
```

To build sequences that include the elements from other sequences, just include the source sequences within the square brackets.

```
var negativePlusEven = [ negativeNumbers,  evenNumbers ];
```

Also, you can use another sequence to create a sequence by using the Boolean operator. Another sequence is used as the source, and a Boolean operator is applied to each element in the source sequence, and the elements from the source that evaluate to true are returned in the new sequence. In the following example, n represents each item in the sequence of positive integers and n mod 2 == 0 is the evaluation.

```
var evenIntegers = positiveIntegers[n | n mod 2 == 0];
```

One can also allocate a sequence from a `for` loop. Each object "returned" from the iteration of the `for` loop is added to the sequence:

```
// creates sequence of Texts
var lineNumbers:Text[]  = for(n in [1..100]) {
     Text { content: "{n}" };
};

// creates Integer sequence, using indexof operator
var indexNumbers = for(n in nodes) {
     indexof n;
};
```

To get the current size of a sequence use the `sizeof` operator.

```
var numEvenNumbers = sizeof evenNumbers;
```

Accessing Sequence Elements

To access an individual element, use the numeric index of the element within square brackets:

```
var firstMonth =  monthNames[0];
```

You can also take slices of sequence by providing a range. Both of the next two sequences are equal.

```
var firstQuarter = monthNames[0..2];
```

```
var firstQuarter = monthNames[0..<3];
```

The following two sequences are also equal. The second example uses a syntax for range to indicate start at an index and return all elements after that index.

```
var fourthQuarter = monthNames[9..11 ];
```

```
var fourthQuarter = monthNames[9.. ];
```

To iterate over a sequence, use the `for` loop:

```
for( month in monthNames) {
    println("{month}");
}
```

Modifying Sequences

To replace an element in a sequence, just assign a new value to that indexed location in the index.

```
var students = [ "joe", "sally", "jim"];
students[0] = "vijay";
```

Developer Note: As we said at the beginning of this chapter, JavaFX is a forgiving language, so if you assign to an element index location outside of the existing size of the sequence, the assignment is silently ignored.

Let's use the students sequence from the previous example:

```
students[3] = "john";
```

The assignment to position 3 would be ignored because the size of students is currently 3, and the highest valid index is 2. Similarly, assignment to the index -1 is silently ignored for the same reason; -1 is outside of the sequence range.

Furthermore, if you access an element location outside of the existing range for the sequence, a default value is returned. For Numbers, this is zero; for Strings, the empty string; for Objects, this is null.

To insert an element into the sequence, use the insert statement:

```
// add "vijay" to the end of students
insert "vijay" into students;

// insert "mike" at the front of students
insert "mike" before students[0];

// insert "george" after the second student
insert "george" after students[1];
```

To delete an element, use the delete statement:

```
delete students[0]; // remove the first student
delete students[0..1]; // remove the first 2 students
delete students[0..<2]; // remove the first 2 students
delete students[1..]; // remove all but the first student
delete "vijay" from students;
delete students; // remove all students
```

Native Array

Native array is a feature that allows you to create Java arrays. This feature is mainly used to handle the transfer of arrays back and forth from JavaFX and Java. An example of creating a Java int[] array is shown in the following code.

```
var ints: nativearray of Integer =
                [1,2,3] as nativearray of Integer;
```

Native arrays are not the same as sequences, though they appear similar. You cannot use the sequence operators, such as insert and delete, or slices. However, you can do assignments to the elements of the array as shown in the following code:

```
ints[2] = 4;
```

However, if you assign outside of the current bounds of the array, you will get an `ArrayIndexOutOfBounds` Exception.

You can also use the `for` operator to iterate over the elements in the native array. The following code shows an example of this.

```
for(i in ints) {
    println(i);
}
for(i in ints where i mod 2 == 0) {
    println(i);
}
```

Functions

Functions define behavior. They encapsulate statements that operate on inputs, function arguments, and may produce a result, a returned expression. Like variables, functions are either script functions or instance functions. Script functions operate at the script level and have access to variables and other functions defined at the script level. Instance functions define the behavior of an object and have access to the other instance variables and functions contained within the function's declaring class. Furthermore, an instance function may access any script-level variables and functions contained within its own script file.

To declare a function, use an optional access modifier, `public`, `protected`, or `package`, followed by the keyword `function` and the function name. If no access modifier is provided, the function is private to the script file. Any function arguments are contained within parentheses. You may then specify a function return type. If the return type is omitted, the function return type is inferred from the last expression in the function expression block. The special return type of `Void` may be used to indicate that the function returns nothing.

In the following example, both function declarations are equal. The first function infers a return type of `Glow`, because the last expression in the function block is an object literal for a `Glow` object. The second function explicitly declares a return type of `Glow`, and uses the `return` keyword.

```
public function glow(level: Number) {
        // return type Glow inferred
        Glow { level: level };
}

public function glow(): Glow { // explicit return type
        return glow(3.0); // explicit return keyword
}
```

The return keyword is optional when used as the last expression in a function block. However, if you want to return immediately out of an if/else or loop, you must use an explicit return.

In JavaFX, functions are objects in and of themselves and may be assigned to variables. For example, to declare a function variable, assign a function to that variable, and then invoke the function through the variable.

```
var glowFunction : function(level:Number):Glow;
glowFunction = glow;
glowFunction(1.0);
```

Functions definitions can also be anonymous. For example, for a function variable:

```
var glowFunction:function(level:Number): Glow =
    function(level:Number)  {
        Glow { level: level };
    };
```

Or, within an object literal declaration:

```
TextBox {
    columns: 20
    action: function() {
        println("TextBox action");
    }
}
```

Use override to override a function from a superclass.

```
class MyClass {
        public function print() { println("MyClass"); }
}
class MySubClass extends MyClass {
        override function print() { println("MySubClass"); }
}
```

Strings

String Literals

String literals can be specified using either double (") or single (') quotes. The main reason to use one over the other is to avoid character escapes within the string literal—for example, if the string literal actually contains double quotes.

By enclosing the string in single quotes, you do not have to escape the embedded double quotes. Consider the following two examples, which are both valid:

```
var quote = "Winston Churchill said:
          \"Never in the field of human conflict was
          so much owed by so many to so few.\""

var quote = 'Winston Churchill said:
          "Never in the field of human conflict was
          so much owed by so many to so few."'
```

Expressions can be embedded within the string literal by using curly braces:

```
var name = "Jim";
// prints My name is Jim
println ( "My name is {name}" );
```

The embedded expression must be a valid JavaFX or Java expression that returns an object. This object will be converted to a string using its `toString()` method. For instance:

```
println ( "Today is {java.util.Date{}}" );

var state ="The state is {
                    if(running) "Running" else "Stopped"}";

println(" The state is {getStateStr()}" );

println("The state is {
            if(checkRunning()) "Running" else "Stopped"}");
```

Also, a string literal may be split across lines:

```
var quote = "Winston Churchill said: "
"\"Never in the field of human conflict was so much owed "
"by so many to so few.\"";
```

In this example, the strings from both lines are concatenated into one string. Only the string literals within the quotes are used and any white space outside of the quotes is ignored.

Unicode characters can be entered within the string literal using \u + *the four digit unicode*.

```
var thanks = "dank\u00eb"; // dankë
```

Formatting

Embedded expressions within string literals may contain a formatting code that specifies how the embedded expression should be presented. Consider the following:

```
var totalCountMessage = "The total count is {total}";
```

Now if `total` is an integer, the resulting string will show the decimal number; but if `total` is a Number, the resulting string will show the number formatted according to the local locale.

```
var total = 1000.0;
```

produces:

```
The total count is 1000.0
```

To format an expression, you need a format code within the embedded expression. This is a percent (%) followed by the format codes. The format code is defined in the `java.util.Formatter` class. Please refer to its JavaDoc page for more details (http://java.sun.com/javase/6/docs/api/index.html).

```
println("Total is {%f total}");      // Total is 1000.000000
println("Total is {%.2f total}");    // Total is 1000.00
println("Total is {%5.0f total}");   // Total is  1000
println("Total is {%+5.0f total}");  // Total is +1000
println("Total is {%,5.0f total}");  // Total is 1,000
```

Developer Note: To include a percent (%) character in a string, it needs to be escaped with another percent (%%). For example:

```
println("%%{percentage}"); // prints %25
```

Internationalization

To internationalize a string, you must use the "Translate Key" syntax within the string declaration. To create a translate key, the String assignment starts with ## (sharp, sharp) combination to indicate that the string is to be translated to the host locale. The ## combination is before the leading double or single quote. Optionally, a key may be specified within square brackets ([]). If a key is not specified, the string itself becomes the key into the locale properties file. For example:

```
var postalCode = ## "Zip Code: ";
var postalCode = ##[postal]"Zip Code: ";
```

In the preceding example, using the first form, the key is "Zip Code: ", whereas for the second form, the key is "postal". So how does this work?

By default, the localizer searches for a property file for each unique script name. This is the package name plus script filename with a locale and a file type of .fxproperties. So, if your script name is com.mycompany.MyClass, the localizer code would look for a property file named com/mycompany/MyClass_xx. fxproperties on the classpath, where xx is the locale. For example, for English in the United Kingdom, the properties filename would be com/mycompany/ MyClass_en_GB.fxproperties, whereas French Canadian would be com/mycompany/MyClass_fr_CA.fxproperties. If your default locale is just English, the properties file would be MyClass_en.fxproperties. The more specific file is searched first, then the least specific file is consulted. For instance, MyClass_en_GB.fxproperties is searched for the key and if it is not found, then MyClass_en.fxproperties would be searched. If the key cannot be found at all, the string itself is used as the default. Here are some examples:

Example #1:

```
println(##"Thank you");
```

French – MyClass_fr.fxproperties:

```
"Thank you" = "Merci"
```

German – MyClass_de.fxproperties:

```
"Thank you" = "Danke"
```

Japanese – MyClass_ja.fxproperties:

```
"Thank you" - "Arigato"
```

Example #2:

```
println(##[ThankKey] "Thank you");
```

French – MyClass_fr.fxproperties:

```
"ThankKey" = "Merci"
```

German – MyClass_de.fxproperties:

```
"ThankKey" = "Danke"
```

Japanese – MyClass_ja.fxproperties:

```
"ThankKey" = "Arigato"
```

When you use a string with an embedded expression, the literal key contains a %s, where the expression is located within the string. For example:

```
println(##"Hello, my name is {firstname}");
```

In this case, the key is "Hello, my name is %s". Likewise, if you use more than one expression, the key contains a "%s" for each expression:

```
println(##"Hello, my name is {firstname} {lastname}");
```

Now, the key is "Hello, my name is %s %s".

This parameter substitution is also used in the translated strings. For example:

French – MyClass_fr.fxproperties:

```
"Hello, my name is %s %s" = "Bonjour, je m'appelle %s %s"
```

Lastly, you can associate another Properties file to the script. This is done using the javafx.util.StringLocalizer class. For example:

```
StringLocalizer.associate("com.mycompany.resources.MyResources",
"com.mycompany");
```

Now, all translation lookups for scripts in the com.mycompany package will look for the properties file com/mycompany/resources/MyResources_xx.fxproperties, instead of using the default that uses the script name. Again, xx is replaced with the locale abbreviation codes.

Expressions and Operators

Block Expression

A block expression is a list of statements that may include variable declarations or other expressions within curly braces. If the last statement is an expression, the value of a block expression is the value of that last expression; otherwise, the block expression does not represent a value. Listing 3.6 shows two block expressions. The first expression evaluates to a number represented by the *subtotal* value. The second block expression does not evaluate to any value as the last expression is a println() function that is declared as a Void.

Listing 3.6 Block Expressions

```
// block expression with a value
var total = {
    var subtotal = 0;
    var ndx = 0;
    while(ndx < 100) {
        subtotal += ndx;
        ndx++;
    };
    subtotal; // last expression
};

//block expression without a value
{
    var total = 0;
    var ndx = 0;
    while(ndx < 100) {
        total += ndx;
        ndx++;
    };
    println("Total is {total}");
}
```

Exception Handling

The throw statement is the same as Java and can only throw a class that extends java.lang.Throwable.

The try/catch/finally expression is the same as Java, but uses the JavaFX syntax:

```
try {
} catch (e:SomeException) {
} finally {
}
```

Operators

Table 3.2 contains a list of the operators used in JavaFX. The priority column indicates the operator evaluation precedence, with higher precedence operators in the first rows. Operators with the same precedence level are evaluated equally. Assignment operators are evaluated right to left, whereas all others are evaluated left to right. Parentheses may be used to alter this default evaluation order.

Table 3.2   Operators

Priority	Operator	Meaning
1	++/-- (Suffixed)	Post-increment/decrement assignment
2	++/-- (Prefixed)	Pre-increment/decrement assignment
	-	Unary minus
	not	Logical complement; inverts value of a Boolean
	sizeof	Size of a sequence
	reverse	Reverse sequence order
	indexof	Index of a sequence element
3	/, *, mod	Arithmetic operators
4	+, -	Arithmetic operators
5	==, !=	Comparison operators (Note: all comparisons are similar to `isEquals()` in Java)
	<, <=, >, >=	Numeric comparison operators
6	instanceof, as	Type operators
7	and	Logical AND
8	or	Logical OR
9	+=, -=, *=, /=	Compound assignment
10	=>, tween	Animation interpolation operators
11	=	Assignment

Conditional Expressions

if/else

if is similar to if as defined in other languages. First, a condition is evaluated and if true, the expression block is evaluated. Otherwise, if an else expression block is provided, that expression block is evaluated.

```
if (date == today) {
        println("Date is today");
}else {
        println("Out of date!!!");
}
```

One important feature of if/else is that each expression block may evaluate to an expression that may be assigned to a variable:

```
var outOfDateMessage = if(date==today) "Date is today"
                                    else "Out of Date";
```

Also the expression blocks can be more complex than simple expressions. Listing 3.7 shows a complex assignment using an if/else statement to assign the value to outOfDateMessage.

Listing 3.7   Complex Assignment Using if/else Expression

```
var outOfDateMessage = if(date==today) {
        var total = 0;
        for(item in items) {
            total += items.price;
        }
        totalPrice += total;
        "Date is today";
    } else {
        errorFlag = true;
        "Out of Date";
    };
```

In the previous example, the last expression in the block, the error message string literal, is the object that is assigned to the variable. This can be any JavaFX Object, including numbers.

Because the if/else is an expression block, it can be used with another if/else statement. For example:

```
var taxBracket = if(income < 8025.0) 0.10
        else if(income < 32550.0)0.15
        else if (income < 78850.0) 0.25
        else if (income < 164550.0) 0.28
        else 0.33;
```

Looping Expressions

For

for loops are used with sequences and allow you to iterate over the members of a sequence.

```
var daysOfWeek : String[] =
                    [ "Sunday", "Monday", "Tuesday" ];
for(day in daysOfWeek) {
    println("{indexof day}). {day}");
}
```

To be similar with traditional for loops that iterate over a count, use an integer sequence range defined within square brackets.

```
for( i in [0..100]} {
```

The for expression can also return a new sequence. For each iteration, if the expression block executed evaluates to an Object, that Object is inserted into a new sequence returned by the for expression. For example, in the following for expression, a new Text node is created with each iteration of the day of the week. The overall for expression returns a new sequence containing Text graphical elements, one for each day of the week.

```
var textNodes: Text[] = for( day in daysOfWeek) {
    Text {content: day };
}
```

Another feature of the for expression is that it can do nested loops. Listing 3.8 shows an example of using nested loops.

Listing 3.8   Nested For Loop

```
class Course {
    var title: String;
    var students: String[];
}
var courses = [
```

```
    Course {
        title: "Geometry I"
        students: [ "Clarke, "Connors", "Bruno" ]
    },
    Course {
        title: "Geometry II"
        students: [ "Clarke, "Connors",  ]
    },
    Course {
        title: "Algebra I"
        students: [ "Connors", "Bruno" ]
    },
];

for(course in courses, student in course.students) {
   println("Student: {student} is in course {course}");
}
```

This prints out:

```
Student: Clarke is in course Geometry I
Student: Connors is in course Geometry I
Student: Bruno is in course Geometry I
Student: Clarke is in course Geometry II
Student: Connors is in course Geometry II
Student: Connors is in course Algebra I
Student: Bruno is in course Algebra I
```

There may be zero or more secondary loops and they are separated from the previous ones by a comma, and may reference any element from the previous loops.

You can also include a where clause on the sequence to limit the iteration to only those elements where the where clause evaluates to true:

```
var evenNumbers = for( i in [0..1000] where i mod 2 == 0 ) i;
```

while

The while loop works similar to the while loop as seen in other languages:

```
var ndx = 0;
while ( ndx < 100) {
    println("{ndx}");
    ndx++;
}
```

Note that unlike the JavaFX for loop, the while loop does not return any expression, so it cannot be used to create a sequence.

Break/Continue

break and continue control loop iterations. break is used to quit the loop altogether. It causes all the looping to stop from that point. On the other hand, continue just causes the current iteration to stop, and the loop resumes with the next iteration. Listing 3.9 demonstrates how these are used.

Listing 3.9   Break/Continue

```
for(student in students) {
    if(student.name == "Jim") {
        foundStudent = student;
        break; // stops the loop altogether,
               //no more students are checked
    }
}

for(book in Books ) {
        if(book.publisher == "Addison Wesley") {
            insert book into bookList;
            continue; // moves on to check next book.
        }
        insert book into otherBookList;
        otherPrice += book.price;
}
```

Type Operators

The instanceof operator allows you to test the class type of an object, whereas the as operator allows you to cast an object to another class. One way this is useful is to cast a generalized object to a more specific class in order to perform a function from that more specialized class. Of course, the object must inherently be that kind of class, and that is where the instanceof operator is useful to test if the object is indeed that kind of class. If you try to cast an object to a class that that object does not inherit from, you will get an exception.

In the following listing, the printLower() function will translate a string to lowercase, but for other types of objects, it will just print it as is. First, the generic object is tested to see if it is a String. If it is, the object is cast to a String using the as operator, and then the String's toLowerCase() method is used to convert the output to all lowercase. Listing 3.10 illustrates the use of the instanceof and as operators.

Listing 3.10   Type Operators

```
function printLower(object: Object ) {
    if(object instanceof String) {
```

```
        var str = object as String;
        println(str.toLowerCase());
    }else {
        println(object);
    }

}
printLower("Rich Internet Application");
printLower(3.14);
```

Accessing Command-Line Arguments

For a pure script that does not declare exported classes, variables, or functions, the command-line arguments can be retrieved using the `javafx.lang.FX` `.getArguments():String[]` function. This returns a `Sequence` of `Strings` that contains the arguments passed to the script when it started. There is a another version of this for use in other invocations, such as applets, where the arguments are passed using name value pairs, `javafx.lang.FX.getArguments(key:String)` `:String[]`. Similarly, there is a function to get system properties, `javafx.lang.FX` `.getProperty(key:String):String[]`.

If the script contains any exported classes, variables, or functions, arguments are obtained by defining a special run function at the script level.

```
    public function run(args:String[] ) {
        for(arg in args) {
            println("{arg}");
        }
    }
```

Loose Expressions with Exported Members: Variables, functions, and expressions at the script level (not within a class declaration) are called *loose expressions*. When these variables and functions are private to the script, no specific run function is required if the script is executed from the command line. However, if any of these expressions are exported outside of the script using public, public-read, protected, package access, a run function is required if the script is to be executed directly. This run method encapsulates the exported variables and functions.

Built-in Functions and Variables

There are a set of functions that are automatically available to all JavaFX scripts. These functions are defined in `javafx.lang.Builtins`.

You have already seen one of these, `println()`. `Println()` takes an object argument and prints it out to the console, one line at a time. It is similar to the Java method, `System.out.println()`. Its companion function is `print()`. `Print()` prints out its argument but without a new line. The argument's `toString()` method is invoked to print out a string.

```
println("This is printed on a single line");
print("This is printed without a new line");
```

Another function from `javafx.lang.Builtins` is `isInitialized()`. This method takes a JavaFX object and indicates whether the object has been completely initialized. It is useful in variable triggers to determine the current state of the object during initialization. There may be times that you want to execute some functionality only after the object has passed the initialization stage. For example, Listing 3.11 shows the built-in, `isInitialized()` being used in an on `replace` trigger.

Listing 3.11   isInitialized()

```
public class Test {
    public var status: Number on replace {
        // will not be initialized
        // until status is assigned a value
        if(isInitialized(status)) {

            commenceTest(status);
        }
    }
    public function commenceTest(status:Number) : Void {
        println("commenceTest status = {status}:);
    }
}
```

In this example, when the class, `Test`, is first instantiated, the instance variable, `status`, first takes on the default value of 0.0, and then the on `replace` expression block is evaluated. However, this leaves the status in the `uninitialized` state. Only when a value is assigned to `status`, will the state change to `initialized`. Consider the following:

```
var test = Test{}; // status is uninitialized
test.status = 1; // now status becomes initialized
```

In this case when `Test` is created using the object literal, `Test{}`, status takes on the default value of 0.0; however, it is not `initialized`, so commenceTest will not be invoked during object creation. Now when we assign a value to status, the state changes to initialized, so commenceTest is now invoked. Please note that if we had assigned a default value to status, even if that value is 0, then status immediately is set to initialized. The following example demonstrates this.

```
public class Test {
    public var status: Number = 0 on replace {
        // will be initialized immediately.
        if(isInitialized(status)) {
            commenceTest(status);
        }
    }
}
```

The last built-in function is isSameObject(). isSameObject() indicates if the two arguments actually are the same instance. This is opposed to the == operator. In JavaFX, the == operator determines whether two objects are considered equal, but that does not mean they are the same instance. The == operator is similar to the Java function isEquals(), whereas JavaFX isSameObject is similar to the Java == operator. A little confusing if your background is Java!

The built-in variables are __DIR__ and __FILE__. __FILE__ holds the resource URL string for the containing JavaFX class. __DIR__ holds the resource URL string for directory that contains the current class. For example,

```
println("DIR = {__DIR__}");
println("FILE = {__FILE__}");
// to locate an image
var image = Image { url: "{__DIR__}images/foo.jpeg" };
```

The following examples show the output from a directory based classpath versus using a JAR-based class path.

Using a Jar file in classpath
```
$javafx -cp Misc.jar misc.Test


DIR = jar:file:/export/home/jclarke/Documents/
    Book/FX/code/Chapter3/Misc/dist/Misc.jar!/misc/


FILE = jar:file:/export/home/jclarke/Documents/
    Book/FX/code/Chapter3/Misc/dist/Misc.jar!/misc/Test.class
```

continues

```
Using directory classpath
$ javafx -cp . misc.Test

DIR = file:/export/home/jclarke/Documents/Book/
    FX/code/Chapter3/Misc/dist/tmp/misc/


FILE = file:/export/home/jclarke/Documents/Book/
    FX/code/Chapter3/Misc/dist/tmp/misc/Test.class
```

!!!
• • •

Notice the Trailing Slash on __DIR__: Because the tailing slash already exists on __DIR__, *do not* add an extra trailing slash when using __DIR__ to build a path to a resource like an image. `Image{ url: "{__DIR__}image/foo.jpeg"}` is correct.

`Image{ url: "{__DIR__}/image/foo.jpeg"}` *is wrong*. If you add the trailing slash after __DIR__, the image will not be found and you will be scratching your head trying to figure out why not.

Chapter Summary

This chapter covered key concepts in the JavaFX Scripting language. You were shown what constitutes a script and what constitutes a class. You were shown how to declare script and instance variables, how to create and modify sequences, and how to control logic flow.

You now have a basic understanding of the JavaFX Script language syntax and operators. Now, it is time to put this to use. In the following chapters, we will drill down into the key features of JavaFX and show how to leverage the JavaFX Script language to take advantage of those features. In the next chapter, we start our exploration of JavaFX by discussing the data synchronization support in the JavaFX runtime.

4

Synchronize Data Models—Binding and Triggers

*"Associate reverently and as much as you can,
with your loftiest thoughts."*

—Henry David Thoreau

We've discussed how JavaFX lends itself to separating the UI design from program logic. Ultimately though, you'll need to establish relationships between these two worlds if you want to create an application of any significance. So how is this association achieved in JavaFX? The answer is through *binding*. In this chapter, we'll describe the principle of Java FX binding, explore the semantics of the bind keyword with various JavaFX expressions, and furnish examples demonstrating how binding can and cannot be used. In addition, as they are in many ways related, we'll touch on *triggers* and how they work within JavaFX too.

Binding

It is no mystery that the skill set required by the traditional programmer is often times vastly different than the graphic designer. Yet, expertise in both areas is necessary to create effective Rich Internet Applications. JavaFX encourages a division of labor along these lines such that the graphic designer and programmer could—and arguably should—be different individuals, each with different areas of expertise, working on distinct parts of a problem set. But somewhere along the line the fruits of their labors must be synchronized. This is where the concept of binding comes into play.

If, for example, you want the appearance of your user interface to reflect some state change in your logic, or vice versa, you'll need a way for those differences to percolate over to one another. In JavaFX, the bind keyword is introduced to facilitate this capability. The act of binding a variable associates that variable with an expression, such that whenever the value of the expression changes, its bound variable will automatically change too. This simple yet powerful principle is all that's needed to connect previously disparate models together.

More formally stated, the bind keyword associates the value of a target variable with the value of a remote variable. Binding in JavaFX follows this general syntax:

```
var v = bind expression;
```

where *expression* can be as trivial as another variable or can include a range of legal JavaFX expressions. When the expression on the right hand side of the bind statement changes, a minimal recalculation takes place. We'll examine how binding affects each type of expression and what actually gets calculated on update.

Binding to Variables

Starting with the simplest case first and working our way toward the more complex, the code that follows demonstrates binding in perhaps its most trivial case, namely binding of a variable to another variable:

```
var x : Integer = 10;
var y = bind x;
var z = x;      // z is not bound to x
println("x={x}, y={y}, z={z}");
x = 20;
println("x={x}, y={y}, z={z}");
```

In the preceding example, the variable x is declared as an Integer and assigned an initial value of 10. A second variable y is declared and bound to variable x. Because it is bound to x, the type of y is inferred to be Integer without having to actually declare it as such. When the value of x changes, it forces y to be recalculated—in this instance, reassigned the new value of x.

The statement binding y to x is an example of *unidirectional binding*, meaning that there is a one-way relationship between x and y. When x changes, y changes, but y on the other hand has no influence on x whatsoever. By default, all binds are unidirectional in nature unless they are specified as bidirectional. This is achieved by including the with inverse keywords as part of the bind expression. We'll discuss *bind with inverse* later on in this chapter; suffice it to say, it is traditionally used far less often than the default bind behavior.

In order to contrast between a bound variable and regularly defined variable, a third variable z is introduced. It too is assigned the value of x, but as it is unbound, its value will not change as x changes. Compiling and running this chunk of code produces output as follows:

```
x=10, y=10, z=10
x=20, y=20, z=10
```

Binding to Instance Variables

Variables inside classes can also be bound. To demonstrate, let's make a few modifications to the preceding example code. Instead of having y and z variables defined at the script level, this time they're placed inside a class called myClass. In this case, an instance of myClass has to be created, where within the object literal the binding of instance variable y takes place. Line 6 in the following listing creates the binding.

```
var x : Integer = 10;
class myClass {
    var y : Integer;
    var z : Integer;
};
var m = myClass { y: bind x, z: x };
println("x={x}, m.y={m.y}, m.z={m.z}");
x = 20;
println("x={x}, m.y={m.y}, m.z={m.z}");
```

Not unlike the previous example, an additional instance variable, z, is also defined but unbound to demonstrate that its value does not change as the value of x does. Compiling and running this code block produces this output:

```
x=10, m.y=10, m.z=10
x=20, m.y=20, m.z=10
```

A best effort has been made to assure that the included code blocks contained in this chapter can be compiled and executed in a standalone fashion. When dealing with class definitions, more than likely you'll want to declare them as public. For our examples, we declare the classes without preceding them with the public keyword. Although not ideal, this will facilitate you being able to cut, paste, and execute these code blocks into an IDE without having to modify the code.

When Can a Variable Be Bound?

With the default bind behavior, a variable can only be bound when it is being defined. In JavaFX, this takes place either with a var or def declaration or during object instantiation via object literals. (The topic of binding and object literals, being a bit more complicated, will be discussed later on in this chapter.) Endeavoring to bind in any other fashion will either result in a compiler or runtime error. For example, declaring a variable first and then trying to use bind in an assignment statement like

```
var x : Integer = 10;
var y : Integer;
y = bind x;           // <-- Illegal
```

produces the following compilation error, shortened for the sake of brevity:

```
JavaFX compilation
executing commandline: ...
main.fx:3: Sorry, I was trying to understand an
expression but I got confused when I saw 'bind' which is a
 keyword.
y = bind x;           // <-- Illegal
```

Furthermore, after a variable has been bound, by default it cannot be subsequently reassigned. Attempting to do so will throw an AssignToBoundException when the guilty code is actually run. As an example, the following code will compile successfully:

```
var x : Integer = 10;
var y = bind x;
println("x={x}, y={y}");
y = 15;            // Reassigning a bound variable?
x = 20;
println("x={x}, y={y}");
```

But upon execution, when the assignment of the previously bound variable is encountered, a runtime exception is thrown:

```
x=10, y=10
com.sun.javafx.runtime.AssignToBoundException: Cannot
assign to bound variable
```

```
    at com.sun.javafx.runtime.location.IntVariable.setAsInt
(IntVariable.java:115)
    at main.javafx$run$(main.fx:4)
    at main.javafx$run$(main.fx:4)
```

One way to avoid the previously noted exception would be to use the def keyword, rather than var, to define the binding relationship between x and y. If y were to be defined like

```
def y = bind x;
```

the attempt to reassign y would instead be caught by the JavaFX compiler and flagged as an error at compile time. As an aside, we'll see later on in this chapter that the reassignment restrictions mentioned in this section do not apply when using the *bind with inverse* clause.

Finally, you cannot bind to an operation that would produce side effects. For example,

```
var x = bind y++;
```

is not permitted.

A Simple Example Using Binding

We have thus far been highlighting bind's capabilities by examining small chunks of code. This affords us the ability to focus on the task at hand without having to worry about additional clutter; however, it does not necessarily provide the proper context for how bind might be used in a (slightly) more realistic application. So let's apply what we've learned so far to show how binding can affect what will actually show up on the screen.

The program in Listing 4.1 always displays an image, the contents of which will change depending upon where the mouse is currently located. While running, this program has two states:

1. When the mouse is hovering directly over the image, the image displayed will include text that suggests that in order to change this image, move your mouse outside the image.

2. When the mouse is not hovering over the image, the image displayed will include text which suggests that if you want the current image to change, run your mouse over it.

Listing 4.1   A Sample UI Program Demonstrating the Use of Binding

```
import javafx.stage.Stage;
import javafx.scene.Scene;
import javafx.scene.image.*;
import javafx.scene.input.*;

var image1 = Image {
    url: "{__DIR__}images/mouse-over.png"
}
var image2 = Image {
    url: "{__DIR__}images/mouse-outside.png"
}
var currentImage : Image = image2;

Stage {
    title: "Simple bind"
    scene: Scene{
        height: image1.height * 2
        width: image1.width * 2
        content: [
            ImageView {
                image: bind currentImage
                x: image1.width / 2
                y: image1.height / 2
                onMouseEntered:  function(e : MouseEvent)
                : Void {
                    currentImage = image1;
                }
                onMouseExited: function (e : MouseEvent)
                : Void {
                    currentImage = image2;
                }
            }
        ]
    }
}
```

Figure 4.1 visually depicts what this program would look like when run, and its two possible display states. The image changeover is accomplished in this way:

1. The program creates two instances of the JavaFX Image class, image1 and image2. Their bitmaps are read from a file represented by the url instance variable.

2. At any point in time, the variable currentImage will either point to image1 or image2. Its value is updated whenever the mouse pointer either enters

Figure 4.1   The Two Individual Display States for This Application Depend upon Where the Mouse Is Located

or exits the image on the display. When the mouse pointer enters the image, the onMouseEntered handler will be executed setting the currentImage variable to image1. When the mouse leaves the image, the onMouseExited handler will execute setting currentImage to image2.

3. The actual display is updated by binding the value of currentImage to ImageView's image instance variable. In particular, the line of code represented by image: bind currentImage makes this happen.

Binding with Arithmetic and Logical Expressions

When binding to arithmetic and logical expressions, a bind recalculation takes place if any component of the expression appearing to the right of the bind keyword changes. Let's run through an example to demonstrate:

```
var a = 3;
var b = 4;
var c = a * b;
var d = 7;
var total = bind c + d;
println("total={total}");
d = 10;
println("total={total}");
b = 5;
println("total={total}");
```

prints out:

```
total=19
total=22
total=22
```

The definition of the variable total specifies that its value will be recalculated whenever c or d change. The second line of output (total=22) is the result of a bind recalculation because the value of d changed from 7 to 10. As part of the recalculation, c does not change. Its value is stored and re-retrieved for the sake of that recalculation. For the third line of output, even though b changes, the bound variable total is not recalculated because neither c nor d changed.

In the preceding example, you may have noticed that the variable c is assigned the product of variables a and b. Yet when either component of c changes it does not cause total to be recalculated. It's quite possible that the author really meant to have total updated whenever a, b, or c change. This can be accomplished by replacing c's declaration from

```
var c = a * b;
```

to

```
var c = bind a * b;
```

Now whenever a or b change, c will be updated, which in turn causes total to be recalculated too. This cascading of bound variables is a powerful concept and is one that you'll likely encounter often when examining JavaFX code. Re-running our example with the modified statement yields

```
total=19
total=22
total=25
```

Binding and Conditional Expressions

Binding variables to conditional expressions of the form

```
var v = bind if (conditionalExpression) expr1 else expr2
```

produces a change in which branch of the if-else statement, *expr1* or *expr2*, gets evaluated when *conditionalExpression* changes. Again, resorting to sample code

```
var a = 1;
var b = 2;
var max = bind if (a > b) a else b;
println("max = {max}");
a = 3;
println("max = {max}");
b = 4;
println("max = {max}");
```

demonstrates how one could use binding with a conditional expression to, in effect, compute the maximum value between two variables. In this case, the bound variable max will always contain the larger of the values of a and b. Whenever a or b change, the conditional expression (a > b) will be reevaluated potentially resulting in the update of max. The output of the code above yields

```
max = 2
max = 3
max = 4
```

Binding and Block Expressions

A block expression in JavaFX is a sequence of zero or more statements with a terminating expression enclosed in curly braces. Binding to a block expression takes on this general syntax:

```
var v = bind { [statement;]* expression }
```

As will become important when *bound functions* are discussed later, the terminating expression is the block's return value. In reality, bound blocks are quite restricted in functionality in that the statements inside a bound block are limited to variable declarations only. When trying to use any other type of statement (i.e., assignment, insert, delete, etc.), a compilation error will result. So let's run though a few examples to see what can and can't be done with bound block expressions:

```
class Cell {
    var row : Integer;
    var col : Integer;
}

var r : Integer = 0;
var c : Integer = 0;
var extra : Integer = 0;

var cell1 = bind Cell { row: r, col: c }        // legal
var cell2 = bind { Cell {row: r, col: c } }      // legal
var cell3 = bind { var a : Integer = 3;          // legal
                Cell {row: r*a, col: c }
           }
var cell4 = bind { extra = 1;                     // ILLEGAL
                Cell {row: r, col: c }
           }
```

Binding to Function Calls

So far, we've seen how variables can be bound to arithmetic and logical expressions, and in those cases where the bound expression is a relatively simple one, it makes perfect sense to use these facilities outright. But what if your binding expression is a bit more complex? At this point, you could attempt to fabricate a more complicated binding by combining together any number of arithmetic or logical expressions. For example, expanding upon a previous example, this time instead of binding to an expression that finds the maximum of two variables, a and b, let's bind a variable to the maximum value of three variables, a, b, and c. Using if-else expressions, the assignment statement could look something like this:

```
var max1 = bind if ((a > b) and (a > c)) a else
                if ((b > a) and (b > c)) b else c;
```

It's not exactly the prettiest code, and it won't win you many friends when the time comes for a code review. Instead, one preferable substitute might be to delegate the computation elsewhere and bind to that result. In essence, it would be a lot nicer to bind to a function call. Let's take a look at how this can be done.

First, a getMax() function could be defined, which takes three arguments and returns the value represented by the largest of the three arguments. Next, a new variable, called max2, is defined and bound to a call to getMax(). The alternative to the original messy bind expression now looks like

```
function getMax(i1: Integer, i2: Integer, i3: Integer)
: Integer {
    if ((i1 > i2) and (i1 > i3)) { return i1; }
    else if ((i2 > i1) and (i2 > i3)) { return i2; }
    else { return i3; }
}

var max2 = bind getMax(a, b, c);
```

If either a JavaFX function call or a Java method call is preceded by the bind keyword (in the appropriate context), it will be reevaluated when any of its arguments change. In order to show that the two aforementioned bind statements do the same thing, we'll create two bound variables, max1, which is bound to the compound if-else clause, and max2, which is bound to the getMax() function call, and see what happens when the values of a, b, and c are changed. So:

```
var a = 1;
var b = 2;
var c = 3;
```

```
var max1 = bind if ((a > b) and (a > c)) a else
                if ((b > a) and (b > c)) b else c;

function getMax(i1: Integer, i2: Integer, i3: Integer)
: Integer {
    if ((i1 > i2) and (i1 > i3)) { return i1; }
    else if ((i2 > i1) and (i2 > i3)) { return i2; }
    else { return i3; }
}

var max2 = bind getMax(a, b, c);

println("max1={max1}, max2={max2}");
a = 4;
println("max1-[max1], max2-[max2]");
b = 5;
println("max1={max1}, max2={max2}");
c = 2;
println("max1={max1}, max2={max2}");
```

outputs the same values for each bound variable:

```
max1=3, max2=3
max1=4, max2=4
max1=5, max2=5
max1=5, max2=5
```

Binding and For Expressions

You can use the for expression to bind JavaFX sequences. For example, the following lines will create a sequence called seq, of length 5, where the elements are [0, 1, 2, 3, 4].

```
var val = 0;
function incrementVal() : Integer {
    return val++;
}
var start = 0;
var end = 4;
var seq = bind for (x in [start..end]) incrementVal();
println(seq);
```

A change in value for either variable, start or end, will also change the bound sequence seq too. Next, we'll step through changes to start and end to see how that affects what seq looks like. Furthermore, because the incrementVal() function always returns an element with a value one greater than its previous call, we'll be able to determine when elements are recalculated. So on to the changes.

```
start = 1; println(seq);
```

This removes the first element of seq, and will not cause any other recalculations. The contents of seq now look like

```
[ 1, 2, 3, 4 ]
```

Changing the value of end from 4 to 5:

```
end = 5; println(seq);
```

will change the sequence, inserting a new element at index 4. Only the new element (value=5) is recalculated. The contents of seq are now

```
[ 1, 2, 3, 4, 5 ]
```

Finally, let's set start back to 0.

```
start = 0; println(seq);
```

This changes seq once again, this time inserting a new element at index 0. The new element needs a recalculation, but no other recalculation is required. seq now looks like:

```
[ 6, 1, 2, 3, 4, 5 ]
```

One corner case with binding sequences and for expressions involves use of the indexof operator. Combining all of the preceding code, and modifying just the bind statement (emboldened below) to include the indexof expression, yields sequences of the same size, but significantly different contents. In essence, any time the start variable changes, all elements are recalculated. Here's what the set of code looks like now

```
var val = 0;
function incrementVal() : Integer {
    return val++;
}

var start = 0;
var end = 4;
var seq = bind for (x in [start..end] where indexof x >= 0)
                incrementVal();
```

```
println(seq);
start = 1;
println(seq);
end = 5;
println(seq);
start = 0;
println(seq);
```

And here's the output demonstrating how `seq` changes:

```
[ 0, 1, 2, 3, 4 ]
[ 5, 6, 7, 8 ]
[ 5, 6, 7, 8, 9 ]
[ 10, 11, 12, 13, 14, 15 ]
```

Bidirectional Binding

JavaFX binding, by default, is unidirectional in nature—that is, a bound variable is dependent upon its binding expression—whereas conversely, a bound expression has no dependency at all on the variable it binds to. Early on in this chapter we demonstrated that after a variable is bound with the default bind behavior, any attempt to reassign it will result in an `AssignToBoundException`. The classic UI example shown in Listing 4.2 brings this point home.

Listing 4.2   A Simple UI Program Highlighting the Limitations of Unidirectional Binding

```
import javafx.stage.Stage;
import javafx.scene.Scene;
import javafx.ext.swing.SwingTextField;

var str = "Change me";
Stage {
    title: "Unidirectional Binding"
    scene: Scene {
        content: [
            SwingTextField {
                columns: 25
                text: bind str
                editable: true
            }
        ]
    }
}
```

Upon execution, this program displays an editable TextField containing the text "Change me". Unfortunately, if you try and type anything inside that TextField, an AssignToBoundException will be thrown. Why? Because whenever the text inside the TextField is changed, its text instance variable changes automatically too. Because text is bound to str, this activity tries to reassign a bound variable causing the exception. Initially, the application appears like that shown in Figure 4.2.

Figure 4.2   Initial Appearance of the TextField

Figure 4.3 shows what happens when you click on the TextField and clear the string.

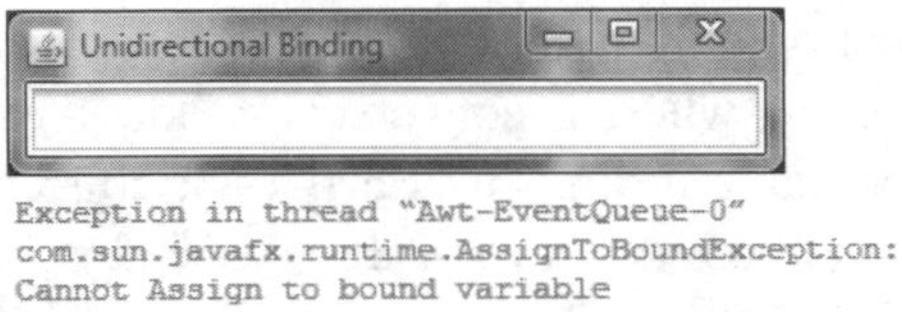

```
Exception in thread "Awt-EventQueue-0"
com.sun.javafx.runtime.AssignToBoundException:
Cannot Assign to bound variable
```

Figure 4.3   Clearing the TextField Throws an Exception

In situations like this, it would be nice if the binding relationship between str and text was bidirectional—that is, a change to *either* variable would automatically update the other. This is possible in JavaFX by using the with inverse phrase when binding. By replacing

```
text: bind str
```

with

```
text: bind str with inverse
```

a bidirectional relationship is created. With this modification, you'll now be able to modify the TextField without worry. When the program begins, the text instance variable is assigned the value of str ("Change me"), and when you change the contents of the TextField, its text instance variable and the str variable will reflect the change. Listing 4.3 contains the new version of the program.

Listing 4.3   A Simple UI Program Demonstrating Bind with Inverse

```
import javafx.stage.Stage;
import javafx.scene.Scene;
import javafx.ext.swing.SwingTextField;

var str = "Change me";
Stage {
    title: "Bind with inverse"
    scene: Scene {
        content: [
            SwingTextField {
                columns: 25
                text: bind str with inverse
                editable: true
            }
        ]
    }
}
```

Not all too different from the first, Figure 4.4 shows what the new program looks like at startup.

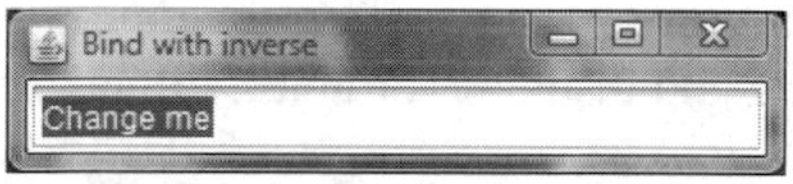

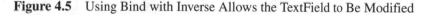

Figure 4.4   Initial Appearance of UI Using Bind with Inverse

This time, the TextField can be modified with no ill effects, as demonstrated by Figure 4.5.

Figure 4.5   Using Bind with Inverse Allows the TextField to Be Modified

One final point worth mentioning about the *bind with inverse* construct is that it is limited to variable declarations. Attempting to use any other type of expression in this context will result in a compile time error.

Advanced Binding Topics

Some of bind options offered in this section are considerably more complex, and in some cases due to side effects and/or limitations, should be used sparingly.

Binding and Object Literals

In JavaFX, the preferred mechanism for instantiating objects is via the object literal. Alongside variable declarations, object literals represent the second and final binding option available for developers. We've already seen how to bind instance variables via object literals. This is normal and expected behavior. But in addition to binding instance variables, it's also possible to bind entire objects. For this section, we'll first state the three possible ways in which object literals can be bound, then follow up with concrete examples.

Object literals can be bound as a whole. In this case, a change to any of an object's instance variables will result in the creation of a new object instance with the recalculated values.

Individual instance variables inside object literals can be bound. When instance variables are bound, recalculations will update the values of bound variables but will *not* result in the creation of a new object instance. Again, this is the expected way in which binding and instance variables will take place.

A combination of individual instance variables or whole objects can be bound. In this scenario, by default, a change to any instance variable will result in the creation of a new object *except* for those instance variables that are themselves bound.

A few examples here should go a long way in illustrating the various binding scenarios that are available to object literals and their instance variables. Included as part of these examples, we'll demonstrate whether the bind recalculations result in the creation of a new object.

First, let's define a simple class that will be used throughout to illustrate object literal binding.

```
class EmpRec {
    public var name : String;
    public var id : Integer;
    public var label : String;
    public function print() : Void {
        println(" obj={label}, name={name}, id={id}");
    }
    init {
```

```
        println(" New instance created for {label}");
    }
};
```

Aside from the definition of the `name` and `id` instance variables, a third called `label`, is utilized. It will not, per se, be one of the variables we'll attempt to bind in the examples that follow, rather it will simply be used to label and differentiate between object instances of the `EmpRec` class. As described by the preceding sidebar, the `init` block gets executed whenever a new object is instantiated. This enables us to output exactly when a new `EmpRec` object is created, and by including the `label` variable in the print statement, we'll know which object was recreated as the result of a bind recalculation. So let's start by declaring a few instances of `EmpRec`:

```
var er1 = bind EmpRec {
    label: "er1"
    name: myName
    id: myID
};
```

The first variable, `er1`, instantiates `EmpRec` and is bound to the object as a whole. A change to any instance variable inside `er1` will result in the creation of a new object. This is accomplished in JavaFX by preceding the `EmpRec` object literal instantiation with the `bind` keyword.

Determining When an Object Has Been Recreated

There may be situations where you'll want to know when new objects are created, possibly due to a bind recalculation. So how can you figure out when this takes place? Unlike the Java programming language, JavaFX does not support constructors; however, within a JavaFX class definition, you can provide a code block preceded by the `init` keyword at the function definition level. The `init` block is executed whenever a new object of this type is instantiated. So by defining a class like

```
class MyClass {
    public var attr : Integer;
    init {
        println(
            "A new instance of MyClass is born"
        );
    }
};
```

you'll be able to see when objects are created because "A new instance of MyClass is born" will be printed out every time **MyClass** is instantiated.

```
var er2 = EmpRec {
    label: "er2"
    name: bind myName
    id: myID
};
```

The second declaration shows how to bind an individual instance variable of an object literal instead of the whole object. Specifically, name is bound to the external variable myName. A change to the value of myName causes a recalculation of the name variable without recreating the er2 object. As the id variable is unbound, a change to the myID external variable will not cause any recalculation at all. Instance variable binding is enabled by placing the bind keyword inside the object literal on the instance variables of interest.

```
var er3 = bind EmpRec {
    label: "er3"
    name: bind myName
    id: myID
};
```

The third declaration combines both whole object and instance variable binding. In this scenario, variables that aren't specifically bound will, when a recalculation takes place, cause a new object to be created. If, on the other hand, an instance variable is bound, a recalculation will update the variable without causing the object to be recreated. In effect, the instance variable bind trumps the overall object literal bind. In the preceding declaration, any update to the myID external variable will trigger an object recreation, whereas any update to myName will cause a recalculation without object recreation. So fleshing this out a little and executing the code snippet

```
var myName : String = "Jack";
var myID : Integer = 123;
var er1 = bind EmpRec {
    label: "er1"
    name: myName
    id: myID
};
var er2 = EmpRec {
    label: "er2"
    name: bind myName
    id: myID
};
var er3 = bind EmpRec {
    label: "er3"
    name: bind myName
    id: myID
};
```

```
er1.print();
er2.print();
er3.print();
```

produces this output:

```
New instance created for er1
New instance created for er2
New instance created for er3
obj=er1, name=Jack, id=123
obj=er2, name=Jack, id=123
obj=er3, name=Jack, id=123
```

Changing the myName external variable from "Jack" to "Jill" causes a bind recalculation on all three EmpRec objects, and in one case an object recreation. Executing this code:

```
myName = "Jill";
er1.print();
er2.print();
er3.print();
```

yields the following:

```
New instance created for er1
obj=er1, name=Jill, id=123
obj=er2, name=Jill, id=123
obj=er3, name=Jill, id=123
```

Finally, changing the myID external variable from 123 to 456 results in a recalculation and object recreation on er1 and er3. For er2, no changes take place at all, because er2's id attribute is unbound. Running this code:

```
myID = 456;
er1.print();
er2.print();
er3.print();
```

outputs this:

```
New instance created for er1
New instance created for er3
obj=er1, name=Jill, id=456
obj=er2, name=Jill, id=123
obj=er3, name=Jill, id=456
```

Bound Functions

Our first brush with `bind` and JavaFX functions demonstrated how to bind to an ordinary function. Bound functions and ordinary functions are similar in that both, when part of a `bind` expression, will be recalculated if their arguments change. However, they differ in one key area, namely how to interpret changes inside the function body. Binding to ordinary functions treats the function body as a black box. An internal change to the function body will *not* cause the function to be re-invoked. A bound function on the other hand will see changes both at the argument level *and* inside the function causing it to get re-invoked. So let's see how this plays out with a concrete example.

```
class Cell {
    public var row : Integer;
    public var col : Integer;
}

var translate = 0;

function moveToUnBound(r : Integer, c : Integer) : Cell {
    return Cell {
        row: r + translate;
        col: c + translate;
    }
}

bound function moveToBound(r : Integer, c : Integer)
    : Cell {
    return Cell {
        row: r + translate;
        col: c + translate;
    }
}

var r = 0;
var c = 0;
var cell1 = bind moveToUnBound(r, c);
var cell2 = bind moveToBound(r, c);
println("cell1: row={cell1.row}, col={cell1.col}");
println("cell2: row={cell2.row}, col={cell2.col}");
r = 5; c = 5;
println("cell1: row={cell1.row}, col={cell1.col}");
println("cell2: row={cell2.row}, col={cell2.col}");
translate = 7;
println("cell1: row={cell1.row}, col={cell1.col}");
println("cell2: row={cell2.row}, col={cell2.col}");
```

Here are two nearly identical functions, the only difference being that moveTo-Bound() is preceded with the bound keyword, whereas moveToUnBound() is not. This subtle difference does affect how the variables cell1 and cell2 are evaluated. First, a change in the value of the arguments (r and c set to 5) causes both functions to be re-invoked (twice) resulting in new and updated cell1 and cell2 instances. However, when the value of translate is changed, the behavior of the bound and unbound functions diverge. The moveToUnBound() function is unaware of any change to the translate variable and is consequently not re-invoked, whereas moveToBound() is re-invoked because the bound function can detect the change in translate. Here's the output of this script:

```
cell1: row=0, col=0
cell2: row=0, col=0
cell1: row=5, col=5
cell2: row=5, col=5
cell1: row=5, col=5
cell2: row=12, col=12
```

An important point regarding bound functions is that the function body is no different than the previously discussed *bound block expression* (with all of its limitations). The last expression—typically the only expression—inside the function body is the bound function's return value. Finally, bound functions may be invoked outside the context of a bind expression. Calling a bound function in this way is no different than calling a regular, plain old function.

Triggers

JavaFX includes a mechanism that facilitates the catching and handling of data modification events. By adding a *trigger* to a variable, you associate a block of code that will be executed every time the variable is modified. A trigger is formally introduced to a variable declaration by appending a phrase starting with the keywords on replace. Although strongly discouraged, a trigger, in its most rudimentary form, can be used to mimic the behavior of *bind*. For example, the following statements:

```
var x : String;
var y = bind x;
```

can be re-written using triggers in a nearly equivalent manner:

```
var x : String on replace {
    y = x;
}
var y : String;
```

Every time that x is modified, it will run the block of code specified by the on replace phrase, essentially keeping y in lock step with x. However, there is one fundamental difference between the two solutions. Recall that earlier in this chapter it was shown that it is illegal to reassign bound variables by default, and with our trigger example, for better or worse, that restriction is removed. For example:

```
class Lyric {
    public var phrase : String on replace {
        s = phrase;
    }
}
var l = Lyric { phrase: "so long" };
var s : String;
println("phrase={l.phrase}, s={s}");
l.phrase = "farewell";
println("phrase={l.phrase}, s={s}");
// would be illegal if s = bind l.phrase
s = "auf Wiedersehen";
println("phrase={l.phrase}, s={s}");
l.phrase = "farewell";
println("phrase={l.phrase}, s={s}");
l.phrase = "good night";
println("phrase={l.phrase}, s={s}");
```

prints out:

```
phrase=so long, s=
phrase=farewell, s=farewell
phrase=farewell, s=auf Wiedersehen
phrase=farewell, s=auf Wiedersehen
phrase=good night, s=good night
```

Among others, a few important things to point out here are

1. Even though the variable s is reassigned every time l.phrase changes, the first line of output shows that they are different. Why? Because l is declared and instantiated first. At the time of instantiation, l is modified, but the trigger can't update s, because s hasn't been defined yet.

2. The variable s can be reassigned, temporarily un-synchronizing it from l.phrase.

3. The on replace block will not be executed *until* the value of the phrase instance variable changes, regardless of whether it subsequently appears on the left hand side of an assignment statement. This is evidenced by the fact that the second assignment of l.phrase="farewell" does not cause s to be resynchronized with l.phrase.

Given a choice between `bind` or `on replace`, you'll almost always want to choose `bind`. In addition to being more efficient, you'll have the added benefit of avoiding the unsynchronized condition identified in the preceding example. In general, `on replace` should only be used when there is no alternative. Triggers are appropriate, for example, when state needs to be synchronized between JavaFX and Java, or when there are ancillary effects that need to be dealt with resulting from a change in the value of a variable. For example, if you need to run an animation sequence, your trigger might look like

```
var image: ImageView = bind ImageView {

    image: currentImage

} on replace {
    imageAnimation.play();
}
```

For the next example, we'll expand on trigger usage by introducing two additional capabilities. First, just like plain variables, triggers can also operate on sequences. Second, the `on replace` phrase can be enhanced so that while executing the trigger code block, you can access the old value of the variable being replaced. In the example that follows, `oldRainbow` is an arbitrarily named variable of the same type as `rainbow`. It appears directly after `on replace`, and upon execution of the code block, it contains the value of rainbow before it is replaced.

Determining If a Variable or Instance Variable Has Been Updated

As explained in an earlier sidebar, there may be times when you want to know when an object has been recreated. Alongside that information, you may also want to know when a variable or instance variable has been updated, possibly due to a bind recalculation. In JavaFX, you can append a trigger with an associated block of code onto a variable declaration such that whenever its value changes that code will be executed. By defining an instance variable to look like

```
class MyClass {
    public var attr : String on replace {
        println("attr updated to {attr}");
    }
}
```

you'll be able to know when `attr` changes because "attr updated to …" will be printed out every time `attr` is modified.

```
var rainbow : String[] = [
    "red", "orange", "yellow", "green", "blue", "violet"
    ] on replace oldRainbow
{
    print("old rainbow: "); println(oldRainbow);
    print("new rainbow: "); println(rainbow);
};
insert "indigo" after rainbow[4];
delete "violet" from rainbow;
insert "purple" into rainbow;
```

The output of this code is as follows:

```
old rainbow: [ ]
new rainbow: [ red, orange, yellow, green, blue, violet ]
old rainbow: [ red, orange, yellow, green, blue, violet ]
new rainbow: [ red, orange, yellow, green, blue, indigo,
  violet ]
old rainbow: [ red, orange, yellow, green, blue, indigo,
  violet ]
new rainbow: [ red, orange, yellow, green, blue, indigo ]
old rainbow: [ red, orange, yellow, green, blue, indigo ]
new rainbow: [ red, orange, yellow, green, blue, indigo,
  purple ]
```

Be Careful When Using Bind/Triggers on Local Variables

When using bind/triggers on local variables, you may come across a situation where the variable is out of scope, yet the trigger still exists. To demonstrate, let's look at the following pseudo code:

```
function doit() {
    var result = SomeAsynchronousFunction { ... };
    var myInput = bind result.data on replace {
        ...
    };
}
```

A call to the SomeAsynchronousFunction() will set the result object's data instance variable. Because, as its name implies, the function is asynchronous, there's a good chance that by the time SomeAsynchronousFunction() returns, the local variable myInput will be out of scope. So what happens here? Theoretically, the bind and trigger should cease to exist after the variable is out of scope. In reality, however, the trigger keeps on working until the variable has been garbage collected. Quite a few already have been bitten by this problem, which is difficult to debug. If at all possible, avoid such a construct.

Our final example demonstrates the full power of triggers as it deals with an assignment of a sequence slice:

```
var s1 : Integer[] = [ 2,4,6,8,10 ] on replace

s1Orig[begin..end]=n
{
    s2[begin..end] = s1[begin..end];
}
var s2 : Integer[];
print("s1: "); println(s1);
print("s2: "); println(s2);
s1[0..2] = [3,6,9];
print("s1: "); println(s1);
print("s2: "); println(s2);
delete s1[0..2];
print("s1: "); println(s1);
print("s2: "); println(s2);
```

The trigger contains five arbitrarily named variables, and in the context of this example, they have the following meanings:

s1 is the sequence after all the changes have been applied.

s1Orig represents the previous value of the s1 sequence. As such, it is the same type as s1.

begin is the first index of the sequence slice that has been updated.

end is the last index of the sequence slice that has been updated. Both begin and end are Integer types.

n represents the sequence of values that will be replacing the slice of s1Orig[begin..end].

The output of this code looks like this:

```
s1: [ 2, 4, 6, 8, 10 ]
s2: [ ]
s1: [ 3, 6, 9, 8, 10 ]
s2: [ 3, 6, 9 ]
s1: [ 8, 10 ]
s2: [ 8, 10 ]
```

For our final example, we'll contrast how bind and on replace behave when instance variables are inherited and overridden from a superclass. The code block that follows contains two classes, the first of which, called MyClass, contains a public name variable that is both bound and has a trigger. The second class, called MyClassExtended, extends MyClass and overrides name with a bind and a trigger too.

```
class MyClass {
public var foo:String = "Jim";
    public var name: String = bind foo on replace {
        println("MyClass: name={name}");
    };
}

class MyClassExtended extends MyClass {
    public var bar:String = "Eric";
    override var name = bind bar on replace {
        println("MyClassExtended: name={name}");
    };
}

var m2 = MyClassExtended {};
m2.bar = "Joe";
```

This is the output when the block is executed:

```
MyClass: name=
MyClassExtended: name=
MyClass: name=Eric
MyClassExtended: name=Eric
MyClass: name=Joe
MyClassExtended: name=Joe
```

From this example, we can glean that triggers and bound variables, when overridden, behave quite differently. To sum it up:

Overridden triggers are cumulative. When an instance variable with a trigger is overridden by a superclass with another trigger, the original trigger is not hidden. It also gets executed along with the overridden trigger. Based on the output, the base class trigger will be executed first, followed by the superclass trigger(s).

Overridden bound variables are hidden. A bound instance variable in a superclass will be re-evaluated by the overridden subclass instance variable. In our example, when MyClassExtended is instantiated, the value of its name instance variable is the same for both the MyClassExtended subclass object and the MyClass base object.

Coming Features

If you had a chance to try pre-release versions of JavaFX, you may have encountered a feature known as *lazy binding*. With the formal release of JavaFX 1.1, references to this aspect of the language have been removed because it was only partially implemented. Specifically, work has yet to be done for sequences. Plans call for full support by the next JavaFX release. In the interim, you can experiment with some of the capabilities of lazy binding, keeping in mind that it is currently not supported.

The primary difference between regular binding and lazy binding lies in how and when updates occur. With lazy binding, an update or bind recalculation *only* takes place when the variable being bound to is being accessed. Whereas with regular binding, any change to the bound expression automatically forces an update. The performance impact of limiting the number of bind calculations can be important. We'll touch more on this in a moment.

Listing 4.4 highlights how these two forms of binding differ.

Listing 4.4   Comparing Lazy Binding to Regular Binding

```
var x : Integer = 1 on replace oldValue {
    println("x: {oldValue} -> {x}")
};
var y : Integer = bind x + 1 on replace oldValue
{
    println("y: {oldValue} -> {y}")
};
var z : Integer = bind lazy y + 1 on replace oldValue
{
    println("z: {oldValue} -> {z}")
};

println("Starting");
println("Reading z"); println("z: {z}");
println("Modify x");
x = 2;
println("Reading z"); println("z: {z}");
```

The listing includes three variables. The first two, x and y, use traditional binding, whereas the third, z, uses lazy binding as specified by the bind lazy keyword sequence. Each variable has a trigger associated with it such that whenever its value changes, it will be printed. When this code is executed, the output validates that z, which is bound lazily, is only updated when it is being accessed via the `println("z: {z}");` statement, while any change to x and y results in an unconditional update.

```
x: 0 -> 1

y: 0 -> 2
Starting
Reading z
z: 0 -> 3
z: 3
Modify x
y: 2 -> 3
x: 1 -> 2
Reading z
z: 3 -> 4
z: 4
```

The performance ramifications of using lazy binding can be significant. Consider the following code that includes a loop that is iterated over 10,000 times.

```
var v1 = 0;
var v2 = bind v1;
for(i in [1..10000]) {
    v1 = i;
}
println(v2);
```

Because v2 is bound to v1, it will be automatically updated for each of the 10,000 loop iterations. Because v2 is not referenced at all within the loop, those recalculations represent a waste of CPU cycles. The developer might have been better served using lazy binding and avoiding all those unnecessary updates.

With the advent of lazy binding, one might ask, why not just have all bindings be lazy? The answer is that there will be occasions where you'll want to know about a change in value when it actually happens. With lazy binding, as updates only occur when the bound variable in question is accessed, this is not possible.

Chapter Summary

In this chapter, we looked at how binding can be used in JavaFX to associate unrelated entities such that changes in one can be reflected in the other. To achieve more clarity, this chapter deliberately focuses more on the language syntax and deals less with the user interface aspects of the platform. Don't worry. As we progress forward, you'll be able to apply what you've learned to solve more realistic problems.

Create User
Interfaces

"One difference between poetry and lyrics is that lyrics sort of fade into the background. They fade on the page and live on the stage when set to music."

—Stephen Sondheim

User Interfaces

The primary focus of JavaFX is to provide a platform to easily and quickly develop cool user interfaces. The goal is to create appealing user interaction that engages the user's full senses and leaves the user with a positive impression. At the core of this is JavaFX's user interface classes.

JavaFX employs a theater metaphor within the JavaFX user interface framework. There is a *stage* that provides space for the action and presents a focal point for the user. A *scene* represents a slice of the action or discrete unit of the application. A *layout* positions the individual components within a scene.

In this chapter, we will cover the key elements required to build a user interface in JavaFX. This chapter covers the basic user interface components, whereas subsequent chapters will discuss animations, special effects, and multimedia features. To begin, you must first define your *stage*.

The Stage

The `javafx.stage.Stage` class is the topmost container for a JavaFX display. It insulates the underlying implementation from the JavaFX developer so it can be readily reused on multiple platforms such as desktop, mobile phone, or a television set top box. In a desktop environment, the Stage parallels a window in the windowing system.

A stage has a title and geometry, may or may not have decorations (the window border, etc.), and may be resizable. The code in Listing 5.1 creates an empty stage that is shown in Figure 5.1.

Listing 5.1   Empty Stage

```
import javafx.stage.Stage;

Stage {
    title: "An empty stage"
    width: 250
    height: 80
}
```

Let's modify this empty stage to place it at position 150,150, change the title, and set resizable to false, so that the stage cannot be resized by the user. Notice that we set visible to true, which is already the default value, but if we did not want to display this stage at a specific instant, we could have set this to false. This is shown in Listing 5.2.

Listing 5.2   Unsizable Stage

```
Stage {
    title: "An empty unsizable stage"
    x: 150
    y: 150
    width: 400
    height: 80
    resizable: false // default is true
    visible: true // default is true
}
```

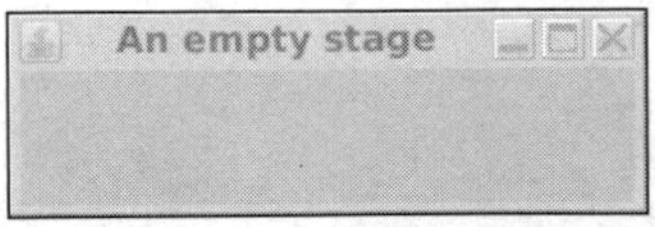

Figure 5.1   Empty Stage

There are also options to set the stage style to DECORATED, UNDECORATED, or TRANSPARENT. DECORATED is the default, and defines a stage with a solid background with platform-specific decorations. On a desktop, this would be the window border and title and the maximize, minimize, and close controls. UNDECORATED is a solid white background with no platform specific decorations. TRANSPARENT defines a stage with a transparent background with no decorations.

```
Stage {
    style: StageStyle.UNDECORATED
    ...
}
```

We have already seen a DECORATED style in Figure 5.1. By setting the style to UNDECORATED, the surrounding decoration, the border, the controls for minimize, maximize, and close, and the title are no longer shown (see Figure 5.2). Just a rectangular area with a white background color appears. In this example, we added the text "JavaFX – Developing Rich Internet Applications".

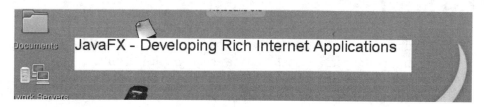

Figure 5.2   Undecorated Stage on Desktop

The TRANSPARENT style sets the window into a transparent mode without any decorations.

```
Stage {
    style: StageStype.TRANSPARENT
    ...
}
```

Here, there is no visible background region. Figure 5.3 shows this.

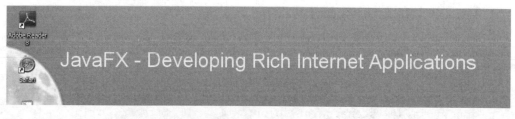

Figure 5.3   Transparent Stage on Desktop

Only the text "JavaFX – Developing Rich Internet Applications" is displayed on the desktop. To achieve this, there was one more thing we had to do. We had to also set the fill for the Scene to null. We will cover this in the next section on the Scene class.

!!!

Developer Warning: TRANSPARENT may not be supported on all platforms. If it is not supported, it will show the same as UNDECORATED.

It is possible to have multiple stages defined for an application. Some may be visible, some not. A stage may acquire the focus and become active. Actions, like mouse presses, may cause a stage to appear or close. If the platform supports it, the stage may fade in or fade out by changing its opacity. The contents of a stage can change during the life of the application. Of course, an empty stage is the same as a dark theater. There is no reason to go there; we need a scene.

The Scene

The Scene, javafx.scene.Scene, is the top-level node within a scene graph. Representing the entire visual scene, a scene graph is a collection of nodes in a hierarchal tree graph. The scene has geometry, a fill paint for the background, a mouse cursor setting, and optionally a set of cascading style sheets (CSS) that may be used by the scene's components.

The scene's geometry represents the area within the stage's region that is available for displaying components. If the stage is resized, the scene will be resized accordingly. Using the scene's geometry, you can position components within the scene to make sure they are fully visible.

Listing 5.3 displays the stage's and scene's geometry, side by side, for comparison (see Figure 5.4). This information is displayed using a Text node that is horizontally centered. As the stage is resized, the display automatically updates with the new geometry for both the stage and scene and repositions the text in the horizontal middle.

Listing 5.3   Stage and Scene Geometry

```
import javafx.stage.Stage;
import javafx.scene.Scene;
import javafx.scene.text.Text;
import javafx.scene.text.TextOrigin;
import javafx.scene.text.Font;
import javafx.scene.paint.Color;
```

```
var scene:Scene;
var text:Text;
var stage:Stage = Stage {
    title: "Stage and Scene Geometry"
    x: 250
    y: 150
    width: 800
    height: 100
    scene: scene = Scene{
        fill: Color.NAVY
        content: text = Text {
            translateX: bind
                (scene.width-text.layoutBounds.width) / 2 -
                text.layoutBounds.minX
            translateY: 24
            fill: Color.YELLOW
            textOrigin: TextOrigin.TOP
            font: Font { size: 24 }
            content: bind
                "Stage: [{stage.x},{stage.y}] , "
                "[{stage.width}, {stage.height}]"
                "Scene: [{scene.x},{scene.y}] , "
                "[{scene.width}, {scene.height}]"
        }
    }
}
```

```
Stage and Scene Geometry                                      _ □ ×

Stage: [250.0,150.0] , [800.0, 100.0] Scene: [5.0,23.0] ,[790.0, 72.0]
```

Figure 5.4   Stage and Scene Geometry

To accomplish the repositioning, we first assigned the Scene instance to the script variable scene. Then we used the instance variable, scene.width, to calculate the start position for the Text. We had to use a bind, because the scene's geometry will change, at least initially, from zero width and height to the width and height based on the stage's geometry.

Notice that the stage's position, [250,150], is relative to the desktop coordinate space, whereas the scene's position, [5, 23], is relative to the stage's coordinate space. Also, the scene's width, (790), and height, (72), is less than the stage's width, (800), and height, (100). This takes into account the border space taken up by the stage that is not available to the scene for rendering graphical nodes.

When the stage is resized, the scene's width and height will also be automatically recalculated and through binding, we quickly see the new geometry and the recalculated text position, to keep it centered (see Figure 5.5).

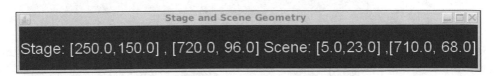

Figure 5.5   Stage and Scene Geometry – Stage Resized

In the preceding example, also notice that we set the stage's fill to navy blue, so the entire background is painted with this color. This is shown as a black background in Figures 5.4 and 5.5. For a full color view of these figures, please check out the book's Web site at http://jfxbook.com. The default color is white. You can also set the fill to null or transparent by using Color.TRANSPARENT. The color displayed when setting it to one of these two values is platform dependent. When we used the StageStype.TRANSPARENT option as shown in Figure 5.3, we also had to set the scene's fill to null so that the default fill of white would not fill the rectangular area represented by the scene. Listing 5.4 shows a TRANSPARENT stage with an invisible background.

Listing 5.4   Transparent Stage

```
Stage {
    title: "TRANSPARENT Stage"
    x: 250
    y: 150
    width: 800
    height: 100
    style: StageStyle.TRANSPARENT
    scene: Scene{
        fill: null
        content: Text {
            fill: Color.YELLOW
            textOrigin: TextOrigin.TOP
            font: Font { size: 36 }
            content:
    "JavaFX - Developing Rich Internet Applications"
        }
    }
}
```

The choice for null or `Color.TRANSPARENT` does not matter for a `Scene`; however, it does matter later on with `Nodes`. The main difference is that mouse events will not be delivered to a node with a null fill when the mouse is over the invisible part of the node. On the other hand, if the fill is `Color.TRANSPARENT`, mouse events will be delivered to the node, even if the mouse is over the invisible part. This is because `Color.TRANSPARENT` is actually a valid color being black with opacity of zero—therefore, it is a color that appears invisible.

In addition to the fill paint, the scene also allows you to set the `Cursor` style for the entire scene. The default is null indicating that the System default cursor will be used. The options from the `javafx.scene.Cursor` class are `default`, `wait`, `crosshair`, `hand`, `move`, and `text`. There is also a set for the resize cursors based on compass direction: `east`, `north`, `northeast`, `northwest`, `west`, `southwest`, `south`, and `southeast`, and `vertical` and `horizontal`. Of course, there is also an option for no cursor at all.

Style Sheets

Cascading style sheets (CSS) are commonly used on the Web to partition content from presentation. This provides flexibility to easily change the presentation qualities without modifying the code that provides the basic content and behavior. A style sheet is a set of rules that control how to display elements. Each rule is made up of a selector that matches an element and a set of properties with values that define the presentation settings for the selected element. JavaFX includes support for style sheets, but there are some minor differences from their HTML cousins.

The most obvious difference is that instead of using HTML or XML elements for the selector, JavaFX uses the JavaFX class names. These can be fully qualified class names enclosed in double quotes, or for the standard JavaFX user interface classes, you can just use the base class name. For example, `javafx.scene.shape.Rectangle` or `Rectangle` will resolve equally.

For CSS ID selectors, instead of using the XML `id` attribute, JavaFX uses the Node's `id` variable. CSS class selectors are similar to the way they are used in HTML. CSS pseudo-classes are defined on certain Boolean instance variables within the JavaFX `Control` and `Skin` classes. To use a style sheet, include its URL in the `Scene`'s `stylesheet` instance variable. There may be zero or more style sheet URL strings.

There are several ways to use a style on a display node. First, you can set the node's `id` attribute to match the CSS ID selector. Secondly, you can include the style in the node's `style` variable. Lastly, you can include the CSS class in the node's `styleclass` variable. Listing 5.5 shows a style sheet that uses a CSS ID selector.

Listing 5.5   Style Sheet CSS ID Selector

```
/* MyStyle.css *./
"javafx.scene.text.Text"#MainText {
    fill: navy;
    font:bold italic 35pt "sans-serif";
}
```

This creates a CSS ID selector for the JavaFX `Text` class, named `MainText`. The fill is navy blue with a bold italic sans serif font. To use this in JavaFX, include the style sheet URL in the `Scene` object literal and add an ID to the `Text` display node to match the ID declaration. Listing 5.6 demonstrates how this is done.

Listing 5.6   JavaFX Class Using Node ID to Match the CSS ID in the Style Sheet

```
/* Main.fx */
Stage {
    title: "Style Sheet Demo"
    width: 500
    height: 80
    scene: Scene {
        stylesheets: ["{__DIR__}MyStyle.css"]
        content: Text {
            id: "MainText"
            x: 10, y: 30
            content: "This shows my style"
        }
    }
}
```

This `Text` node is created with an ID to match the style sheet's ID selector, "MainText". When run, this displays the text in bold italic sans serif font with a size of 35 points (see Figure 5.6).

Figure 5.6   Using Style Sheets

In the style sheet file, besides using the fully qualified class name for `javafx` `.scene.text.Text`, you can also just use the basic class name `Text`. This is true for all the standard JavaFX user interface classes. Notice that when you use the fully qualified class name, it needs to be enclosed in double quotes. This is so the CSS parser can distinguish it from a CSS class selector. The alternative style for our text example is shown in Listing 5.7.

Listing 5.7　Style Sheet – Short Class Name for JavaFX Standard Classes

```
/* MyStyle.css */
Text#MainText {
    fill: navy;
    font:bold italic 35pt "sans-serif";
}
```

Another way to define styles is to use CSS class selectors. You do this by defining a CSS class selector, then by using it with the `styleClass` instance variable of the display node. Listing 5.8 shows how to create a CSS class of `PrimaryText` on the `Text` class.

Listing 5.8　Style Sheet CSS Class Selector

```
/* MyStyle.css */
Text.PrimaryText {
    fill: navy;
    font:bold italic 35pt "sans-serif";
}
```

This is then used in the object literal for the text by initializing the `styleClass` instance variable with the name of the CSS class. Listing 5.9 shows how to use this in a JavaFX object literal.

Listing 5.9　JavaFX styleClass for CSS Class Selector

```
/* Main.fx */
...
...
Text {
    styleClass: "PrimaryText"
    x: 10, y: 30
    content: "This shows my style"
}
...
```

A third alternative is to use an in-line string with the style settings. This is done using the `style` instance variable in the display node's object literal. For instance, Listing 5.10 shows using a `style` with a `Text` node.

Listing 5.10   Node Style Instance Variable

```
/* Main.fx */
...
...
Text {
    style: "fill: navy; "
           "font:bold italic 35pt sans-serif;"
    x: 10, y: 30
    content: "This shows my style"
}
...
```

When using the node's `style` variable, the style is applied to all the nodes in the scene graph starting with the node that contains the style declaration. For example, if the node is a `Group`, the style is applied to the group node and all the nodes defined as children contained in the group's `content` sequence. So, if you have a group that contains many text objects, setting the `fill` style would apply to all the text instances. If you need finer control over this, use either a `styleClass` or ID selector defined in a style sheet.

CSS Pseudo Class

Pseudo classes are supported for classes that extend `javafx.scene.control` `.Control` and `javafx.scene.control.Skin`. The currently supported pseudo classes are :hover, :focused, :disabled, and :pressed. The pseudo class :hover indicates that the style is active when the mouse if over the control; :focused is active when the control has the keyboard focus; :pressed is active when the mouse is pressed while over the control; and :disabled is active when the node is marked as disabled.

Listing 5.11 shows examples of using these CSS pseudo classes with `javafx` `.scene.control.TextBox`.

Listing 5.11   Style Sheet – JavaFX Supported Pseudo Classes

```
TextBox:hover {
    background-fill: red;
    text-fill: yellow;
}
```

```
TextBox:pressed {
    background-fill: navy;
    text-fill: white;
}
TextBox:focused {
    background-fill: purple;
    text-fill: yellow;
}
```

When the TextBox has the focus, it will have a purple background with yellow text. When the mouse moves over the TextBox, the background changes to red, and the text changes to yellow. When the mouse is pressed in the TextBox, the background changes to navy blue and the text to white. (Who chose these colors?)

To implement these pseudo classes in custom controls and skins, the custom code must set the value for the corresponding properties. An example is provided in the section Custom Controls, later in this chapter.

CSS Properties

In the StyleSheet file, the properties map directly to instance variables within the specified JavaFX class. In the preceding example, the CSS properties (fill and font) map directly to the instance variables fill and font in the javafx.scene.text.Text class. CSS type properties like background-fill would map to a JavaFX instance variable backgroundFill. The hyphen is removed and the second word is capitalized.

The allowed property values are decimal number, integer, string, color, paint, or font. Strings are enclosed in quotes.

Colors

Colors may be represented with a color name, (e.g., gray, red, or black), a hexadecimal triplet beginning with a sharp (#) sign, #808080, or using a function-like syntax, rgb (red, green, blue)—for example, rgb(128, 128, 128).

Paint

Paint may either be linear or radial.

linear maps to the javafx.scene.paint.LinearGradient class.

```
linear (startX, startY) to (endX, endY) stops
    (offset, color), (offset, color), ...  [reflect|repeat]
```

For example, the following style sheet entry would create a linear gradient starting with sky blue from the upper-left migrating to white in the lower-right part of the paint area.

```
fill: linear (0%, 0%) to (100%, 100%) stops
      (0.0, skyblue), (1.0, white)
```

For linear, the startX/startY and endX/endY may be expressed as an absolute value or a percent. The only restriction is that all values must be in the same units. reflect and repeat are optional and map to the javafx.scene.paint.Cycle-Methods of REFLECT and REPEAT, respectively. Reflect means the gradient is reflected to fill remaining space. When reflect is used, the gradient colors are painted start to end, then painted end to start, and so on to fill in extra space. Repeat means the start and end colors are repeated to fill in extra space.

radial maps to the javafx.scene.paint.RadialGradient class.

```
radial (startX, startY),100% focus(focusX, focusY) stops
      (offset, color), (offset, color), ...  [reflect|repeat]
```

For example, to create a RadialGradient starting at position 0,0 with a focus a quarter of the way across and down migrating from red to blue, you use a style sheet entry using the following syntax:

```
fill: radial (0%,0%),100% focus(25%,25%)
                        stops (0.00,red),(1.00, blue);
```

For radial, the startX/startY and focusX/focusY may be expressed as an absolute value or a percent. The only restriction is that all values must be in the same units. reflect and repeat are optional and map to the javafx.scene .paint.CycleMethods of REFLECT and REPEAT, respectively. Reflect means the gradient is reflected to fill remaining space. When reflect is used, the gradient colors are painted start to end, then painted end to start, and so on to fill in extra space. Repeat means the start and end colors are repeated to fill in extra space.

Font

Fonts are defined as having optional font weight, a font size, and a font name. Font weight may be bold, italic, or both. Size is a number, either decimal or integer, with units of either pt (point), mm (millimeters), cm (centimeters), pc (pica), or in (inch).

```
font:  bold italic 35pt "sans-serif";
```

Image

There is a special `url` syntax for defining images.

```
background-image: url(http://jfxbook.com/NASA/nasa.jpg);
```

This actually creates a `java.awt.image.BufferedImage` object that can then be used to create a `javafx.scene.Image`. A JavaFX example to handle this is shown in Listing 5.12.

Listing 5.12 JavaFX Example for Creating Image from BufferedImage

```
var image: Image;
public var backgroundImage:
  java.awt.image.BufferedImage on replace {
    if(backgroundImage != null) {
        image = Image{}.
                   fromBufferedImage(backgroundImage);
    }
}
```

Nodes

As we already mentioned, a scene graph is a representation of a display scene. It is represented as a tree data structure with a set of linked nodes. Nodes may be either inner nodes, sometimes called branch nodes or leaf nodes that have no children. The `javafx.scene.Node` class is the base class for all the `scene` graph nodes.

In JavaFX, the `Scene` is the root node and contains a set of direct child nodes; inner nodes are either a `javafx.scene.Group` or `javafx.scene.CustomNode`. The leaf nodes are all the other nodes like shapes, controls, text, and the Swing Extension nodes.

Each node may be given an ID represented as a string. A lookup function is provided to find a node with a specific ID. Already, we saw ID used in conjunction with style sheets and the developer should take care to assign unique IDs when they are used.

Nodes have a set of instance variables of function type that can be assigned and are called when certain input events occur. These include the onKey*XXXX* and onMouse*XXXX* instance variables that hold functions to handle key or mouse events, where *XXXX* represents the specific type of event. The `blocksMouse` instance variable indicates whether mouse events should be delivered to the parent. These will be discussed in more depth in the section Input Events, later in this chapter.

Nodes may also have a set of transforms applied, including translate, scale, rotate, and shear. Transforms may be provided as one sequence of transforms, each being applied in the order they are presented in the transforms sequence. Alternatively, the instance variables, translateX, translateY, scaleX, scaleY, and rotate may be used. When using these instance variables, there is certain default behavior. For example, scaleX/scaleY and rotate use the center point as the anchor. If you need finer control over these kinds of transforms, use the transforms sequence.

The geometry of nodes is contained in four instance variables: boundsInLocal, boundsInParent, boundsInScene, and layoutBounds. boundsInLocal is the rectangular area defined for the node without considering any transformations. boundsInParent is the rectangular area defined for the node after all the transformations have been applied and is in the coordinate space of the node's parent. boundsInScene is the rectangular area defined for the node after all the transformations have been applied and is in the coordinate space of the node's scene or root node if the node is not connected to a scene. layoutBounds is the geometry that should be used in all calculations for node layout and includes all the transformations defined in the nodes transforms sequence.

There are several indicators available with a node: hover, pressed, and focused. The indicator hover indicates that the mouse is over the node. pressed indicates that the mouse is over the node and the mouse button is pressed, focused indicates that the node has the input focus. To programmatically gain the input focus, call the node function requestFocus().

To control the appearance of a node, there are instance variables for opacity and visible. Also, there are functions to move the node forward (in front of other nodes), toFront(), or backward (behind other nodes), toBack(). You can assign a special effect using the effect variable. This will be discussed in depth in Chapter 6, Apply Special Effects. We have already discussed the style and styleClass variables when we discussed style sheets, earlier in this chapter.

Lastly, you can use another node to define a clip region for this node, using the clip attribute. When doing this, only the portion of the node that is contained within the region of the other node is visible.

Custom Nodes

To create a custom node, just extend javafx.scene.CustomNode and implement the abstract function, create(), which returns a node. The following Title class is a CustomNode.

To implement this, Title first extends CustomNode then implements the create() function. In the create function, it creates a rectangle that fills the background, a circle, and a text object to display "JavaFX is Cool". This is shown in Figure 5.7 and Listing 5.13.

Figure 5.7 Title Object Display

Listing 5.13 "JavaFX is Cool" – CustomNode

```
public class Title extends CustomNode {
    public var text:String = "JavaFX is Cool";
    public var width:Number = 200;
    public var height: Number = 100;

    override function create(): Node {
        Group {
            content: [
                Rectangle {
                    width: bind width
                    height: bind height
                    fill: LinearGradient {
                        startX: 0 startY: 0
                        endX: 0    endY: 1
                        stops: [
                            Stop { offset: 0.0
                                color: Color.DODGERBLUE },
                            Stop { offset: 1.0
                                color: Color.WHITE }
                        ]
                    }
                },
                Circle {
                    centerX: bind width / 4 * 3;
                    centerY: bind height / 2
                    radius: bind height / 3
                    fill: Color.CORAL
                },
                Text {
                    translateX: 5
                    translateY: bind height / 2 + 10
```

continues

```
                        content: bind text
                        font: Font{ name: "Times-Roman Bold" ,
                                   size:25}
                        stroke: Color.NAVY
                    }
                ]
            }
        }
    }
```

This custom node is comprised of a group containing a rectangle that fills the entire background with a linear gradient paint, a circle, and a text. The `create()` function returns the group, which is a node. This is the most common way to create a custom node, but this is not the only way. The only requirement is that the returned object extend `javafx.scene.Node`.

javafx.scene.Group

The `Group` (`javafx.scene.Group`) node contains a sequence of child nodes that are displayed in the order reflected in the sequence. It merely displays the nodes as they are defined and will take on the geometric bounds that encapsulate all its children. It does not do any layout for the children and each child node must position itself. Its main purpose is to group together a set of nodes and allow those nodes to be manipulated as a group. For example, you can apply transforms to the group, change its visibility or opacity, and so on.

The order of the nodes in the Group's content sequence dictates which nodes are drawn first and which are drawn last. If there is overlap on the display, nodes at the beginning of the content sequence will be underneath nodes later in the sequence. Actually, the `Node`'s method `toFront()` moves the affected node to the end of the containing Group's content sequence. Likewise, `toBack()` merely moves the affected node to the beginning. Of course, you can always change the order of the nodes assigned to content to achieve the desired layering.

Layout

JavaFX has two layout controls: `javafx.scene.layout.HBox` and `javafx.scene.layout.VBox`. HBox lays out its nodes horizontally, whereas VBox does it vertically.

Listing 5.14 illustrates an example using the horizontal box (HBox) layout.

Listing 5.14   Horizontal Box Layout

```
scene: Scene {
    content: HBox {
        spacing: 10
        content: [
            Rectangle {
                width: 50
                height: 20
                fill: Color.NAVY
                stroke: Color.YELLOW
            },
            Rectangle {
                width: 40
                height: 10
                fill: Color.CORAL
                stroke: Color.BLACK
            },
            Rectangle {
                width: 30
                height: 20
                fill: Color.YELLOW
                stroke: Color.BLACK
            },
            Rectangle {
                width: 30
                height: 20
                fill: Color.RED
                stroke: Color.YELLOW
            },
        ]
```

This produces various rectangles horizontal to each other, as shown in Figure 5.8.

Figure 5.8   HBox Layout

Similarly, the Vertical Box (VBox) code is shown in Listing 5.15.

Listing 5.15   Vertical Box Layout

```
scene: Scene {
    content: VBox {
        spacing: 10
```

continues

```
content: [
    Rectangle {
        width: 50
        height: 20
        fill: Color.NAVY
        stroke: Color.YELLOW
    },
    ...
    ...
```

VBox is shown in Figure 5.9.

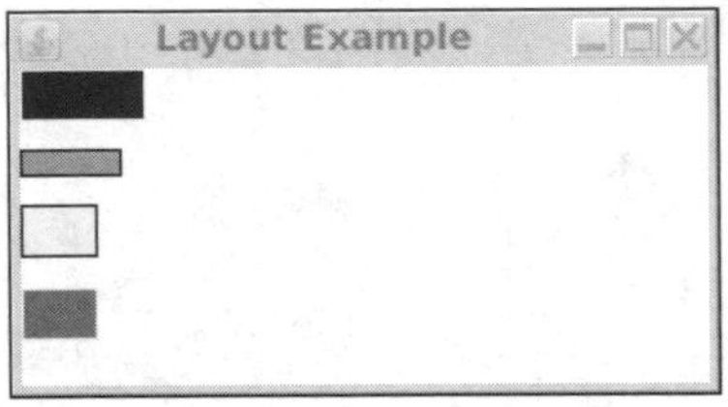

Figure 5.9   VBox Layout

Notice that these two layouts are quite simple. Other than specifying the spacing between the nodes, there is not much else you can do with these layouts. Also notice that the HBox layout justifies the nodes at the top, or North position, whereas VBox aligns the nodes on the left position. You have no control over this.

To get a little more interesting, let's combine the two layouts. First, we create a VBox that contains a set of HBoxes, each using the same set of colored rectangles. This is presented in Listing 5.16.

Listing 5.16   Combined Box Layouts

```
scene: Scene {
    content: VBox {
        spacing: 10
        content: [
            HBox {
                spacing: 20
                content: [
                    Rectangle {
                        width: 50
                        height: 20
                        fill: Color.NAVY
                        stroke: Color.YELLOW
                    },
```

```
            ...
            ...
    },
    HBox {
        spacing: 20
        content: [
            Rectangle {
                width: 50
                height: 20
                fill: Color.NAVY
                stroke: Color.YELLOW
            },
            ...
            ...
```

This lays out the components horizontally in two rows, as shown in Figure 5.10.

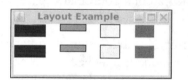

Figure 5.10   VBox Layout of HBoxes

Layout Basics

In JavaFX, layout can be achieved by positioning individual nodes using either their x and y or translateX and translateY variables directly. The other way is to use a layout container that positions nodes in a special way. In the previous sections, we looked at the built-in layout containers for horizontal, HBox, and vertical layout, VBox. In the next section, we will explore custom layout using a grid. But what internal geometry is used in doing layouts?

In JavaFX, rectangular bounds are represented by the javafx.geometry .Rectangle2D class. This class contains variables for minX, minY, maxX, maxY, width, and height. However, there are several geometric properties on each node that represent different geometries. These are boundsInLocal, boundsIn-Parent, boundsInScene, and layoutbounds. How are these related?

Bounds may change depending on a number of variables, including clips, effects, and transformation. So the different bounding rectangles represent the bounds for a node depending on whether some of these effects have been applied yet.

BoundsInLocal defines the bounds before any transformations have been applied. However, boundsInLocal does take into effect any changes required by clipping and special effects. For shapes, this bounded area also includes any non-zero strokes that may fall outside of the shape's geometry. For special effects, added space may be included to achieve the effect. For example, DropShadow includes a radius variable (default is 10.0) that is added to the overall dimensions for the node.

LayoutBounds defines the rectangular bounds after applying any transforms to the node. By design, the transformations specified by translateX and translateY are not included in this calculation. This is because if you are trying to position a node binding translateX and translateY based on the layoutBounds, you would enter into a circular change condition that would create an endless loop. LayoutBounds should be used when laying out nodes in an area.

BoundsInParent defines the rectangular area after applying all transformations to the node. This bounding rectangle is in the parent's coordinate space. However, it is still calculated if there is no parent.

BoundsInScene defines the rectangular area of the node after all its ancestor node's transformations have been applied. If the node is attached to a Scene, this would be in the Scene's coordinate space. Otherwise, it is in the coordinate space or the topmost node in the scene graph.

To illustrate the differences in these, let's look at an example. This example uses a rectangle that is originally 50 by 50 in size. It has a DropShadow effect, and is scaled on the x axis by a factor of 1.2. The rectangle is positioned horizontally in the center of the scene and down 50 along the y axis. The rectangle belongs to a group that is rotated 45 degrees, and this group belongs to a scene. Listing 5.17 shows the code required for this.

Listing 5.17   Layout Geometry

```
scene: scene = Scene {
    content: [
        Group {
            rotate: 45
            content: [
                rect = Rectangle {
                    translateX: bind (scene.width -
                        rect.layoutBounds.width)/2.0 -
                        rect.layoutBounds.minX;
                    translateY: 50
                    transforms: Transform.scale(1.2,1.0)
                    width: 50
```

```
                        height: 50
                        fill: Color.DODGERBLUE
                        effect: DropShadow{}
                }
            ]
        },
```

We have added text objects to display the various layouts and the output for this is shown in Figure 5.11.

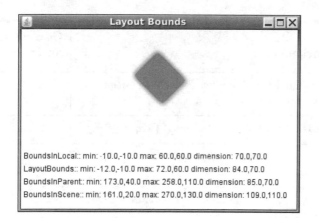

Figure 5.11 Layout Bounds

As you can see, all the bounds are different. So let's examine them and determine why they are the way they are. First, the basic rectangle is a 50 by 50 square, but we added a DropShadow effect, which added a margin area of 10 width around the square. So, boundsInLocal shows a 70 by 70 square starting at position -10, -10. Notice that we are still dealing with a square and not a rectangle. This is because boundsInLocal ignores the scaling transform. Now let's examine the layoutBounds.

In the layoutBounds, the scale transform has been applied and the square has been transformed into an 84 by 70 rectangle. Notice that we had to use the transforms[] sequence as layoutBounds ignores the scaleX and scaleY variables. Also, the other transform variables, rotate, translateX, and translateY are ignored by the layoutBounds. LayoutBounds are different than the other bounds in that the other bounds are read only, whereas layoutBounds can be set programmatically when the node is first created. So, you can force the layout geometry, if desired. Otherwise, it is calculated automatically based on the boundsInLocal augmented with the transforms contained in the transforms sequence variable.

The boundsInParent reflects the Group's coordinate system and also reflects the translateX and translateY transform from the Rectangle node. Notice the dimensions are still 84 by 70 but the minX and minY and maxX and maxY values have changed to reflect the translateX and translateY transformation.

The boundsInScene reflects the Group's rotation, and now the bounding area is a square that encloses the rotated rectangle. This reflects the Group's rotation.

Table 5.1 summarizes the differences between these four bounds.

Table 5.1   Bounds

Bounds	Contribution	Coordinate Space
boundsInLocal	Untransformed local coordinates, including shape stroke, clip, and effect	Node
layoutBounds	BoundsInLocal plus transforms[] sequence	Node
boundsInParent	LayoutBounds plus translateX/translateY, scaleX/scaleY, rotate	Parent
boundsInScene	BoundsInParent plus accumulated transforms of all ancestor nodes	Scene

To position a node, you need to use the Nodes layoutBounds to determine its basic size. If you need to incorporate transformations into this calculation, you should use the transforms[] sequence rather than the standalone transform instance variables, translateX/Y, scaleX/Y, and rotate. Listing 5.18 provides an example to center a node in a scene.

Listing 5.18   Centering a Node in a Scene

```
var rect:Rectangle;
Stage {
    var scene:Scene;
    width: 200
    height: 200
    scene: scene = Scene {
        content:  rect = Rectangle {
                translateX: bind (scene.width -
                    rect.layoutBounds.width)/2.0 -
                    rect.layoutBounds.minX
```

```
        translateY: bind (scene.height -
                    rect.layoutBounds.height)/2,0 -
                    rect.layoutBounds.minY

            ...
        }
    }
}
```

Notice that we need to assign local variables to both the Scene and the Rectangle, and then use those variables within a bind to set the `translateX` and `translateY` variables. Also, notice that we need to include the `minX`/`minY` for each, as this would include any offset due to shape drawing, effects, and clipping.

Custom Layout

If you need more control over layouts, you need to create a custom layout using the `javafx.scene.layout.Container` class. To illustrate this, we will walk through a `GridLayout` class. The `GridLayout` class lays out its nodes in a series of rows and columns. Instead of using a fixed width and height for the rows and columns, this layout class calculates the width of each column to be wide enough to handle the widest node within the column. Likewise, the height for each row is calculated to handle the maximum height to accommodate each node in that row. Therefore, the column widths and row heights vary depending on the nodes contained in each.

Because some nodes will have extra horizontal or vertical space within a row or column, you can specify the alignment of those nodes within the row or column. Either align left, right, or center for columns, and align top, center, or bottom within rows. The actual alignment values are directional with values for North, NorthEast, East, and so on.

To begin, we create the `GridLayout` class extending `javafx.scene.layout.Container`.

```
    public class GridLayout extends Container {
```

`javafx.scene.layout.Container` extends `javafx.scene.Group`, so from there we have access to the `content[]` sequence of Nodes. Also, `Container` extends `javafx.scene.layout.Resizable`, and from there we have access to width, height, minimum width/height, maximum width/height, and preferred width/height. There are also some helper functions defined in `Resizable`; we will use `getNodePreferredWidth/Height()`.

Next, let's add some instance variables as shown in Listing 5.19.

Listing 5.19   Grid Layout Variables

```
/** Specifies the default alignment to use */
public var defaultAlignment = Alignment.CENTER;

/** indicates the number of columns to use,
 *  if this is zero or less and rows is greater than 0,
 *  then the number of columns will be calculated
 *  based on the number of nodes and the number of rows
 */
public var cols: Integer = 1;

/** indicates the number of rows to use,
 *  if this is zero or less and cols is greater than 0,
 *  then the number of rows will be calculated
 *  based on the number
 *  of nodes and the number of columns
 */
public var rows: Integer;

// spacing from left and right margin
public var horizontalMargin = 0.0;

// spacing from top and bottom margin
public var verticalMargin = 0.0;

/** spacing between columns */
public var horizontalSpacing = 2.0 ;

/** spacing between rows */
public var verticalSpacing = 2.0;

/** the horizontal alignments, one for each column,
 *  if the size of this sequence
 *  is less than the number of columns,
 *  then the default alignment will be used
 *  for the remaining columns
 */
public var horizontalAlignments : Alignment[];

/** the vertical alignments, one for each row,
 *  if the size of this sequence
 *  is less than the number of rows,
 *  then the default alignment
 *  will be used for the remaining rows
 */
public var verticalAlignments : Alignment[];
```

Next, we add some functions. First, we need a function to walk through all the nodes and calculate the maximum width for each column and the maximum height for each row. We also use this function to calculate the overall dimensions for the GridLayout object. This function is shown in Listing 5.20.

Listing 5.20   Grid Layout Functions – calcDimensions()

```
function calcDimensions(): Void {
    // calculate either rows or cols
    if(cols <= 0) {
        cols = (sizeof content + rows -1)/rows;
    }else {
        rows = (sizeof content + cols - 1)/cols;
    }
    // calculate the colWidths and rowHeights
    var index = 0;
    colWidths = for(i in [0..<cols]) 0.0;
    rowHeights = for(i in [0..<rows]) 0.0;
    for(node in content) {
        if(node.visible) {
            var w = getNodePreferredWidth(node);
            var h = getNodePreferredHeight(node);
            var row = index / cols;
            var col = index mod cols;
            if(colWidths[col] < w) colWidths[col] = w;
            if(rowHeights[row] < h) rowHeights[row] = h;
            index++;
        }
    }
    // merge the provided alignments with the default
    delete _hAlignments;
    insert horizontalAlignments into _hAlignments;
    while(sizeof _hAlignments < cols) {
        insert defaultAlignment into _hAlignments;
    }
    delete _vAlignments;
    insert verticalAlignments into _vAlignments;
    while(sizeof _vAlignments < rows) {
        insert defaultAlignment into _vAlignments;
    }
    //calculate total width for container
    preferredWidth = horizontalMargin;
    for(i in [0..<cols]) {
        if(i > 0) preferredWidth += horizontalSpacing;
        insert preferredWidth into colOffsets;
        preferredWidth += colWidths[i];
    }
```

continues

```
    preferredWidth += horizontalMargin;
    //calculate total height for container
    preferredHeight = verticalMargin;
    for(i in [0..<rows]) {
        if(i > 0) preferredHeight += verticalSpacing;
        insert preferredHeight into rowOffsets;
        preferredHeight += rowHeights[i];
    }
    preferredHeight += verticalMargin;
    maximumWidth = minimumWidth = preferredWidth;
    maximumHeight = minimumHeight = preferredHeight;
    }
```

Next, we need a function to actually position each node within the Grid. The layout() function is shown in Listing 5.21.

Listing 5.21   Grid Layout Functions – layout()

```
function layout() {
    inCalc = true; //do not call layout from layout
    calcDimensions();
    var index = 0;
    for(node in content) {
        if(node.visible) { // only layout visible nodes
            var w = getNodePreferredWidth(node);
            var h = getNodePreferredHeight(node);
            var row = index / cols;
            var col = index mod cols;
            var x = colOffsets[col];
            var y = rowOffsets[row];
            // adjust based on Alignment
            x += alignX(node, col);
            // adjust based on Alignment
            y += alignY(node, row);
            node.translateX = x;
            node.translateY = y;
            index++;
        }
    }
    inCalc = false;
}
```

alignX and alignY adjust the nodes position depending on the alignment value for that column and row, respectively. The Alignment class is just a Java Enum type. These two functions are presented in Listing 5.22.

Listing 5.22   Grid Layout Functions – alignX()/alignY()

```
function alignX(node:Node, col:Integer): Number {
    var alignment = _hAlignments[col];
    if(alignment == Alignment.NORTHEAST or
        alignment == Alignment.EAST or
        alignment == Alignment.SOUTHEAST) {
            return 0.0;
    } else if(alignment == Alignment.NORTHWEST or
        alignment == Alignment.WEST or
        alignment == Alignment.SOUTHWEST) {
        return colWidths[col] -
            getNodePreferredWidth(node);
    } else { // CENTER
        return (colWidths[col] -
            getNodePreferredWidth(node))/2;
    }
}
function alignY(node:Node, row:Integer): Number {
    var alignment = _vAlignments[row];
    if(alignment == Alignment.NORTHEAST or
        alignment == Alignment.NORTH or
        alignment == Alignment.NORTHWEST) {
            return 0.0;
    } else if(alignment == Alignment.SOUTHEAST or
        alignment == Alignment.SOUTH or
        alignment == Alignment.SOUTHWEST) {
        return rowHeights[row] -
                getNodePreferredHeight(node);
    } else { // CENTER
        return (rowHeights[row] -
                getNodePreferredHeight(node))/2;
    }
}
```

To kick start the layout, we add a `postinit` block to do the layout. This does the layout after all the instance variables in the class have been through the initialization process. We added a Boolean variable `postInitted` to indicate that this step has completed.

```
postinit {
    layout();
    postInitted = true;
}
```

Now, we have to do one more thing. Whenever any of the public instance variables change, we need to recalculate the layout. We do this by adding on replace triggers to these variable declarations. For example:

```
public var cols:Integer = 1 on replace {
    if(postInitted and not inCalc) {
        layout();
    }
};
```

To do a layout on the Group's content instance variable, we need to add an override declaration.

```
override var content
    on replace oldValues [lo..hi] = newValues {
    if(postInitted and not inCalc) {
        layout();
    }
}
```

The following is an example of how to create a GridLayout object literal with some example nodes, using the default CENTER alignment. Listing 5.23 shows how to use the GridLayout class.

Listing 5.23　　Grid Layout – Object Literal

```
scene: Scene {
    width: 200
    height: 200
    content: GridLayout {
        cols: 3
        content: [
                    Rectangle {
                        width: 50
                        height: 20
                        fill: Color.NAVY
                        stroke: Color.YELLOW
                    },
                    ...
```

When we run this, we see the display as shown in Figure 5.12.

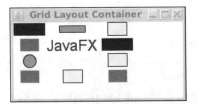

Figure 5.12　　Custom Container for Grid Layout

There is a trick that this lets us do for empty cells. Notice the empty space in column 2, row 3, right below the "JavaFX" text. To achieve this, all we had to do was assign an empty Group, `Group{}`, node to this position. Because the column width and row height will be sized to hold the maximum width and height for the column and row, respectively, then this row and column appears to be empty. This is because an empty Group is essentially dimensionless.

The full listing is on the book's Web site at http://www.jfxbook.com.

Input Events

JavaFX supports two types of input events: `javafx.scene.input.MouseEvent` and `javafx.scene.input.KeyEvent`. Mouse events are generated by actions with the mouse and include mouse button actions like clicked, pressed, and released. Also, events are generated for mouse movement like moved, dragged, enter, and exit and for mouse wheel move events.

Key events are generated when the user presses, releases, and "types" keys from the keyboard. Key type events are at a higher level than press and release events and multiple key pressed/released events may map to one typed event.

There is an important attribute in `javafx.scene.Node`, `blocksMouse`, that controls delivery of mouse events. Normally, when a mouse event is generated, the runtime system delivers the event to all the nodes that intersect with the mouse coordinate. If you set `blocksMouse` to true on a node, that node will consume the mouse event and it will no longer propagate up the scene graph tree. If you do not want mouse events sent to other nodes that are visually blocked by a node, set `blocksMouse` to true on that node.

Mouse Events

`javafx.scene.Node` defines eight mouse event actions; these are

Mouse Actions

```
onMouseClicked: function(e:MouseEvent): Void

onMousePressed: function(e:MouseEvent): Void

onMouseReleased function(e:MouseEvent): Void

onMouseEntered: function(e:MouseEvent): Void

onMouseExited: function(e:MouseEvent): Void

onMouseMoved: function(e:MouseEvent): Void

onMouseDragged: function(e:MouseEvent): Void

onMouseWheelMoved: function(e: MouseEvent): Void
```

Listing 5.24 shows an example of defining a mouse clicked action.

Listing 5.24   Using onMouseClicked

```
Rectangle {
    width: 50
    height: 20
    fill: Color.NAVY
    stroke: Color.YELLOW
    onMouseClicked: function(e:MouseEvent) : Void {
        println("clicked at {e.x}, {e.y}");
    }
}
```

To properly implement a drag action, you need to capture and save the drag node's initial x and y coordinate when the mouse drag is started and use it later to calculate the ending coordinates. Then when the mouse is dragged or released, you use the MouseEvent's dragX and dragY variables as a delta to the original position to calculate the new position for the node. The MouseEvent's dragX and dragY variables hold a relative value to when the most recent drag event started. Therefore, it can be used to do a relative change to the original position of a node. Listing 5.25 is an example for a circle that is to be dragged.

Listing 5.25   Mouse Drag

```
var origCX: Number; // hold the original centerX
var origCY: Number; // hold the original centerY
var x: Number; // center x for circle
var y: Number; // center y for circle

circle1 = Circle {

    centerX: bind x
    centerY: bind y
    radius: 5

    fill: Color.DODGERBLUE

    blocksMouse: true

    // save the position at the start of a drag
    onMousePressed: function(e:MouseEvent):Void {
        origCX = circle1.centerX;
        origCY = circle1.centerY;
    }
```

```
onMouseReleased: function(e:MouseEvent):Void {
    x = e.dragX + origCX;
    y = e.dragY + origCY;
}

onMouseDragged: function(e:MouseEvent):Void {
    x = e.dragX + origCX;
    y = e.dragY + origCY;
}

}
```

When the mouse is pressed, we save the original coordinates of the center of the circle in the origCX and origCY variables. When a drag event is delivered, we adjust the center of the circle by setting the bound variables x and y based on the delta change in the mouse position. This shows the circle being moved while dragging. Finally, we do the same thing on release so that the circle is moved to its final position.

Key Events

Key events are generated from the keyboard, when a key is pressed and released, and when a typed key is recognized. A typed key may be the result of multiple key press and release events. The key actions defined are

Key Actions

```
onKeyPressed: function(e:KeyEvent): Void

onKeyReleased: function(e:KeyEvent): Void

onKeyTyped: function(e:KeyEvent): Void
```

In Listing 5.26, the example displays a Text item in the center of the scene. As you type characters, the text is updated by appending the typed character. A backspace key erases the last character typed. Notice that the backspace is handled in the onKeyReleased function. This is because the key code is always VK_UNDEFINED in a key typed event.

Listing 5.26 Key Events

```
var text: Text;
var scene:Scene;

Stage {
  title: "Key Event Example"
```

continues

```
width: 250
height: 80
scene: scene = Scene {
  content: Group {
    content: [
        Rectangle {
          width: bind scene.width
          height: bind scene.height
          fill: Color.LIGHTBLUE
          onKeyTyped: function(e:KeyEvent):Void {
            if(java.lang.Character.isLetterOrDigit(
                      e.char.charAt(0)) or
              java.lang.Character.isWhitespace(
                      e.char.charAt(0)) ) {
                text.content = "{text.content}{e.char}";
            }
          }
          onKeyReleased: function(e:KeyEvent):Void {
            if(e.code == KeyCode.VK_BACK_SPACE) {
              text.content = text.content.substring(
                      0, text.content.length()-1);
            }
          }
        },
        text = Text {
          // center text in scene
          translateX: bind
            (scene.width - text.layoutBounds.width)/2 -
                          text.layoutBounds.minX;
          translateY: bind
            (scene.height - text.layoutBounds.height)/2 -
                          text.layoutBounds.minY;
          font : Font {size : 24}
            textOrigin: TextOrigin.TOP
            fill: Color.NAVY
        }
    ]
  }
 }
}
```

Another way to handle the backspace key is to look at the key event char directly.

```
if(java.lang.Character.isLetterOrDigit(
                        e.char.charAt(0)) or
        java.lang.Character.isWhitespace(
                        e.char.charAt(0)) ) {
```

```
        text.content = "{text.content}{e.char}";
    }else if(e.char == "\b") {
        text.content = text.content.substring(0,
                        text.content.length()-1);
    }
```

However, this may not be portable across different locales and languages.

Text Display

There are two ways to handle text display in JavaFX. First, to merely display text to the screen, use the `javafx.scene.text.Text` class. However, if you need user editable text, it is easiest to use the `javafx.scene.control.TextBox` class.

Text

A Text is a shape that displays a string. A text has a font, geometry with a Text Origin setting, and instance variables to control line wrapping. Newline characters within the string cause the line to wrap; otherwise, wrapping is governed by the `wrappingWidth` variable.

A bare bones Text uses the default font and size and is black (see Figure 5.13). It is declared as

```
Text {
    translateX: 10, translateY: 30
    content: "This is my Text"
}
```

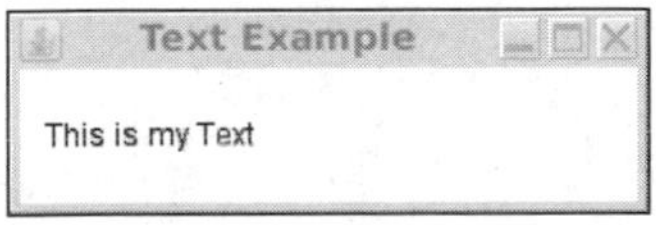

Figure 5.13   Bare Bones Text

It is necessary to move the text to see it, and this will be explained in the section on TextOrigin a little later in this chapter.

To make this more interesting, let's adjust the font size, and instead of using the default fill of black, let's set the fill to transparent and the stroke to black (see Figure 5.14).

```
Text {
    translateX: 10, translateY: 30
    content: "This is my Text"
    font: Font { size: 36 }
    fill: Color.TRANSPARENT
    stroke: Color.BLACK
}
```

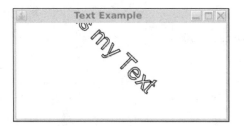

Figure 5.14   Outline Text

Now let's rotate it 45 degrees (see Figure 5.15).

```
Text {
    translateX: 10, translateY: 30
    content: "This is my Text"
    font: Font { size: 36 }
    fill: Color.TRANSPARENT
    stroke: Color.BLACK
    rotate: 45
}
```

Figure 5.15   Rotated 45 Degrees

What happened? When we use the rotate variable, the rotation is anchored on the center point. This is also true if we had used the scaleX and scaleY variables; the scaling would have been from the center point, which is not always desired. If we want to rotate at the origin point, 0,0, we need to use a Rotate transform, javafx.scene.transform.Rotate (see Figure 5.16).

```
Text {
    translateX: 10, translateY: 30
    content: "This is my Text"
```

```
    font: Font { size: 36 }
    fill: Color.TRANSPARENT
    stroke: Color.BLACK
    transforms: Rotate {
        angle: 45
        pivotX: 0 // default is 0
        pivotY: 0 // default is 0
    }
}
```

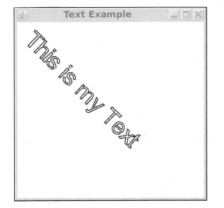

Figure 5.16   Rotated 45 Degrees from Origin

Adding the `pivotX`/`pivotY` is not absolutely necessary because their default values are zero anyway, but this does show you that you can control the pivot point when using a `javafx.scene.transform.Rotate` transform. `javafx.scene.transform` `.Scale` also has `pivotX`/`pivotY` variables to anchor the scaling at a particular point.

TextOrigin

If you were paying close attention, you may have noticed something a little different with this last rotation, which brings us to the next topic, text origin. Text origin is the origin point, where the text is placed. There are three options for the text origin: baseline, top, and bottom.

Baseline is the line on which the font places its characters. Some characters may descend this line, like j, p, and y. Top means the origin is at the top of the font, and bottom means the origin is at the bottom.

Figure 5.17 shows the three options. Each text is outlined to show its bounding region, and the dot indicates the origin point (0,0) with a horizontal line. Notice that the baseline option shows the origin at the baseline, the top option shows the origin at the top, and the bottom at the bottom. Also, notice that each dot representing the origin is equidistant from each other; however, the placement of the text is quite different.

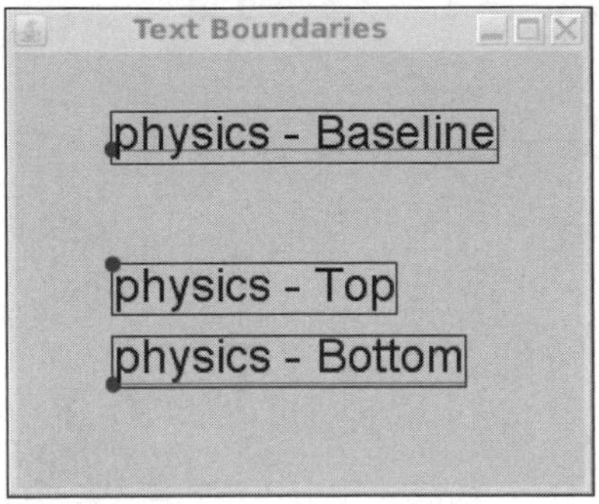

Figure 5.17   Text Origin Options

The only difference between the three text nodes is the `textOrigin` variable. The first one uses the default, which is `TextOrigin.BASELINE`, the second, `TextOrigin.TOP`, and the third, `TextOrigin.BOTTOM`. When placing text on the display, it is important to consider these settings.

The code for this example is shown in Listing 5.27.

Listing 5.27   Text Placement

```
var t1: Text;
var t2: Text;
var t3: Text;
    ...
    ...
    scene: Scene {
        fill: Color.LIGHTGRAY
        content: VBox {
            translateX: 50
            translateY: 50
            spacing: 30
            content: [
                Group {
                    content: [
                        Line {
                            endX: bind t1.boundsInParent.width
                            stroke: Color.RED
                        },
```

```
            Rectangle {
                x: bind t1.boundsInParent.minX
                y: bind t1.boundsInParent.minY
                width:
                        bind t1.boundsInParent.width
                height:
                        bind t1.boundsInParent.height
                stroke: Color.NAVY
                fill: Color.TRANSPARENT
            },
              Circle {
                radius: 4
                fill: Color.BLUE
              }
              t1 = Text {
                  font : Font {size : 24}
                  content: "physics - Baseline"
              }
          ]
        },
        Group {
            content: [
                Line {
                    ...
                },
                Rectangle {
                    ...
                },
                Circle {
                    ...
                }
                t2 = Text {
                    font : Font {size : 24}
                    textOrigin: TextOrigin.TOP
                    content: "physics - Top"
                }
            ]
        },
        Group {
            content: [
                Line {
                    ...
                },
                Rectangle {
                    ...
                },
                Circle {
                    ...
                }
```

continues

```
            t3 = Text {
                font : Font {size : 24}
                textOrigin: TextOrigin.BOTTOM
                content: "physics - Bottom"
            }
        ]
    },
    ]
}
}
```

Text Wrapping

There are several settings to control text wrapping. First, if we insert newline characters into the content string, the display will present each line separately (see Figure 5.18).

```
Text {
    font: Font { size: 24 }
    x: 10,
    y: 30
    content: "Hello\nWorld"
}
```

Figure 5.18   Wrapping with Newline Character

The next option is to set the wrapping width to justify the text between the margins as defined by the wrappingWidth variable (see Figure 5.19).

```
Text {
    font: Font { size: 24 }
    x: 10,
    y: 30
    wrappingWidth: 150
    textAlignment: TextAlignment.JUSTIFY
    content:
"Goodbye cruel World now is the time to leave thee"
}
```

Figure 5.19   Wrapping Width with Justify Alignment

Also, if we change the alignment to left, we get what is shown in Figure 5.20.

```
textAlignment: TextAlignment.LEFT
```

Figure 5.20   Wrapping Width with Left Alignment

Using RIGHT alignment, we get what is shown in Figure 5.21.

```
textAlignment: TextAlignment.RIGHT
```

Figure 5.21   Wrapping Width with Right Alignment

Font

One final topic is font. The easiest way to create a font is to use a `javafx.scene`
`.text.Font` object literal giving it a size and a font name.

```
var font = Font { name:  "Lucida Grande Bold" size: 36 };
    font: Font { name:  "Arial"  size: 24 }
    font: Font { name:  "Arial Bold"  size: 12 }
    font: Font { name: "Book Antiqua Bold Italic" size: 14}
var defaultFont = Font {};
```

The font names vary per platform and the function `Font.getFontNames()`
retrieves the set of available names in the form of a sequence of string.

Programmer Tip: With JDK 1.6, it is possible to programmatically install your
own font. However, for JavaFX to know about these fonts, you need to register them
with Java before the first JavaFX font is created. Here is an example code fragment:

```
var fontResource = "{__DIR__)myFont.ttf";

var fontDef =         fontRes.getClass().getResourceAsStream(fontRes);

var awtFont: java.awt.Font =  if(fontDef != null) {
    java.awt.Font.creatFont(
            java.awt.Font.TRUETYPE_FONT, fontDef
);
    } else {
        null;
    };
if(awtFont != null) {
    // this requires JRE 1.6

    GraphicsEnvironment.getLocalGraphicsEnvironment().
                            registerFont(awtFont);
}
```

This only works with True Type Fonts and only works with JDK 1.6. The other
option is to install the font into the JRE lib/fonts directory.

TextBox

The `javafx.scene.control.TextBox` class provides a means for user text input
and editing. An example of a `TextBox` is shown in Figure 5.22.

A `TextBox` can be editable or not using the `editable` Boolean variable and you
can specify the number of columns with the `columns` variable. Also, you can

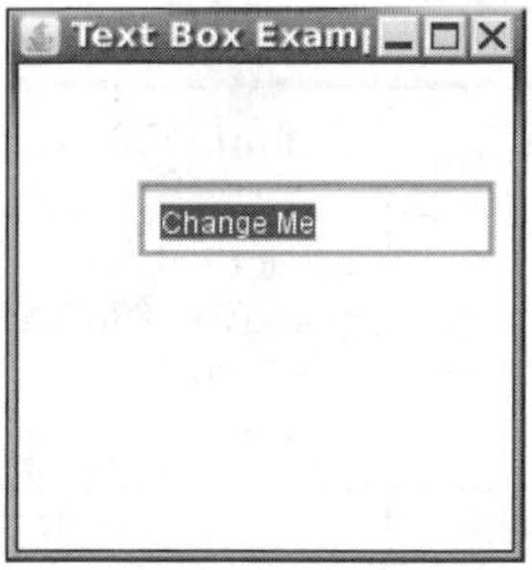

Figure 5.22 TextBox

indicate that the entire text will be selected when the `TextBox` gains the focus, using the `selectOnFocus` Boolean variable. In addition, you can specify an `action` function that is invoked when an action is fired on the `TextBox`. Typically, this is done when the user presses the Enter key.

There are two variables that hold the text, `text` and `value`. On supported platforms, the variable text is updated as the user types. The variable value is updated when the user commits the changed text on the `TextBox`. Typically, this is when the user presses the Enter key or changes focus.

The `TextBox` skin implements the visual appearance for the `TextBox` and Table 5.2 defines the CSS attributes that are supported by the `TextBox` skin. The only way to change these from the default is to use one of the CSS style sheet mechanisms previously discussed. You can either use a style sheet and give its URL location to the `Scene` object, or include a style string using the `TextBox`'s `style` variable.

Table 5.2 TextBox CSS Attributes

CSS Attribute	JavaFX Attribute	Type	Default Value
padding-left	paddingLeft	Number	4
padding-top	paddingTop	Number	4
padding-bottom	paddingBottom	Number	4
padding-right	paddingRight	Number	4
border-radius	borderRadius	Number	0
border-width	borderWidth	Number	1

continues

Table 5.2   TextBox CSS Attributes (*Continued*)

CSS Attribute	JavaFX Attribute	Type	Default Value
border-fill	borderFill	paint	linear (0, 0) to (0, 4) stops (0.0, #8d8e8f), (0.75, #b3b3b), (1.0, #b8b8b9);
background-fill	backgroundFill	paint	linear (0, 1) to (0, 4) stops (0.0, #cbcbcc), (0.66, #f8f8f8), (1.0, white);
text-fill	textFill	paint	#0b1621;
selected-text-fill	selectedTextFill	paint	#0b1621;
font	font	font	12pt Dialog;
focus-fill	focusFill	paint	#73a4d1;
focus-size	focusSize	paint	1.4
caret-fill	caretFill	paint	black
caret-stroke	caretStroke	paint	black
highlight-fill	highlightFill	paint	null;

The pseudo classes :hover, :pressed, :disabled, and :focused are supported for the TextBox control.

Listing 5.28 shows how to create a TextBox.

Listing 5.28   javafx.scene.control.TextBox

```
Stage {
    title: "Text Box Example"
    scene: Scene {
        width: 200
        height: 200
        content: [
            TextBox {
                translateX: 50
                translateY: 50
                text: "Change Me"
                columns: 12
```

```
                        selectOnFocus: true
                        style: "padding-left: 5; padding-right: 5; "
                                "text-fill: navy; "
                                "background-fill: skyblue; "
                                "font: bold 14pt arial;"
                    }
                ]
            }
        }
}
```

In this example, we used the `TextBox`'s `style` variable to specify the visual aspects for the `TextBox`.

JavaFX 1.2 Controls

With the release of JavaFX 1.2, many new controls have been added to the JavaFX platform. Table 5.3 lists these. Because these new controls are just being finalized as the book is going to press, please visit the book's Web site, http://jfxbook.com, for more detailed information.

Table 5.3 JavaFX Controls

Control	Purpose
Button	A simple push button.
CheckBox	A tri-state selection control typically shown with a check mark.
ComboBox	A control that allows one to pick from a list of pre-defined strings or optionally enter a custom string.
Hyperlink	An HTML-like text label that responds to rollovers and clicks.
Label	A control useful for displaying text that is required to fit within a specific space.
ListView	A control to show a list of items that is scrollable.
ProgressBar	A control to show progress.
ProgressIndicator	An indicator to show the user that an operation is in progress.
RadioButton	A `ToggleButton` that belongs to a group.
Slider	A control that allows a user to adjust values within a range.

continues

Table 5.3   JavaFX Controls (*Continued*)

Control	Purpose
ScrollBar	A control that allows the user to control scrolling.
ToggleButton	A control with a Boolean indicating whether it has been selected.

Custom Controls

TextBox is a control—that is, it extends `javafx.scene.control.Control` and has a companion class that is a Skin, `javafx.scene.control.Skin`. The advantage of controls is that the Skin, or display characteristics, are separated from the actual control. The other main advantage is that controls implement full style sheet support including the pseudo classes :hover, :pressed, and :focused. Creating a custom control is easy.

First, create the `Control` by extending `javafx.scene.control.Control`. Within this control, you need to assign a `Skin` to the `skin` variable inherited from `javafx.scene.control.Control`. Let's look at an example that creates a control for hypertext. HyperText is a `Text`-like object that displays text; when you click it, some action is taken on a URL. This is similar to links in a Web page. If the link has not been visited, the text is displayed in one color, and after it has been visited, it is displayed in another color. Also, typically these links are underlined. The beauty of using a `Control` is that all these appearance attributes can be set using a style sheet.

The `HyperText` object extends `Control` and assigns a `HyperTextSkin` object to its `skin` variable. This is detailed in Listing 5.29.

Listing 5.29   Custom Control

```
public class HyperText extends Control {
    public var url:String;
    public var content: String;
    public var action: function(url:String):Void;
    public var textOrigin: TextOrigin =
                HyperTextSkin.defaultText.textOrigin;
    public var textAlignment: TextAlignment =
                HyperTextSkin.defaultText.textAlignment;

    init {
        skin = HyperTextSkin{};
    }
}
```

The variable, url, holds the URL, content holds the displayed text, and action is called when the user clicks on the text. The variables textOrigin and textAlignment are used for the underlying Text object defined in HyperTextSkin.

The skin variable can either be assigned in the init block, or using an override declaration on skin.

```
protected override var skin = HyperTextSkin {};
```

The only caution in using the override approach is that the Control may not have been fully initialized when the Skin is created, thus certain values may not be available to the Skin when it is first created.

The HyperTextSkin object has the bulk of the logic as shown in Listing 5.30.

Listing 5.30 Custom Skin

```
// used to get default values
package def defaultText = Text{};

public class HyperTextSkin extends Skin {
    var hypertext : HyperText = bind control as HyperText;

    // Stylesheet settings
    public var wrappingWidth: Number =
                        defaultText.wrappingWidth;
    public var underline: Boolean = true;
    public var overline: Boolean = defaultText.overline;
    public var strikethrough: Boolean =
                        defaultText.strikethrough;
    public var unvisitedFill: Paint = Color.BLUE;
    public var visitedFill: Paint = Color.PURPLE;
    public var font = Font {};

    // local variables
    var text: Text;
    package var visited: Boolean = false;
    ...
    ...
```

The first item in the Skin is to declare a local variable that casts the control to the specific type. This is just a convenience for later when we have to access variables from the HyperText control. The bind is necessary as the control may not be set when this local variable is declared.

Second, there is a set of variables that can be set from the style sheet. These must all be public and remember that a word with a capital letter within the variable name is translated on the style sheet. For example, `unvisitedFill` is unvisited-fill in the style sheet. Table 5.4 shows the available CSS properties for this control.

Table 5.4   HyperText CSS Attributes

CSS Attribute	JavaFX Attribute	Type
`wrapping-width`	`wrappingWidth`	Number
`underline`	`underline`	Boolean
`overline`	`overline`	Boolean
`strikethrough`	`strikethrough`	Boolean
`unvisited-fill`	`unvisitedFill`	paint
`visited-fill`	`visitedFill`	paint
`font`	`font`	font
`:hover`		Boolean
`:pressed`		Boolean
`:focused`		Boolean

The last part of the `Skin` source is the actual creation of the node that will be displayed. This is similar to the `CustomNode` example; however, instead of returning a node in the `create()` function, you actually have to assign the node to the `scene` variable inherited from `javafx.scene.control.Skin`. Notice the mouse handling for the enclosing rectangle. When the user does a mouse action over the hypertext, this sets the corresponding variables on the `Skin` so that the CSS pseudo variables, :focused, :hover, and :pressed, are operational. This is shown in Listing 5.31.

Listing 5.31   Custom Skin – Node Creation

```
var enclosingRect: Rectangle;

protected override function requestFocus():Void {
    enclosingRect.requestFocus();
}
var _focus = bind enclosingRect.focused on replace {
    focused = _focus;
}
```

```
init {
    scene = Group {
        content: [
            enclosingRect = Rectangle {
                translateX: bind text.layoutBounds.minX
                translateY:
                        bind text.boundsInLocal.minY;
                width: bind text.layoutBounds.width
                height: bind text.layoutBounds.height
                fill: Color.TRANSPARENT
                onMouseClicked: function(e) {
                    visited = true;
                    hypertext.action(hypertext.url);
                }
                onMouseEntered: function(e) {
                    hover = true;
                }
                onMouseExited: function(e) {
                    hover = false;
                }
                onMousePressed: function(e) {
                    pressed = true;
                    if(not control.focused and
                                control.focusable)
                        then control.requestFocus();
                }
                onMouseReleased: function(e) {
                    pressed = false;
                }
            },
            text = Text {
                content: bind hypertext.content
                fill: bind if(visited)
                        visitedFill else unvisitedFill
                wrappingWidth: bind wrappingWidth
                underline: bind underline
                overline: bind overline
                strikethrough: bind strikethrough
                content: bind hypertext.content
                textOrigin: bind
                    if(hypertext.textOrigin != null)
                        hypertext.textOrigin
                    else defaultText.textOrigin
                textAlignment: bind if
                  (hypertext.textAlignment != null)
                    hypertext.textAlignment
                  else defaultText.textAlignment
                font: bind font
            }
        ]
    };
}
```

Developer Tip: The Rectangle shape encapsulates the Text object and allows for the user to have a larger area to click the mouse. This area is the full width and height of the entire text. If this Rectangle were not present, then the user would have been restricted to clicking the mouse right over the painted parts of the individual letters of the Text. For example, clicking inside the letter O would not work; you would have to click on the black part of the letter O. Otherwise, the mouse events would not be delivered to the HyperText object.

Shapes

The javafx.scene.shapes package contains numerous shape types. We have already seen Rectangle and Circle in action in some of the previous examples. The other shapes are Line, Arc, Ellipse, Polygon, CubicCurve, and QuadCurve.

Polygon

An example of a triangle using a polygon centered within the scene is shown in the following code and in Figure 5.23.

```
Polygon {
    translateX: bind scene.width/2
    translateY: bind scene.height/2
    scaleX: 4
    scaleY: 4
    rotate: 45
    points: [ 0, -10, 10, 10, -10, 10, 0, -10]
    fill: Color.RED
}
```

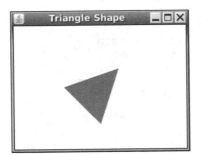

Figure 5.23   Triangle – Scaled 4×, Rotated 45 Degrees

Line

A line draws a line between two points (see Figure 5.24).

```
Line {
    startX: 10   startY: 10
    endX: 100   endY: 100
    stroke: Color.RED
    strokeWidth: 2
}
```

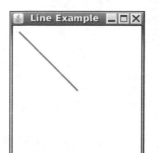

Figure 5.24 Line

Arc

An Arc draws a curved area between two points based on a radius, starting angle, and length in degrees. The Arc type may be open, meaning the two end points are not closed (see Figure 5.25); chord, meaning the end points are closed by drawing a straight line between the two end points (see Figure 5.26); and round, meaning the arc is closed by drawing straight lines to the center point of the ellipse that contains the arc (see Figure 5.27).

```
Arc {
    centerX: 100 centerY: 100
    radiusX: 50   radiusY: 50
    startAngle: -45 length: 180
    type: ArcType.OPEN
    stroke: Color.RED
    strokeWidth: 2
    fill: null
}
```

Figure 5.25 Arc – OPEN

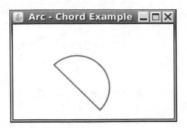

Figure 5.26   Arc – CHORD

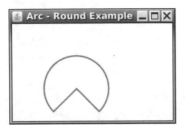

Figure 5.27   Arc – ROUND

Ellipse

An Ellipse shape is defined using a center point with radii for both the x and y axis. The following listing shows how to create an ellipse centered at point 100, 50 with an x axis radius of 50 and a y axis radius of 10. This example creates an outlined ellipse as shown in Figure 5.28. If you need to create a filled ellipse, you can set the fill variable to a color or gradient.

```
Ellipse {
    centerX: 100   centerY: 50
    radiusX: 50   radiusY: 25
    stroke: Color.RED
    strokeWidth: 2
    fill: null
}
```

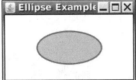

Figure 5.28   Ellipse

CubicCurve

A CubicCurve defines a cubic Bézier parametric curve segment used to model smooth curves. The startX, startY, endX, and endY points mark the ends of the curve. The variables controlX1, controlY1, controlX2, and controlY2 specify the Bézier controls points that shape the curve. The following listing shows how to create a curved line as shown in Figure 5.29. If you want a filled shape, set the fill variable to a color or gradient.

```
CubicCurve {
    startX: 10   startY: 10
    endX: 100   endY: 100
    controlX1: 20 controlY1: 0
    controlX2: 80 controlY1: 110
    stroke: Color.RED
    strokeWidth: 2
    fill: null
}
```

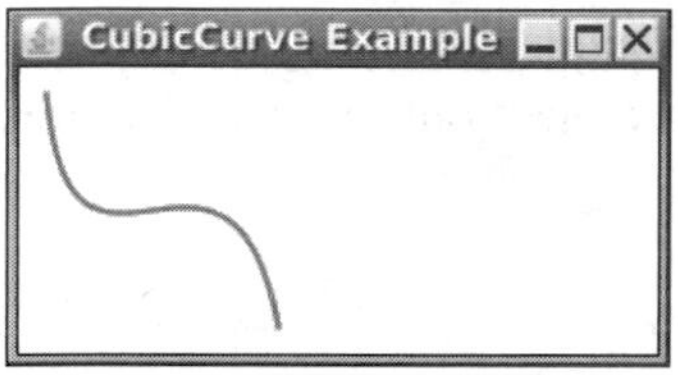

Figure 5.29   CubicCurve

QuadCurve

A QuadCurve defines a quadratic Bézier parametric curve segment. It is similar to the CubicCurve, but it only uses one control point. The following listing shows how to create a QuadCurve starting at point 10,20 and ending at point 100,100. The control point is 75,0. The output for this curve is shown in Figure 5.30.

```
QuadCurve {
    startX: 10   startY: 20
    endX: 100   endY: 100
    controlX: 75 controlY: 0
    stroke: Color.RED
    strokeWidth: 2
    fill: null
}
```

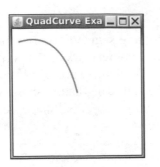

Figure 5.30   QuadCurve

Paths

Paths let you draw arbitrarily complex shapes. There are two path shapes: Path and SVGPath. Paths take a set of elements that draw the outline of a shape. The Path may be either open or closed. The class javafx.scene.shape.Path takes a set of PathElements, whereas SVGPath is built using a standard SVG Path encoded string as defined at http://www.w3.org/TR/SVG/paths.html. The following example shows a triangular shape with a circular chunk taken out of it (see Figure 5.31).

```
Path {
    translateX: 50
    translateY: 50
    fill: Color.RED
    elements: [
        MoveTo { x: 0 y: 0},
        LineTo { x: 100 y: 0 },
        ArcTo { x: 200 y: 0 radiusX: 25 radiusY: 20 },
        LineTo { x: 300 y: 0 },
        LineTo { x: 150 y: 100 },
        ClosePath{}
    ]
}
```

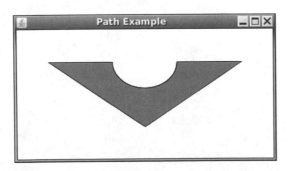

Figure 5.31   Path Example

Here is the same shape using an SVGPath, using a stroke color instead of a fill (see Figure 5.32).

```
SVGPath {
    translateX: 50
    translateY: 50
    fill: Color.TRANSPARENT
    stroke: Color.RED
    content:
            "M0,0 L100,0 A25,20 0 0,0 200,0 L300,0 150,100z"
}
```

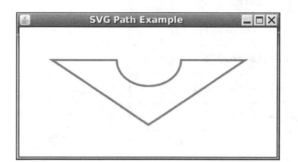

Figure 5.32   SVG Path Example

Programmer Tip: Remember when we discussed using a scene fill of either null or Color.TRANSPARENT? Let's reexamine this using the preceding shape. Because the fill is Color.TRANSPARENT, when you click anywhere inside the shape, the onMouseClicked function will be called if defined for the shape. However, if you change the fill to null, now when you click inside the shape, there is no mouse event generated for the shape. You have to click on the outlined stroke to generate the event. Though both shapes look the same, there is a big difference when processing mouse events. Either way is valid; it all depends on what you are trying to do with mouse events for the shape.

Java Swing Extension

The javafx.ext.swing package contains numerous JavaFX classes that support Java Swing components. It is important to note that the Swing extension is not supported on all platforms, so if you use Swing extensions your application may not run on a platform like JavaFX Mobile or JavaFX TV.

The Swing components supported are listed in Table 5.5.

Table 5.5   javafx.ext.swing to javax.swing class Mapping

javafx.ext.swing class	javax.swing class
SwingButton	javax.swing.JButton
SwingCheckBox	javax.swing.JCheckBox
SwingComboBox	javax.swing.JComboBox
SwingIcon	javax.swing.Icon
SwingLabel	javax.swing.JLabel
SwingList	javax.swing.JList
SwingRadioButton	javax.swing.JRadioButton
SwingScrollPane	javax.swing.JScrollPane
SwingSlider	javax.swing.JSlider
SwingTextField	javax.swing.JTextField
SwingToggleButton	javax.swing.JToggleButton

All the JavaFX Swing classes also extend javafx.scene.Node, so they can be added to a scene or other node container such as javafx.scene.Group. The scene graph can freely intermix these nodes with non-Swing nodes.

All the JavaFX Swing classes extend javafx.scene.SwingComponent. This class has an abstract function, createJComponent(): JComponent, that the subclass uses to actually instantiate the corresponding Java Swing class. In addition, the SwingComponent class has a function, getJComponent(): JComponent, that returns the underlying javax.swing.JComponent object. This object can then be cast to the specific Java Swing class. For example, when using a SwingTextField object stored in the variable jtextfield:

```
var jtextfield = textfield.getJComponent() as JTextField;
```

Most of the JavaFX Swing classes implement a function that does this conversion. For example, in SwingTextField there is a function, getJTextField(): JTextField, that does this.

If you have a Java class that extends JComponent, you can use that class in JavaFX by wrapping it via the SwingComponent.wrap() function. For example,

```
var myFXcomponent = SwingComponent.wrap(myJavaJComponent);
```

This merely allows the Swing component to participate in the JavaFX scene graph, but does not provide any other functionality. For instance, you do not have any mapping of your JComponent's attributes with corresponding JavaFX variables, so you do not realize any benefits from binding. If you wish to go one step further, you need to implement a Custom Swing Component.

Custom Swing Component

As we mentioned, all JavaFX Swing classes extend javafx.ext.swing.Swing-Component. These classes then must implement the function, createJComponent() : javax.swing.JComponent. This is easy enough, but what we really want to do is connect the Java Swing class's attributes to a JavaFX instance variable. Let's work through an example using the JTextArea class.

First, our class extends SwingComponent and implements the createJComponent() method to create the Swing component object.

```
public class TextArea extends SwingComponent {
    override function createJComponent() : JComponent {
        new JTextArea();
    }
}
```

Next, add the helper function to cast the component returned by SwingComponent's getJComponent() function to a JTextArea.

```
public function getJTextArea() : JTextArea {
    getJComponent() as JTextArea;
}
```

Now, we are ready to add some attribute support. Let's start with JTextArea's text attribute, which is of course the text that is displayed on the screen.

```
public var text:String;
```

This is not enough though. What happens if the user types into the JTextArea? How does this field update? What if the program sets this value; how does the JTextArea update? We need two more things. One is an on replace trigger so that when the JavaFX text instance variable changes, a corresponding change is made to the JTextArea. We will add an initialization to get the default value from the JTextArea.

```
public var text:String = getJTextArea().getText() on replace {
    getJTextArea().setText(text);
};
```

Next, to update the JavaFX text variable, when the JTextArea text attribute changes, we need to install a JavaBeans property change listener on the JTextArea.

```
init {
    var textArea = getJTextArea();
    textArea.addPropertyChangeListener(
                PropertyChangeListener {
        public override function propertyChange(
                ev: PropertyChangeEvent) : Void {
            var property = ev.getPropertyName();
            if(property == "text") {
                text = textArea.getText();
            }
            ...
```

Now, whenever the JTextArea text changes, a JavaBeans property change event will be fired, and the JavaFX corresponding instance variable can be set.

However, we have a problem. If the JavaFX program changes the JavaFX text instance variable, it will in turn call the JTextArea.setText() method, which causes the JavaBeans property change event to fire, which in turn sets the JavaFX text instance variable. We are stuck in an infinite circle and eventually our program will crash.

To overcome this, we need to add a flag indicating this condition to our JavaFX class. This indicates that the JavaFX text variable change caused the property change event to fire, so there is no need for the JavaBeans property change listener to update the companion JavaFX variable. We added the private Boolean variable, inChange.

```
var inChange = false;

public var text:String = getJTextArea().getText()
  on replace {
    if(not text.equals(getJTextArea().getText())){
        try {
            inChange = true;
            getJTextArea().setText(text);
        }finally {
            inChange = false;
        }
    }
};
...
```

```
    ...
        textArea.addPropertyChangeListener(
                PropertyChangeListener {
        public override function propertyChange(
                rev:PropertyChangeEvent) : Void {
                    if(inChange) {
                        return;
                    }
                    var property = ev.getPropertyName();
                    if(property == "text") {
                        text = textArea.getText();
    ...
    ...
```

This pattern can be repeated for any other Java attributes to JavaFX instance variable mappings.

In Chapter 12, JavaFX Code Recipes, we will discuss this pattern in more detail.

You may have realized that a JTextField is usually shown in a JScrollPane because the number of rows and columns may be more than the screen can accommodate; so we add one last tweak to our example. Instead of directly extending javafx.ext.swing.SwingComponent, we extend javafx.ext.swing.SwingScrollableComponent.

```
    public class TextArea extends SwingScrollableComponent {
```

That's it! Now, we have scroll bar support.

To use our text area class, just use an object literal just like any other JavaFX node.

```
Stage {
    title: "TextArea custom component"
    width: 475
    height: 425
    scene: Scene {
        content: TextArea {
            text: "Enter data here!"
            columns: 40
            rows: 24
            lineWrap: true
            wrapStyleWord: true
        }
    }
}
```

The full example is on the book's Web site, http://www.jfxbook.com.

Chapter Summary

JavaFX makes developing user interfaces straightforward and easy. By laying out the scene graph nodes using JavaFX object literals, the JavaFX language supports a top-down view of the scene graph. This is more intuitive to the developer. JavaFX also provides a robust set of user interface nodes and controls that facilitate developer productivity.

In this chapter, we discussed the stage, the scene, style sheets, JavaFX nodes, creating custom nodes, layout options, and using Java Swing Components. This all provides the foundation for creating rich user interfaces. Now we are ready to delve into some really cool stuff. The next set of chapters cover topics from special effects, animation, multimedia presentation, and creating RESTful applications.

6

Apply Special Effects

*"You know, my dear
My father used to say to me
Nando, don't be a schnook
It's not how you feel
It's how you look"*

—Billy Crystal

Sometimes, the task of constructing modern Rich Internet Applications ends up being more an exercise in integration and less a focus on what's really important: namely, creating interfaces that are intuitive and visually appealing. As part of an ongoing project, development teams will need to enlist the talents of graphic designers along with one or more graphics editing software packages. Additionally, they may require experts intimate with the intricacies of 2D and 3D graphics. Furthermore, someone well versed in a specific windowing platform (e.g., Java Swing) may be desired too.

One of the goals of the JavaFX platform is to increase the efficiency and ease by which a certain class of images and effects can be introduced into an application. Graphic designers will continue to perform the complex and interesting work with their image editing software. But why not incorporate many of the more common effects available in their toolbox right into the application platform? It could ease the designer's burden, and be a boon to developer productivity.

JavaFX offers, as an integral part of the platform, a wealth of *effects*, enabling developers in many instances to duplicate in a few lines of JavaFX script, what may have taken more effort with one of the popular graphics editing software packages. These effects also serve as the same classes used by the JavaFX Production Suite (i.e., Adobe Photoshop and Adobe Illustrator plug-ins) to import graphics into a JavaFX application. This chapter will cover many of the built-in effects that are available, and how they can be applied to your application to make a more compelling visual experience. They include

- **Shadowing** including DropShadow, InnerShadow, and Shadow.
- **Lighting** including DistantLight, PointLight, and SpotLight.
- **Gradients** including LinearGradient and RadialGradient. Technically, these do not belong to the effects package, but are used in a similar fashion and are thus grouped with this chapter.
- **Blurs** including GaussianBlur and MotionBlur.
- **Reflection.**
- **Blending** including Blend and BlendMode.
- **PerspectiveTransform.**
- **Glow.**
- **Bloom.**
- **DisplacementMap.**
- **Color Adjustment Effects** including SepiaTone and ColorAdjust.

Effects

In the JavaFX node-centric approach, the library classes that are used to create content (e.g., Text, Rectangle, ImageView, CustomNode, etc.) are all ultimately derived from the javafx.scene.Node class. As a result, they all share a set of common instance variables defined by Node, one of the most important being a variable called effect. By assigning a value to an instance's effect variable, you, in essence, apply an effect to that object.

The JavaFX runtime, by default, contains packages and classes under the javafx.scene.effect hierarchy, which represent the range of available effects that can be applied. They include, among others, classes for 2D and 3D lighting, blurring, shadowing, color adjusting, blending, glowing, toning, inverting, reflecting, blooming, and flooding operations. They are suitable for those of us who are not artistically inclined and offer an alternative in many cases to utilizing sophisticated image manipulation software.

In an effort to expose you to as many of the classes as possible, we'll spend a good part of this chapter applying individual effects first to simple shapes and later on to images and see how their appearance changes. It should, at minimum, serve as a reference for how to use a particular effect. Of course in the real world, you'll likely want to combine a host of effects together. So let's get started.

Shadowing

Adding a shadow to content is likely one of the things that you'll want to per-form regularly. To help make the task of showing straightforward, JavaFX has seen fit to include the `Shadow`, `DropShadow`, and `InnerShadow` effects. To demon-strate their usage, we'll first display some simple text as a baseline and see what happens as various permutations of the effects are applied. Figure 6.1 displays a simple `Text` node.

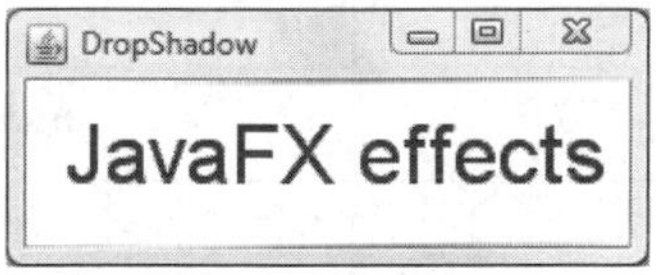

Figure 6.1   Initial Baseline Text

It is represented by the following code:

```
import javafx.stage.Stage;
import javafx.scene.Scene;
import javafx.scene.paint.*;
import javafx.scene.text.*;

Stage {
    width: 250
    height: 100
    scene: Scene {
        content: [
            Text {
                font: Font {
                    size: 32
                }
                x: 15, y: 40
                fill: Color.DARKRED
                content: "JavaFX effects"
            }
        ]
    }
}
```

DropShadow

The first effect we'll investigate is `DropShadow`, which enables you to render a shadow behind your content. Most effects provide one or more instance variables that allow you to control the visual appearance of the effect. For example, the `DropShadow` class provides five such variables, as described in Table 6.1.

Table 6.1   Instance Variables for DropShadow

Variable	Description	Default Value	Min Value	Max Value
color	The color of the shadow	BLACK	n/a	n/a
offsetX	The offset (in pixels) in the x direction	0.0	n/a	n/a
offsetY	The shadow offset (in pixels) in the y direction	0.0	n/a	n/a
radius	The radius of the shadow blur in pixels	10.0	1.0	63.0
spread	The spread of the shadow	0.0	0.0	1.0

It is not necessary to define all of these variables each time you want to use DropShadow, as they default to values that you may find acceptable. As we run through examples of other effects, explaining each of the instance variables in detail would result in a very lengthy and cumbersome chapter. Instead, we'll stick to easy-to-understand sample usages and suggest that for additional detail, you consult the JavaFX API documentation.

So let's apply a DropShadow effect to our sample code. To do so, only two easy insertions are required. The first involves letting the compiler know that the JavaFX effects classes will be brought into play. This is done by including the following import statement alongside your other imports:

```
import javafx.scene.effect.*;
```

Next, comes the more interesting modification of setting the Text node's effect instance variable. So, for example, if you want to add a DropShadow effect to the Text node referenced earlier, the effect instance variable could look something like

```
effect: DropShadow { offsetX: 3, offsetY: 3 }
```

Listing 6.1 shows the code for the original Text node enhanced to include a DropShadow effect, where the shadow offset is 3 pixels in the x and y direction. The remaining unreferenced instance variables of the DropShadow effect are assigned their default value.

Listing 6.1 Adding a DropShadow to a Text Node

```
import javafx.stage.*;
import javafx.scene.*;
import javafx.scene.paint.*;
import javafx.scene.text.*;
import javafx.scene.effect.*;

Stage {
    title: "DropShadow"
    width: 250
    height: 100
    scene: Scene {
        content: [
            Text {
                font: Font {
                    size: 32
                }
                x: 15, y: 40
                fill: Color.DARKRED
                content: "JavaFX effects"
                effect: DropShadow {
                    offsetX: 3
                    offsetY: 3
                }
            }
        ]
    }
}
```

Figure 6.2 depicts what would be displayed if the code in Listing 6.1 were to be compiled and executed.

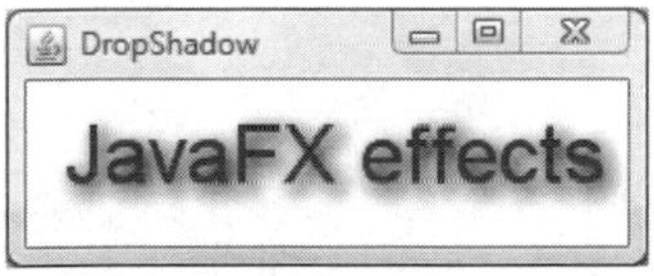

Figure 6.2 Text with DropShadow

Figure 6.3 demonstrates how, by changing the values of the instance variables of DropShadow, you can achieve different shadow effects.

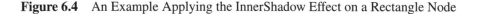

```
effect: DropShadow {              effect: DropShadow {
        offsetX: 3                        offsetX: 5
        offsetY: 15                       offsetY: 20
    }                                     radius: 3
                                      }
```

Figure 6.3   Two Different DropShadow Instances

InnerShadow

Similar to DropShadow, InnerShadow instead renders a shadow inside, rather than behind the content. It has the same instance variables as DropShadow, and introduces one other called choke, which gives additional control over the shadow effect. This time, we'll do our rendering on a Rectangle node to demonstrate how InnerShadow might be used. The following chunk of code demonstrates how a Rectangle instance might use InnerShadow.

```
Rectangle {
    x: 10, y: 10
    width: 200, height: 100
    arcWidth: 20, arcHeight: 20
    fill: Color.GRAY
    effect: InnerShadow { offsetX: 3, offsetY: 3 }
}
```

Figure 6.4 displays what the content would look like.

Figure 6.4   An Example Applying the InnerShadow Effect on a Rectangle Node

Shadow

The last of the built-in shadow effects is Shadow, which can be used to create a shadowy version of the original content. For example, if we replace the Drop-Shadow effect found in Listing 6.1 with

```
effect: Shadow { radius: 10 }
```

the resulting output would look like Figure 6.5.

Figure 6.5   An Example of the Shadow Effect on Text

Here, we see that the content *becomes* the shadow without including the original pre-effect text. Using Shadow, we could mimic the DropShadow effect seen in Figure 6.2 by including two Text nodes, one using the Shadow effect with the x and y coordinates offset by 3 pixels, the other node just displaying the text at the original coordinates. Nodes are displayed in the order they appear in the code, so the node with the Shadow effect must appear before the plain Text node. Here's how the JavaFX code segment would look:

```
Stage {
width: 250
    height: 100
    scene: Scene {
        var xStart = 15;
        var yStart = 40;
        content: [
            Text {
                font: Font {
                    size: 32
                }
                x: xStart+3, y: yStart+3
                content: "JavaFX effects"
                effect: Shadow { radius: 10 }
            }
            Text {
                font: Font {
                    size: 32
                }
                x: xStart, y: yStart
                fill: Color.DARKRED
                content: "JavaFX effects"
            }
        ]
    }
}
```

Lighting

The shadowing effects mentioned in the previous section represent one of many options available that can be used to give ordinary two-dimensional objects a three-dimensional look and feel. Another technique found in the JavaFX toolbox is *lighting*. The `Lighting` effect introduces a configurable light source that can be shone onto your content to produce a sense of depth. To use lighting, you must assign your content's `effect` variable with an instance of the `javafx .scene.effect.Lighting` class. Let's elaborate by offering up a straightforward example. The code snippet that follows shows how a `Lighting` effect can be added to a Rectangle.

```
Rectangle {
    width: 150,
    height: 100
    fill: Color.WHITE
    effect: Lighting {
        light: PointLight {
            x: 0, y: 200, z: 35
        }
    }
}
```

To be of any real use, the `Lighting` object literal needs to, at minimum, define its `light` instance variable. Derived from the base `javafx.scene.effect .light.Light` class, JavaFX provides three lighting effects, out of the box, for this purpose. Table 6.2 describes these lighting effects.

Like many of its relatives, the lighting effects come along with a good deal of configurable parameters. Instead of regurgitating verbatim what is already in the

Table 6.2   Lighting Effects

Lighting Effect	Description
DistantLight	Represents a distant light source by defining an azimuth and elevation in degrees relative to the content.
PointLight	Demonstrated above, defines a light source in 3D space with x, y, and z coordinates.
SpotLight	A subclass of `PointLight`, in addition to defining a light source in 3D space, `SpotLight` allows for configuration of the light source's direction and focus.

JavaFX API documentation, we'll show a few example usages and suggest again that the API documentation is the definitive source for further details. It turns out that using text, with all its nooks and crannies, shows off the capabilities of lighting quite nicely. For example, Listing 6.2 is a complete code listing for displaying text with a `DistantLight` effect.

Listing 6.2   Displaying Text with a DistantLight Effect

```
import javafx.stage.*;
import javafx.scene.*;
import javafx.scene.effect.*;
import javafx.scene.effect.light.*;
import javafx.scene.paint.*;
import javafx.scene.shape.*;
import javafx.scene.text.*;

function run() : Void {
    Stage {
        scene: Scene {
            var text:Text;
            content: [
                Rectangle {
                    width: bind
                        text.layoutBounds.width + 30
                    height: bind
                        text.layoutBounds.height + 20
                    fill: Color.BLACK
                },
                text = Text {
                    x: 10, y: 10, textOrigin: TextOrigin.TOP
                    content: "DistantLight"
                    fill: Color.YELLOW
                    font: Font {
                        size: 72
                    }
                    effect: Lighting {
                        light: DistantLight {
                            azimuth: 90
                            elevation: 45
                        }
                    }
                }
            ]
        }
    }
}
```

In addition to specifying a `Text` node with a `DistantLight` effect, Listing 6.2 also includes a black `Rectangle` node, which serves as a background to better contrast the lighting effect. By wrapping the content inside a `run()` function as defined in the preceding code, you can use the Design Preview feature of Net-Beans to make changes to your code and interactively see how those changes affect your display.

Adding a run() Function to Your Source Files

It is not uncommon for Java programmers to add `main()` methods inside their class definitions. Even though many individual classes are never meant to be run by themselves, including a `main()` method gives the developer an opportunity to test and debug a class separate from the whole application. JavaFX has a somewhat analogous capability with the `run()` function. By placing a `run()` function at the script level in your source, which follows this form:

```
function run() : Void {
    //Put your code here
}
```

you'll have the ability to quickly modify and visualize whatever content appears inside the body of the function by using the Design Preview capability within Net-Beans. Listing 6.2 contains a sample `run()` function.

Figure 6.6 shows what is produced when the code in Listing 6.2 is compiled and executed.

Figure 6.6   Demonstrating a Text Node with a DistantLight Lighting Effect

For our next two lighting examples, we'll use the same basic content, a `Text` node inside a black `Rectangle`; this time changing the text string and the lighting effect to see how the rendering of the image is affected. Figure 6.7 illustrates an instance of `PointLight` being applied to text. The light source for `PointLight` has an (x,y,z) coordinate of (0, -500, 100).

As part of the demonstration, an additional instance variable that can be utilized with `PointLight`, called `surfaceScale`, is assigned a value of 5. The range of

Figure 6.7   Demonstrating a Text Node with a PointLight Lighting Effect

acceptable values for this variable is from 0 to 10, the default value being 1.5. The `PointLight` effect for Figure 6.7 looks like this in JavaFX:

```
effect: Lighting {
    light: PointLight {
        x: 0 y: -500 z: 100
    }
    surfaceScale: 5
}
```

Finally, as `SpotLight` extends `PointLight`, it takes in the same instance variables as its parent and adds a few extras including the ability to define a vector—a light source direction—in 3D space. `SpotLight` also lets you set the value of a variable called `specularExponent`, which controls the focus of the light source and accepts a value from 0 to 4. Figure 6.8 shows one example of how a `SpotLight` effect can be applied to text.

Figure 6.8   Demonstrating a Text Node with a SpotLight Lighting Effect

In this case, the light source has been directed toward the end of the text, by virtue of assigning the `pointsAtX`, `pointsAtY`, and `pointsAtZ` instance variables to (400, 0, 0). This causes the dim letters at the beginning of the text. The preceding effect is represented in JavaFX as follows:

```
effect: Lighting {
    light: SpotLight {
        x: 0 y: 150 z: 40
        pointsAtX: 400 pointsAtY: 0 pointsAtZ: 0
        specularExponent: 4
    }
    surfaceScale: 5
}
```

Gradients

Gradients, as defined by the W3C *Scalable Vector Graphics Specification*, "consist of continuously smooth color transitions along a vector from one color to another" (http://www.w3.org/TR/SVG/pservers.html). Once defined, a gradient can be used as a fill pattern for graphical content. It could be a simple transition from one color to another, or it may involve multiple transitions and multiple colors. JavaFX mimics the functionality stated in the SVG spec by implementing classes that represent the two types of SVG gradients: `LinearGradient` and `RadialGradient`.

Technically, gradients do not belong to the built-in effects subclasses. It just so happens though that they are oftentimes used to produce effects similar to those discussed throughout this chapter. For this reason we include gradients here. Our samples that follow demonstrate, for example, how gradients can be used to make shapes look more three dimensional.

In keeping with our policy, we'll explain by example. Let's say you want to render a rectangle where the fill pattern starts out as white on the left side and transitions to black on the right. The rectangle might look something similar to what is seen in Figure 6.9.

Figure 6.9   A Rectangle Filled with a LinearGradient

Isolating the JavaFX script code, which describes the rectangle and this particular fill pattern, would look like this:

```
Rectangle {
x: 10, y: 10
width: 250, height: 50
stroke: Color.BLACK
fill: LinearGradient {
    proportional: true
    startX: 0.0, startY: 0.0, endX: 1.0, endY: 0.0
    stops: [
        Stop {offset: 0.0 color: Color.WHITE},
        Stop {offset: 1.0 color: Color.BLACK}
    ]
}
}
```

Let's dissect what's taking place here. First, gradients do not operate on the `effect` instance variable. Rather, they are assigned to the content's `fill` instance variable. As mentioned, gradients are not part of the javafx.scene.effect package, but instead they belong to `javafx.scene.paint`.

The `stops` variable is a sequence used for defining the overall gradient effect. Within the sequence, a series of `Stop` instances are used to describe individual transitions. Its `offset` variable, ranging in value from 0 to 1, describes where, within the content, this gradient should be placed, 0.0 being the beginning of the content, 1.0 being the end, 0.33 being approximately a third of the way in, and so on. Alongside the `offset` variable, a `Stop` instance should also specify the `color` too. In our preceding example, we, in effect, define the simplest of transitions, a beginning `Stop` (offset is set to 0.0) with a white color, and an end `Stop` (offset 1.0) set to black. With this information, the JavaFX runtime will fill in the content interpolating all of the colors in between the stops.

Lastly, in our example, the gradient was defined with the `proportional` variable set to true. By doing so, the start and end coordinates are defined relative to the shape where, again, 0.0 specifies the beginning of the shape, 1.0 specifies the end. By setting `proportional` to false instead, the start and end points would have to be defined in absolute pixels.

LinearGradient

Sticking with our 3D theme, gradients, among many other uses, could be employed to add perspective to content. Let's see how a `LinearGradient` can be applied to an ordinary shape to make it look more realistic. First, we'll combine two simple shapes together, a triangle and an ellipse, to create a cone. Figure 6.10 displays the particulars; later on we'll supply the complete code.

The resulting cone uses a class called `ShapeIntersect`, which is part of the `javafx.scene.shape` package, to construct one logical shape from a number of previously independent ones. The `ShapeIntersect a[]` instance variable forms a union of the shapes included in the sequence—in this case a triangle and an ellipse—while the `b[]` sequence (not used in this example) could be used to add additional shapes that are intersected with `a[]` to form yet a more complex shape. The big advantage of using `ShapeIntersect` here is that you can apply an effect to the entire object, rather than having to do so on each individual component.

```
Polygon {                Ellipse {                ShapeIntersect {
   points : [               centerX: 85             fill: Color.PURPLE
      10, 190                centerY: 190           a: [
      80, 10                 radiusX: 75               Polygon {
      160, 190               radius:  20                  points: [
   ]                         fill: Color.PURPLE              10, 190
   fill: Color.PURPLE     }                                  85, 10
}                                                            160, 190
                                                          ]
                                                       }
                                                       Ellipse {
                                                          centerX: 85
                                                          centerY: 190
                                                          radiusX: 75
                                                          radiusY: 20
                                                       }
                                                    ]
```

Figure 6.10   Combining Two Basic Shapes Together to Form a Cone

Let's add a LinearGradient to the entire cone. The code describing our desired fill pattern looks like this:

```
fill: LinearGradient {
    startX: 30, startY: 190
    endX: 190, endY: 170
    proportional: false
    stops: [
        Stop { offset: 0.0 color: Color.PURPLE },
        Stop { offset: 0.5 color: Color.WHITE },
        Stop { offset: 1.0 color: Color.PURPLE },
    ]
}
```

This time, we set the proportional instance variable to false and use pixel coordinates to specify the start and stop locations. To give a realistic perspective to the cone, the LinearGradient is centered slightly to the right of the cone tip, and its angle is not vertical, but to some extent diagonal. A third `Stop` is included in the `stops` sequence, to add gradient transitions from purple to white back to purple again. Figure 6.11 shows the rendered cone.

Figure 6.11 Adding a LinearGradient to a Compound Shape

Combining all of the snippets together, Listing 6.3 contains the complete set of code required to generate the image found in Figure 6.11.

Listing 6.3 A Cone with a LinearGradient

```
import javafx.stage.*;
import javafx.stage.*;
import javafx.scene.*;
import javafx.scene.paint.*;
import javafx.scene.shape.*;

function run(args : String[]) : Void {
    Stage {
        scene: Scene {
            width: 170
            height: 220
            content: ShapeIntersect {
                fill: LinearGradient {
                    startX: 30, startY: 190
                    endX: 190, endY: 170
                    proportional: false
                    stops: [
                        Stop {
                                offset: 0.0
                                color: Color.PURPLE
                        },
```

continues

```
                    Stop {
                        offset: 0.5
                        color: Color.WHITE
                    },
                    Stop {
                        offset: 1.0
                        color: Color.PURPLE
                    },
                ]
            }
            a: [
                Polygon {
                    points: [
                        10, 190,
                        85, 10,
                        160, 190
                    ]
                }
                Ellipse {
                    centerX: 85, centerY: 190
                    radiusX: 75, radiusY: 20
                }
            ]
        }
    }
  }
}
```

RadialGradient

A LinearGradient can be employed to augment the appearance of a shape, making it look more 3D-like. However, it is only effective for a certain class of objects. For example, if you want to add some perspective to a circle to make it look more sphere-like, using LinearGradient would likely not result in a very realistic image. You could make use of the RadialGradient class. Rather than filling shapes with linear patterns, a RadialGradient gives you a way to fill content with circular or radial patterns. Here's a segment of code demonstrating the use of RadialGradient with a Circle node.

```
Circle {
    centerX: 100, centerY: 60
    radius: 50
    fill: RadialGradient {
        centerX: 125, centerY: 45,
        radius: 50
        proportional: false
```

```
        stops: [
            Stop {offset: 0.0 color: Color.WHITE},
            Stop {offset: 1.0 color: Color.DARKORANGE},
        ]
    }
}
```

A `RadialGradient` is typically instantiated by defining a center (x,y) point and a radius size. Like its `LinearGradient` cousin, a `RadialGradient` gives the developer the choice of either using absolute or relative coordinates as defined by the `proportional` instance variable. In the preceding case, absolute coordinates are used where the center of the gradient appears in the upper-right quadrant of the circle, giving the illusion of a light source shining down on the upper-right part of a sphere. Executing the preceding code within an appropriate stage and scene results in an image depicted in Figure 6.12.

Figure 6.12　Adding a RadialGradient to a Circle to Make It Look Like a Sphere

Blurs

The ability to blur your content is available in JavaFX via the `GaussianBlur` and `MotionBlur` effects.

GaussianBlur

The `GaussianBlur` effect defines one primary instance variable, `radius`, which is used to specify the extent of the blur in pixels. Of its many possible uses, `GaussianBlur` could serve as yet another mechanism for shadowing. Let's see how we might use it to add a shadow to our cone image. First, create a simple triangle, which is shown in Figure 6.13.

Figure 6.13　A Simple Triangle

Then, apply a `GaussianBlur` effect to the triangle as demonstrated in Figure 6.14.

Figure 6.14   GaussianBlur Applied to Triangle

Here's the JavaFX code snippet.

```
Polygon {
    points : [
        10, 190,
        10, 110
        150, 190
    ]
    fill: Color.BLACK
    effect: GaussianBlur { radius: 15 }
}
```

Finally, let's add this shape to our cone found in Figure 6.11 to produce the image displayed in Figure 6.15.

Figure 6.15   Cone with GaussianBlur Shadow

MotionBlur

`MotionBlur` allows you to employ a blur effect in a particular direction, in essence, simulating motion. This can be brought about by adding an instance variable, called `angle`, which is stated in degrees, to control the direction of the blur. The following block of code defines a series of chevron shapes in succession, and applies a `MotionBlur` effect giving the appearance that the chevrons are moving quickly to the right.

```
Scene {
    var numChevrons = 8;
    height: 50
    width: (numChevrons+2)*20
    content: [
        Group {
            effect: MotionBlur { radius: 12 angle: 0 }
            content:  for (i in [0..numChevrons]) {
                Polyline {
                    points: [ 10+i*20, 10,
                              25+i*20, 25,
                              10+i*20, 40 ]
                    strokeWidth: 4
                    stroke: Color.RED
                }
            }
        }
    ]
}
```

Figure 6.16 portrays what our chevron shapes look like before and after the `MotionBlur` effect, which is in bold in the preceding code, is applied to them.

Figure 6.16   Chevron PolyLine Shapes Before and After a MotionBlur Effect Is Applied

Reflection

JavaFX comes equipped with an effect called `Reflection`, which, as its name implies, renders a mirror image of your content below the original image. So, if you want to add a reflection effect to the sphere represented by Figure 6.12, you could do so with this single line of JavaFX code:

```
effect: Reflection { fraction: .75, topOffset: 3 }
```

This object literal defines two of Reflection's instance variables. The `fraction` variable represents what percentage of the original image is reflected below the original image, in our case, 75%. The second variable, `topOffset`, defines where, in numbers of pixels, the reflection effect should begin below the content. Figure 6.17 shows what happens to our sphere when the effect is added to it.

Figure 6.17   Sphere with Reflection Effect

Blending

Blending enables you to combine two inputs together to form a composite output by selecting one of the predefined `BlendModes`. The JavaFX API spells out approximately 20 of these; we'll demonstrate a few with straightforward examples so that you get a feel for how blending can be used in practice.

For our first sample, we'll compare and contrast the `ADD` and `MULTIPLY` `BlendModes` by intersecting a magenta-filled rectangle with some green-colored text. The rationale for choosing these two colors will become apparent as we differentiate between `ADD` and `MULTIPLY`, which are described in Table 6.3.

Table 6.3   ADD and MULTIPLY BlendModes

BlendMode	Description
ADD	The individual color components (R, G, B) and alpha value (transparency) are *added* together to form new component values. In the case where the sum of any component exceeds the maximum component value, it is capped to the maximum value.
MULTIPLY	The individual color components (R, G, B) and alpha value (transparency) are *multiplied* together to form new component values. In the case where the product of any component exceeds the maximum component value, it is capped to the maximum value.

Listing 6.4 demonstrates how to blend two inputs together using the `ADD` `BlendMode`.

Listing 6.4   Demonstrating BlendMode.ADD

```
import javafx.scene.shape.*;
import javafx.scene.paint.*;
```

```
import javafx.stage.*;
import javafx.scene.*;
import javafx.scene.effect.*;
import javafx.scene.text.*;

Stage {
    scene: Scene {
        width: 150
        height: 150
        content: [
            Group {
                blendMode: BlendMode.ADD
                content: [
                    Rectangle {
                        x: 35 y: 50
                        width: 75 height: 50
                        fill: Color.rgb(255, 0, 255, 1)
                    }
                    Text {
                        font: Font {
                            size: 52
                        }
                        x: 5, y: 95
                        content: "Blend"
                        fill: Color.rgb(0, 255, 0 , 1)
                    }
                ]
            }
        ]
    }
}
```

Figure 6.18 displays the resulting output.

Figure 6.18   BlendMode.ADD Effect

The resulting image shows, even in grayscale, that the text appearing inside the rectangle is white. This happens because the rectangle color, specified in (R, G, B), is (255, 0, 255), whereas the text has a color of (0, 255, 0). If we add each of the individual components up, we get a resulting color of (255, 255, 255).

For our next example, we'll make one small code change to Listing 6.4 to demonstrate a different `BlendMode` effect. Replace the `BlendMode.ADD` occurrence with `BlendMode.MULTIPLY` as follows:

```
blendMode: BlendMode.MULTIPLY
```

Figure 6.19 shows the result.

Figure 6.19   BlendMode.MULTIPLY Effect

This time, the text enclosed within the rectangle is black. Why? Because the individual color components are multiplied with one another rather than added. The resulting (R, G, B) color is now (0, 0, 0).

For our next example, we'll utilize the `Blend` effect to demonstrate two additional `BlendMode`s. `Blend` includes, among others, two instance variables called `topInput` and `bottomInput` which, as their names imply, let you identify both top and bottom inputs, respectively, for blending. We'll specify the `topInput` variable to show how the `SRC_OUT` and `SRC_IN` `BlendMode`s can be used and how they differ.

Our code for this segment furthermore introduces a new effect called `Flood`, which "floods" a rectangular region with an effect denoted by its `paint` instance variable (in this case, a `LinearGradient` instance). This could be used as a potentially more efficient alternative to rendering a `Rectangle`. Before showing the listing and the resulting output, Table 6.4 describes the available `SRC BlendMode`s.

Just in case you're a little confused by the descriptions, let's show how an example usage of `SRC_OUT` might be coded. Listing 6.5 has the specifics.

Table 6.4   SRC BlendModes

BlendMode	Description
SRC_ATOP	The part of the top input that is lying inside the bottom input is blended with the bottom input
SRC_IN	The part of the top input that is lying inside the bottom input is kept inside the resulting image
SRC_OUT	The part of the top input that is lying outside the bottom input is kept inside the resulting image
SRC_OVER	The top input is blended over the bottom input

Listing 6.5   Demonstrating SRC_OUT BlendMode

```
import javafx.scene.shape.*;
import javafx.scene.paint.*;
import javafx.stage.*;
import javafx.scene.*;
import javafx.scene.effect.*;
import javafx.scene.text.*;

Stage {
    scene: Scene {
        width: 160 height: 80
        content: [
            Text {
                effect: Blend {
                    mode: BlendMode.SRC_OUT
                    topInput: Flood {
                        paint: LinearGradient {
                            proportional: true
                            startX: 0.0, startY: 0.0
                            endX: 1.0, endY: 0.0
                            stops: [
                                Stop {
                                    offset: 0.0
                                    color: Color.WHITE
                                },
                                Stop {
                                    offset: 1.0
                                    color: Color.BLACK
                                }
                            ]
                        }
                    }
```

continues

```
                    width: 100 height: 25
                    x: 30 y: 25
               }
          }
          x: 10 y: 55
          content: "Blend"
          font: Font.font(null, FontWeight.BOLD,
                          FontPosture.REGULAR, 48);
     }
  ]
}
}
```

Figure 6.20 displays the output generated by executing the code found in Listing 6.5.

Figure 6.20   BlendMode.SRC_OUT Effect

Figure 6.21 shows what happens when the `SRC_OUT` `BlendMode` found in Listing 6.5 is replaced with `SRC_IN` as represented by the following line of code:

```
mode: BlendMode.SRC_IN
```

Figure 6.21   BlendMode.SRC_IN Effect

PerspectiveTransform

Thus far, the effects examples in this chapter revolved around basic shapes, neglecting a whole universe of content available to JavaFX in the form of images. For the remainder of this chapter, we'll switch gears and use images rather than shapes to demonstrate that effects can be applied to this type of content in the same fashion.

The first of these effects, `PerspectiveTransform`, gives us a mechanism to render an artificial 3D effect to content that is otherwise two-dimensional. It is accomplished by mapping the original content to an arbitrary four-sided polygon to provide perspective. The instance variables that must be defined represent the (x,y) coordinates of the new polygon, namely the upper-left (`ulx`, `uly`), upper-right (`urx`, `ury`), lower-left (`llx`, `lly`), and lower-right (`lrx`, `lry`) corners. Let's begin with an image as shown in Figure 6.22.

Figure 6.22 Base Image Before PerspectiveTransform

Let's apply a `PerspectiveTransform` on it, using this code:

```
ImageView {
    image: Image {
        url: "{__DIR__}liberty.jpg"
    }
    effect: PerspectiveTransform {
        ulx:  10 uly: 50
        urx: 200 ury: 10
        llx:  10 lly: 100
        lrx: 200 lry: 160
    }
}
```

The resulting image is transformed into the output displayed by Figure 6.23.

Figure 6.23 Base Image After PerspectiveTransform Has Been Applied

Glow and Bloom

The `Glow` and `Bloom` effects are comparable in function and usage. In this section, we'll supply examples of both, ultimately contrasting the subtle differences that `Glow` and `Bloom` provide for the JavaFX developer.

Glow

To show the `Glow` effect, we'll borrow an idea from our sample Sudoku application. While playing the Sudoku game, when you click on a space on the board, the number inside that space will glow for the duration of the mouse click. So applying a `Glow` effect to one of the numbers, which are represented as images, is as easy as this:

```
ImageView {
    effect: Glow { level: .9 }
    image: Image {
        url: "{__DIR__}8-bold.png"
    }
}
```

The `level` instance variable that is part of `Glow` is responsible for setting the intensity of the glow effect. It takes a number ranging in value from 0 to 1. Figure 6.24 shows what the number image looks like under normal conditions and how it appears when a `Glow` effect with intensity level .9 is applied.

Figure 6.24   Before and After a Glow Effect Has Been Applied

To provide slightly more context within the Sudoku application, the `Glow` effect is achieved by catching and handling the mouse events that occur on the node represented by the board space. When the mouse is pressed on a space, a `Glow` effect is assigned to the image occupying that space. When the mouse is released, the effect is taken away. The `onMousePressed` and `onMouseReleased` handlers of the Sudoku `SpaceNode` look as follows:

```
override var onMousePressed = function(me : MouseEvent)

: Void {
    me.node.effect = Glow { level: 0.9 };
}
```

```
override var onMouseReleased = function(me : MouseEvent)
: Void {
    me.node.effect = null;
}
```

Bloom

Very similar to Glow, instead of operating on the entire image, the Bloom effect focuses on the brighter aspects of an image and makes them appear to glow. The primary instance variable associated with Bloom is called threshold and can be assigned a value between 0 and 1. Here's how it might be applied to a sample image with embedded text:

```
Group {
    effect: Bloom { threshold: .9 }
    content: [
        ImageView {
            image: Image {
                width: 250, height: 166
                url: "{__DIR__}flower.jpg"
            }
        },
        Text {
            font: Font {
                size: 28
                embolden: true
            }
            x: 70, y: 22
            content: "Bloom .9"
            fill: Color.WHITE
        }
    ]
}
```

Figure 6.25 depicts three separate images and the subtle differences that result as the Glow and Bloom effects are utilized. The first image is rendered with no effects; the second includes a Glow effect and the third a Bloom effect. Again, the original images are in color. Rendering them in grayscale here may further reduce the details.

Figure 6.25   Applying Glow and Bloom Effects to an Image

DisplacementMap

One of the more sophisticated effects, you can use a `DisplacementMap` to change the appearance of your content in some very unique ways. For each pixel, a corresponding user-supplied `FloatMap` entry is retrieved, and along with optional `scale` and `offset` instance variables, applied to the content to produce a new output.

For this effect, we'll lean heavily on the JavaFX API documentation. As explained there, each individual `FloatMap` entry contains per-pixel offset information in the x and y direction. Filling `FloatMap` entries with values of (0, 0) would signify no offset change, whereas a `FloatMap` full with values of (0.5, 0.5) would yield an offset half the original source size.

Taken in good part from the API documentation, the next example fills a `FloatMap` with data produced by a mathematical function (a sine wave). The result of using it inside a `DisplacementMap` produces a wavy effect on your content. The API example uses shapes and text as input. If instead we use the image of, for example, a flag, the `DisplacementMap` effect could be construed to produce an image of a flag flapping in the wind. Listing 6.6 has the details.

Listing 6.6 An Example Usage of DisplacementMap

```
import java.lang.Math;
import javafx.scene.*;
import javafx.stage.*;
import javafx.scene.effect.*;
import javafx.scene.image.*;

function run (args : String[]) : Void {
    var w = 200;
    var h = 140;
    var map = FloatMap { width: w height: h }
    for (i:Integer in [0..<w]) {
        var v = (Math.sin(i/35.0*Math.PI)-0.5)/30.0;
        for (j:Integer in [0..<h]) {
            map.setSamples(i, j, 0.0, v);
        }
    }
    Stage {
        scene: Scene {
            content: [
                ImageView {
                    effect: DisplacementMap { mapData: map }
                    image: Image {
                        url: "{__DIR__}brazilflag.jpg"
                    }
```

```
            }
        ]
    }
  }
}
```

Figure 6.26 shows the before and after effect on an image representing the flag of Brazil.

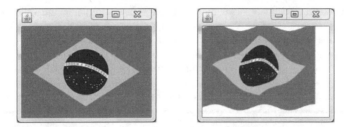

Figure 6.26   Before and After Effects of Applying a DisplacementMap on an Image

Miscellaneous Color Adjustment Effects

The final two effects described in this chapter revolve primarily around the manipulation of color. Because the publishing process converts images to gray-scale, effectively defeating the intended outcome of these effects, we'll forego furnishing sample images for this section.

SepiaTone

One such effect, called SepiaTone, can be used to simulate the look of a faded antique photo. It includes a level instance variable that takes a value ranging from 0 to 1 controlling the intensity of the effect. Using our original Statue of Liberty image and applying a SepiaTone to it can be described as follows:

```
ImageView {
    image: Image {
        url: "{__DIR__}liberty.jpg"
    }
    effect: SepiaTone { level: .7 }
}
```

We suggest you create a simple example or two to get a feel for how this effect might be used.

ColorAdjust

JavaFX provides the ability to adjust the contrast, hue, saturation, and brightness of your content via the `ColorAdjust` effect. Table 6.5 describes the available instance variables.

Table 6.5   ColorAdjust Instance Variables

Variable	Description
contrast	The contrast adjustment value, ranging from (0.25 – 4). The default value is 1.
hue	The hue adjustment value, ranging from (-1 – 1). The default value is 0.
saturation	The saturation adjustment value, ranging from (-1 – 1). The default value is 0.
brightness	The brightness adjustment value, ranging from (-1 – 1). The default value is 0.

Chapter Summary

For this chapter, we've touched on the effects that come as part of the JavaFX platform, and included straightforward examples of how these can be utilized, stressing simplicity. This should serve as a quick reference as you delve into making your content more eye-catching.

Add Motion with JavaFX Animation

"Animation is not the art of drawings that move
but the art of movements that are drawn."

—Norman McLaren

Computer Animation

In traditional hand-drawn animation, a lead animator draws key drawings in a scene. These are the most important actions and represent the extremes of the action. The idea is to provide enough detail to present the main elements of movement. Next, the animator decides how long each action should last on the screen. After this is done, these key drawings are passed to assistant animators who draw the inbetween frames to achieve smooth movement. The action duration dictates how many inbetween frames are needed. This process is called tweening, which is short for inbetweening.

Borrowing from the traditional animation process, computer animation is a time period sliced with *key frames*. However, instead of using assistant animators, the computer does the tweening process by applying mathematical formulas to adjust the position, opacity, color, or other aspects required for the action. The computer decides how many inbetween frames are required based on the timing constraints placed between two key frames.

The primary property of animation is time, so JavaFX supports the time period of an animation sequence with a timeline. The JavaFX class that represents animation actions spread across a time duration is `javafx.animation.Timeline`. Key frames, `javafx.animation.KeyFrame`, are interspersed across the timeline at specified intervals, represented by time durations, `javafx.lang.Duration`. These key frames may contain key values, `javafx.animation.KeyValue`, that represent the end state of the specified application values such as position, opacity, and color, and may also include actions that execute when the key time occurs. Key values also contain a declaration of which mathematical formula, or interpolator, `javafx.animation.Interpolator`, should be used in the tweening process.

Figure 7.1 demonstrates the key frames within a timeline that mimics the rise and setting of the sun or moon. Each disc is at a specific location at the respective key frame time. At the start, 0 seconds, the disc is on the left hand side at its lowest position. At 200 seconds, the next key position is a little further right and higher. At 500 seconds, the disc shape is at its zenith. At 800 seconds, the disc is lower and to the right, then at 1,000 seconds, it is setting off the horizon. In the actual animation, the disc smoothly moves in an arc from left to right, over 1,000 seconds.

The timeline represents the animation sequence, and can be started, paused, resumed, and stopped. It is also possible to choose the point in time to start or resume the animation, which enables an application to implement features found in a Videocassette Recorder (VCR) or Digital Video Recorder (DVR) such as play, pause, stop, rewind, and fast forward.

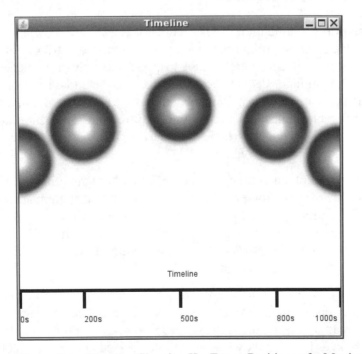

Figure 7.1   Timeline Showing KeyFrame Positions of a Moving Disc Shape

The next few sections cover these animation classes and demonstrate their use. After that, we will revisit our Eclipse animation example based on the graphical objects we created with the JavaFX Production Suite in Chapter 2, JavaFX for the Graphic Designer.

Timelines

A timeline provides the ability to update animation associated properties over a period of time. A timeline is defined by one or more sequential key frames ordered by their respective time within the timeline. The animation properties are then changed over the time period using a mathematical formula to a new target value.

A timeline may move either forward or backward in time. Also, it may play its cycle one or more times, or even indefinitely. You can specify that it alternates direction for each cycle so that it plays forward then backwards. You can also speed up or slow down the rate of play. Timelines can also be paused, resumed, or stopped. In addition, you can set when to start or restart, either at the beginning or at some intermediate point within the timeline.

A sample `Timeline` object literal is shown in Listing 7.1 with the key points highlighted. The `KeyFrame` syntax will be covered in the next section.

Listing 7.1   Timeline Object Literal

```
import javafx.animation.*;

// point on screen
var x: Integer;
var y: Integer;

var timeline = Timeline {
    // go forward, then backward on alternating cycle
    autoReverse: true
    repeatCount: Timeline.INDEFINITE // run until stopped
    // normal time, 2x would be 2.0, half speed is 0.5
    rate: 1.0
    keyFrames: [
        // at 0 milli seconds, set x/y to initial value
        at(0ms) {
            x => 0;
            y => 0;
        },
```

continues

```
        // at 10 seconds, set x/y to target value
        at(10s) {
            x => 1000 tween Interpolator.LINEAR;
            y => 1000 tween Interpolator.LINEAR;
        }
    ]

};

// play from current position, which at start is 0
timeline.play();
timeline.pause();        // pause
timeline.play();         // resume at pause point
timeline.pause();
timeline.time = 1s;      // set the current time to 1 second
timeline.play();         // resume play at 1 second
// stop and reset start time to the Start Time

timeline.stop();
```

When the timeline plays, it starts, by default, at time zero; then, while it progresses to the next specified time (10 seconds in the preceding example), the interpolators for each target value are repeatedly invoked so that the animation can provide a smooth transition from the original value to the final target value. The runtime system decides how to break up the interval between key frames in order to have smooth movement; however, this can be influenced by load and capabilities of the client's machine. Insufficient compute power may result in jerky animations.

The function play() starts the timeline from its current position. There is also a playFromStart() function that always starts at the initial position. The function, pause(), stops the play at the current position, and a subsequent play() resumes the timeline from that position. Finally, the stop() function stops the play and resets the timeline to the initial position.

By default, autoReverse is turned off, so the timeline only progresses forward, repeatCount is 1.0, so that the timeline only cycles once, and the rate is 1.0, so the animation runs at normal speed.

You can examine several instance variables to determine the current state of the timeline. First, the instance variable, running, indicates whether the timeline has been started or stopped. Notice that a paused timeline is still in the running state, but the paused instance variable is true. To detect that the timeline is playing, it is necessary to check running for true and paused for false.

The currentRate instance variable indicates the current speed and direction of play. A negative currentRate indicates the timeline is playing backwards. Therefore, if autoReverse is set to true, you can determine whether the timeline is currently playing forward or backward from the currentRate value. To set the play rate, use the rate instance variable. Again, if the rate is negative, the timeline will play in reverse.

You can tell the current instant of playback using the time instance variable. Also use this instance variable to set the specific time to resume play. If you want to resume play halfway through the time sequence, then you can set the time value to one half the total duration. Then when you instruct the timeline to play, it will play from that point. Another way to use the time variable is to increment the time to jump forward or decrement it to jump backward in the animation. For example, if you define a button to skip forward 10 seconds, you can increment the time by 10 seconds or actually by 10,000 milliseconds. To set the timeline to the beginning, you can set the time variable to zero (0). To set it to the end, set the time variable to the end duration for the timeline. This is useful if you want to play the timeline in reverse from the end.

The instance variable, interpolate, is by default set to true and means that when the timeline plays, the system will split up the interval between time frames and invoke the key target value interpolators. If the timeline is not using interpolations, but perhaps only uses actions, there may be a performance improvement to set interpolate to false. This is because when interpolate is false, the timeline does not have to do the tweening steps between key frames.

Key Frames

A key frame defines a pivotal timing event with values that are tweened, or interpolated, along the timeline. The key frame contains a time value within the timeline, along with optional items. These items are associated target values called key values, an *action* that is executed when the time is reached within a play, or a sub timeline that starts when the key frame's time within the timeline is reached. There is also an indicator identifying whether the action function can be skipped if the timeline is running behind schedule.

A KeyFrame may be defined using the object literal syntax for creating any JavaFX object, or may use a special short-cut syntax. First, let us cover a few basics.

Duration

A javafx.lang.Duration is an object that defines a time interval. To simplify creating durations, JavaFX supports *time literals*. In the previous timeline example, there were two time literals, 0ms, zero milliseconds, and 10s, for ten seconds. To declare a time literal, use a number followed by a time unit. The possible units of time are ms for milliseconds, s for seconds, m for minutes, and h for hours. The number may be either an integer or a decimal number. For example, 1500ms is equal to 1.5s.

You can also do arithmetic functions on time literals. For example:

```
println(2h + 30m + 3s + 10ms); // 9003010.0ms
println(1m - 30s);             //   30000.0ms
println(10ms * 2);             //      20.0ms
println(10ms / 2);             //       5.0ms
```

Duration objects are immutable, so they cannot be changed once created. In the preceding examples, each time literal argument within the arithmetic expression represents a distinct Duration instance and another distinct instance represents the result.

Besides using the time literals as shown here, you can also create Duration objects using the function valueOf(), passing in milliseconds as the parameter. The following all equal a duration of 10 seconds:

```
var duration = Duration.valueOf(10000);
var duration = 10000ms;
var duration = 10s;
var duration = 0.166666m; // approximates 10 seconds
```

Sometimes, it is useful to declare a Duration object that can later be bound within an expression. This is useful if you want to dynamically change the time of the timeline. Perhaps you want to allow the user to change the animation from 5 seconds to 15 seconds. When doing this within a timeline, this duration object is automatically bound. This is illustrated in Listing 7.2.

Listing 7.2 Duration Variable

```
public var duration = 10s;
var x:Number;
var y:Number;
var timeline = Timeline {
    keyFrames: [
        // at 0 milli seconds, set x/y to initial value
        at(0ms) {
            x => 0;
            y => 0;
        },
```

```
KeyFrame {
    time: duration
    values: [
        x => 1000 tween Interpolator.LINEAR,
        y => 1000 tween Interpolator.LINEAR,
    ]
}
]
}
```

Now, if the application needs to change the duration of the timeline, one merely has to change the `duration` variable to a new duration. Please note that it is important to declare the `duration` variable before the timeline is declared.

Key Values

Key values are declared using a special syntax:

```
target => value tween interpolator
```

`Target` is the target variable that will be changed, `value` is the target value that the target variable assumes when the key frame time arrives, and `interpolator` is the `Interpolator` to use. So in the preceding example, the x variable is zero at 0 seconds, and then 1000 at 10 seconds. This value uses a *linear*, or constant rate of change, interpolator over the 10-second interval. The `=>` operator indicates that the variable will transition to the value during the time slice. The `tween` keyword identifies the `Interpolator` to use during tweening. If no `tween` and `interpolator` is given, a discrete interpolator is the default. This means the value instantly changes from 0 to 1000 when the key frame's time is reached.

Key Frames

The class, `javafx.animation.KeyFrame`, represents a key frame within the timeline. Each key frame has a time in the form of a duration, zero or more key values, an optional action function that is executed when the play arrives at the key frame's time, and zero or more sub timelines that start to play when the key frame's time is reached.

As previously mentioned, there are two ways to declare a key frame. One way is to use the normal JavaFX object literal syntax for the `KeyFrame` object.

```
KeyFrame {
    time: 10s
    values: [
        x => 1000 tween Interpolator.LINEAR,
        y => 1000 tween Interpolator.LINEAR,
    ]
    action: function():Void {
        println("Key frame @10 seconds");
    }
    timelines: [
        subTimeline1,
        subTimeline2
    ]
}
```

The time instance variable contains the duration within the timeline that the key frame represents. Next, there are the set of zero or more key values, followed by an optional action function. Lastly, there is an optional sequence of sub time-lines represented by the timelines instance variable. By default, time is set to 0 seconds, values and timelines are empty, and the action instance variable is null. There is another instance variable, canSkip, that indicates that the timeline can skip the defined action if it is running behind schedule.

Sub timelines allow you to nest timelines within other timelines and allow you to break up complex animations into smaller, more manageable parts. Each sub time-line's starting point is relative to the parent timeline's key frame time. Sub timelines are useful if you have several discrete animations controlled by a master anima-tion. Also, sub timelines are useful if you want more than one animation to start at exactly the same time—for example, if you want to animate two motions at once.

The second form for declaring a KeyFrame is a shortcut version of the object lit-eral syntax. This takes the form of using the at keyword with a time literal within parenthesis. The key values are contained within the following curly braces. Notice the semicolon rather than a comma after the key value statements.

```
at(10s) {
    x => 1000 tween Interpolator.LINEAR;
    y => 1000 tween Interpolator.LINEAR;
}
```

This is a concise way for declaring the majority of KeyFrames. However, there are limitations. First, when using this syntax, there is no way to include an action function nor include sub timelines. Second, the syntax only allows time literals, so another duration variable cannot be used for specifying the time. Nonetheless, when creating timelines, you can intersperse this concise syntax with the full object literal syntax for those key frames requiring the extra features. The following code snippet shows this.

```
var timeline = Timeline {
    keyFrames: [
        at(0ms) {
            x => 0;
            y => 0;
        },
        KeyFrame {
            time: duration
            values: [
                x => 1000 tween Interpolator.LINEAR,
                y => 1000 tween Interpolator.LINEAR,
            ]
            action: function():Void {
                println("Key frame @10 seconds");
            }
        }
    ]
}
```

Interpolation

Interpolation is the process of estimating values between two known values. This section describes how interpolation is applied to animation and discusses how interpolation is supported in JavaFX. Let's start by examining the "tweening" process and how it is applied to computer animation.

Tweening

As we already mentioned, tweening is the process of filling in the "inbetween" frames between two key frames. In JavaFX, the runtime system takes the time interval between two key frames and breaks it up into smaller periods so that the animation appears smooth. Each of these smaller chunks of time is represented as a percentage of the overall time period using the value range 0.0 to 1.0. Interpolation is based on calling a mathematical function for each of these discrete time chunks, increasing the percentage of elapse time with each invocation.

When the runtime system invokes the interpolation function, it passes the starting value for the variable being interpolated, the ending value, and the fractional time percentage. Based on these input values, the interpolator calculates the value that the variable should contain at that instant.

A common way to interpolate is to provide a mathematical function that represents a drawn curve between 0.0 and 1.0 for the time, and 0.0 and 1.0 for the value. The output of this function represents the fractional change in the value between the start value and the end value for the target variable. This pattern of interpolation is quite common; to facilitate it, JavaFX provides the `javafx.animation.SimpleInterpolator` abstract class. All the standard interpolators extend `SimpleInterpolator`, and later in this chapter we will show an example of creating a custom interpolator based on it.

Standard Interpolators

The JavaFX platform provides a set of standard interpolators that handles most types of animation. The standard interpolators are defined in `javafx.animation.Interpolator`. They are

```
Interpolator.DISCRETE

Interpolator.LINEAR

Interpolator.EASEIN

Interpolator.EASEOUT

Interpolator.EASEBOTH

Interpolator.SPLINE
```

The next few sections discuss each of these interpolators.

Discrete

A `DISCRETE` interpolator jumps instantaneously from one value to the next. The target variable instantly assumes the target value when the key frame's time is reached. This is the default interpolator if none is provided.

```
x => 1000 tween Interpolator.DISCRETE
```

Linear

A `LINEAR` interpolator changes the variable from the start value to the target value at a constant rate of change over the time period. Using a vehicle's velocity as an analogy, this would be the same as the vehicle traveling at a constant speed over the time frame.

```
x => 1000 tween Interpolator.LINEAR
```

Ease In

An EASE IN interpolator initially accelerates the rate of change in the target value until a constant rate is achieved, then maintains that constant rate of change. This is analogous to a vehicle accelerating after stopping at a traffic signal and then reaching the speed limit; then, it maintains the speed limit.

```
x => 1000 tween Interpolator.EASEIN
```

In the JavaFX implementation, the acceleration phase is during the first 20 percent of the time period.

Ease Out

An EASE OUT interpolator is the opposite of the ease in interpolator. It initially starts with a constant rate of change; then, toward the end of the time period, it decelerates. This is analogous to a vehicle operating at the speed limit, then applying the brakes as it comes to a traffic light.

```
x => 1000 tween Interpolator.EASEOUT
```

In the JavaFX implementation, the deceleration phase is during the last 20 percent of the time period.

Ease Both

An EASE BOTH interpolator is the combination of ease in and ease out. The rate of change increases until a constant rate of change is achieved, then near the end of the time period, the rate of change decelerates. This is similar to a vehicle accelerating from one traffic signal to the speed limit, travelling at a constant speed, then braking and decelerating as it approaches the next traffic signal.

```
x => 1000 tween Interpolator.LINEAR
```

In the JavaFX implementation, the acceleration phase is the first 20 percent of the time period and the deceleration phase is during the last 20 percent of the time period.

Spline

A SPLINE interpolator uses a cubic spline shape to dictate the acceleration and deceleration phases over the time period. SPLINE() returns an interpolator based on the control points that are specified as parameters to the SPLINE function. The anchor points are statically defined as (0.0, 0.0) and (1.0, 1.0). The control points range in value from 0.0 to 1.0.

```
x => 1000 tween Interpolator.SPLINE(x1, y1, x2, y2)
```

When the cubic spline is plotted, the slope of the plot defines the acceleration at that point. As the slope approaches vertical, the acceleration increases; when the slope of the plot approaches horizontal, the motion decelerates. If the slope of the line at a point is 1.0, the interpolation is moving at a constant rate of change.

Figure 7.2 shows the spline plot equivalent to the LINEAR built-in interpolator. This reflects a constant rate of change, as the slope for the entire line is 1.0.

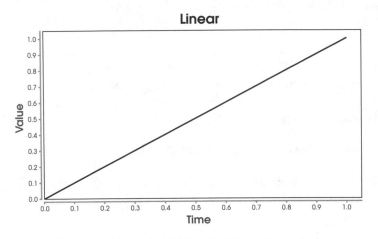

Figure 7.2   Linear – Cubic Spline for Linear Interpolation

The control points for the spline are (0.25, 0.25) and (0.75, 0.75), which results in a straight line with a slope of 1. This represents a constant speed from the start of the time period to the end.

```
x => 1000 tween Interpolator.SPLINE(0.25, 0.25, 0.75, 0.75)
```

Figure 7.3 represents the plot for an ease both interpolation. Here the control points are (0.2, 0.0) and (0.8, 1.0).

```
x => 1000 tween Interpolator.SPLINE(0.2, 0.0, 0.8, 1.0)
```

Notice that the slope is flat near the beginning and end of the plot. So the motion will start slow and accelerate for the first 20% of the time period, stay at a constant speed until the last 20% of the time period, when it will decelerate.

By using the Interpolator SPLINE() function, you can easily create unique interpolation behavior. However, for performance reasons, stick to the predefined interpolators if that is what you want.

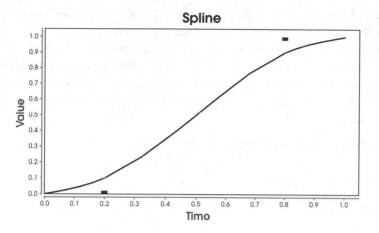

Figure 7.3   Ease Both (%20) – Cubic Spline

As part of the software available on the book's Web site (http://jfxbook.com), there is a `SplineDemo.fx` file that lets you play with the spline parameters and immediately see the resulting impact on the animation.

While using a cubic spline affords much flexibility, there are times where even that does not satisfy the animation requirements. This is when a custom interpolator comes into play.

Writing a Custom Interpolator

Besides providing support for the built-in interpolators and the cubic spline interpolator, if you need custom interpolation, you can either extend `javafx.animation.SimpleInterpolator` or `javafx.animation.Interpolator`.

SimpleInterpolator

`SimpleInterpolator` does more of the internal pluming for you. All you have to do is implement the `curve` function. The implementation of curve returns a fraction of the amount to change the start value as it migrates to the target value.

```
public function curve(t:Number) : Number
```

The parameter, `t`, represents the fraction of time that has elapsed in the current interval, where 0.0 is the start of the interval and 1.0 is the end of the interval. This result centers around the range, [0.0..1.0]. Nonetheless, this number is not constrained by this range—for example, the curve function could return -0.1 or 1.1 if the interval movement fluctuates beyond the original start and end values.

To demonstrate this, we will go through an Elastic Interpolator based on the elastic interpolator defined in the The Yahoo! User Interface Library (YUI) (http://developer.yahoo.com/yui/docs/Easing.js.html). The main difference between the two implementations is that the Yahoo JavaScript version translates directly to the actual values based on the elapsed time, whereas the JavaFX version deals with the percentage of elapsed time, and therefore returns a percentage change for the target value.

The actual implementation is shown in Listing 7.3.

Listing 7.3 Elastic Interpolator

```
package animation;

import javafx.animation.SimpleInterpolator;
import java.lang.Math;

// Elastic period is at start of animation
public def IN = 0;
// Elastic period is at end of animation
public def OUT = 1;
// Elastic period is at start and end of animation
public def BOTH = 3;

public class Elastic extends SimpleInterpolator  {
    public-init var type = BOTH;
    public-init var amplitude = 1.0;
    public-init var period = if(type == BOTH)
                        {0.3*1.5} else { 0.3}
        on replace {
            if(amplitude < Math.abs(period)) {
                amplitude = period;
                s = period/4.0;
            }
    };

    var s: Number;

    init {
        if(s == 0.0) {
            s = period/(2*Math.PI) *
                    Math.asin (1.0/amplitude);
        }
    }
```

```
public override function curve(t: Number) : Number {
    if( t == 0.0 or t == 1.0) {
        return t;
    }
    if(type == IN) {
        var xt = t - 1;
        return -(amplitude*Math.pow(2,10*xt) *
            Math.sin( (xt-s)*(2*Math.PI)/period ));
    } else if(type == OUT) {
        var xt = t;
        return amplitude*Math.pow(2,-10*xt) *
            Math.sin( (xt-s)*(2*Math.PI)/period )
                        + 1.0;
    } else { // type == BOTH
        var dt = t * 2.0;
        if(dt < 1.0) {
            var xt = dt -1;
            return -.5 * amplitude*Math.pow(2,10*(xt)) *
                Math.sin( (xt-s)*(2*Math.PI)/
                            period );
        } else {
            var xt = dt-1;
            return (0.5 * amplitude*
                Math.pow(2,-10*(xt)) *
                Math.sin(
                    (xt-s)*(2*Math.PI)/period )) + 1.0;
        }
    }
}
```

Elastic is similar to bounce or spring effects, but gives a snap out/in effect. There are three flavors for Elastic: IN focuses the elastic movement at the start of the animation, OUT focuses on the end of the animation, and BOTH focuses on both ends of the animation.

The elastic graphs are shown in the following three figures. Figure 7.4 shows the Elastic IN graph where the animated movement snaps into its final location.

Figure 7.5 shows the Elastic OUT graph where the movement jumps out of its original position then smoothly moves to its final location.

Figure 7.6 shows the Elastic BOTH graph where the movement jumps out of its original position and then snaps into its final position.

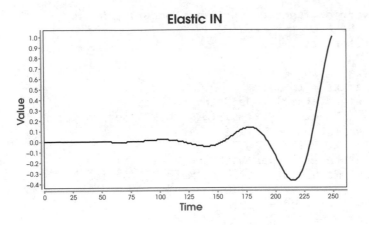

Figure 7.4   Elastic IN

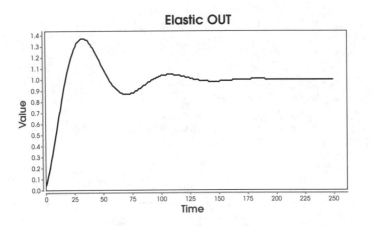

Figure 7.5   Elastic OUT

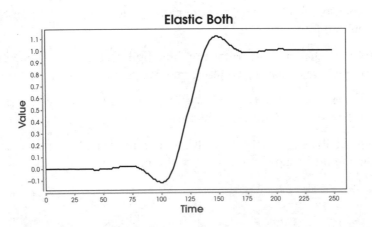

Figure 7.6   Elastic BOTH

Interpolator

One of the constraints of the SimpleInterpolator is that target and start values need to differ by a certain amount to actually see any movement. This is because the curve() value is fractional from 0.0 to 1.0 and is multiplied by this difference to obtain the actual change in value. Obviously, if the start value is the same as the target value, the fractional result would always be multiplied by the zero difference, so there would be no movement at all.

What if you want a shaking effect, without the object actually ending at a new location? In this case, the start values and end values are the same, but during the time interval, the object shakes back and forth. This is exactly what happens with the eQuake Alert plug-in to the Firefox browser. With eQuake Alert, when an earthquake of a certain magnitude occurs, the entire Firefox browser shakes with an amplitude based on the magnitude of the earthquake. You cannot use Simple-Interpolator for this kind of animation. You must create a custom interpolator that extends javafx.animation.Interpolator and implements the function interpolate().

```
public function interpolate(startValue:Object,
            endValue:Object, fraction:Number):Object
```

The parameter startValue is the starting value for the target variable at the beginning of the time slice represented by the KeyFrame, endValue is the ending value, and fraction is a number from 0.0 to 1.0, which represents the fraction of time within the time period. This function returns the interpolated value for that instant. Actually, SimpleInterpolator, itself, extends Interpolator and implements its own version of interpolate() that ends up calling the abstract curve() function. Let's examine an example for shaking.

A perfect mathematical formula for doing a shake is a Bessel function. Figure 7.7 shows the graph of the Bessel function, where the shaking effect is greatest at the beginning of the animation and calms down as the animation progresses.

Basically, we need to call the Bessel function when the animation runtime calls the interpolate() method. However, it is not that straightforward, and there is a little plumbing that needs to be created. The following code snippet in Listing 7.4 illustrates this. (The full listing is on the book's Web site, http://jfxbook.com.)

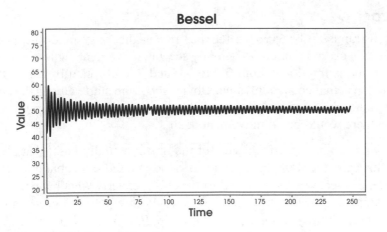

Figure 7.7   Bessel Function

Listing 7.4   Bessel Interpolator

```
package animation;

import javafx.animation.Interpolator;
import javafx.animation.Interpolatable;
import java.lang.Math;

public class Bessel extends Interpolator  {
    // Bessel integer order
    public-init var order:Integer = 0;
    // Amplitude of resulting wave
    public-init var amplitude = 40.0;
    // frequency of resulting wave
    public-init var frequency = 600;

    public override function interpolate(startValue:Object,
            endValue:Object, fraction:Number):Object {
        if(fraction == 1.0) {
            return endValue;
        }
        if(startValue instanceof java.lang.Number and
                endValue instanceof java.lang.Number) {
            var start : Number = startValue as Number;
            var end: Number = startValue as Number;
            var val = start + j(frequency * fraction) *
                                                amplitude;
            if(startValue instanceof java.lang.Integer and
                    endValue instanceof java.lang.Integer) {
                (val + 0.5).intValue();
            }else {
```

```
                    val;
                }
        } else if( startValue instanceof Interpolatable) {
            (startValue as Interpolatable).ofTheWay(
                    (endValue as Interpolatable),
                    j(frequency * fraction) * amplitude);
        } else {
            // discrete
            if (fraction == 1.0) endValue else startValue;
        }
    }
```

The function, j(), is the Bessel function.

Interpolatable

You may have noticed that we checked for the start and end value types and if they were not numeric, we checked to see if they implemented Interpolatable. The abstract class javafx.animation.Interpolatable allows a class to participate in Interpolation even if that class is not inherently numerical. To do this, the class must implement the function

```
ofTheWay(endVal:Object, t:Number) : Object
```

The classes javafx.scene.paint.Color and javafx.scene.shape.Shape are two examples of JavaFX classes that implement Interpolatable. Color allows the color to morph from the starting color to the end color by changing its red, green, blue, and opacity a fractional amount toward the end color. Shape allows the beginning shape to morph into the end shape.

Path-Based Animation

Path-based animation is the concept of a graphical asset traveling along a path. An example is a race car traveling along a race track, or a car driving within a city.

Conceptually, path-based animation has two components: a graphical asset that will travel the path, represented by a javafx.scene.Node class, and a route, represented by a Path, javafx.scene.shape.Path or javafx.scene.shape.SVGPath. To create the actual animation, use the javafx.animation.transistion.Path-Transition class. To illustrate this, let's use an example of an automobile travelling the streets of midtown Manhattan in New York City.

First, locate an image for the map of midtown Manhattan, the image in the example is from the United States Census Bureau and is located from http://www.census.gov/geo/www/tiger/tigermap.html. Next, calculate a route on the map for the animation. One way to do this is to display the map using JavaFX, and then add an onMouseClicked function to print the coordinates where the mouse is clicked. Then, mark the route by clicking at major transition points along the route. Include these points either in a javafx.scene.shape.Path or javafx.scene.shape.SVGPath. The example uses an SVGPath.

```
var route = SVGPath {
    fill: Color.TRANSPARENT
    stroke: Color.TRANSPARENT
    content: "M21.5,330.0 L186.5,421.0 235.5,335.0 "
             "293.5,368.0 407.5,167.0 287.5,103.0 "
             "181.5,302.0 68.5,244.0 z"
};
```

In an SVGPath, the code letter M means *moveto*, L means *lineto*, and z means *closepath*. After a lineto code is entered, it automatically applies to adjacent uncoded point coordinate pairs. In this example, the route is made invisible with the TRANSPARENT fill and stroke instance variables. If desired, you can use the stroke to visibly show a route. For example, to demonstrate a yellow highlighter, use

```
var route = SVGPath {
    fill: Color.TRANSPARENT
    stroke: Color.rgb(255,255,0, .5)
    strokeWidth: 15
...
...
```

Next, we need a graphical asset that will move along the path, and this is defined generically as a javafx.scene.Node. In the example, we used an image of an automobile.

```
var racecar = ImageView {
    scaleX: 0.5
    scaleY: 0.5
    image: Image{ url: "{__DIR__}images/racecar.gif" }
}
```

Lastly, we need to define a path animation using javafx.animation.transition.PathTransition.

```
def animation = PathTransition {
        node: racear
        path: AnimationPath.createFromPath(route)
        orientation: OrientationType.ORTHOGONAL_TO_TANGENT
        interpolate: Interpolator.LINEAR
        duration: duration
        repeatCount: Timeline.INDEFINITE
};
```

Notice the orientation instance variable. By setting this to ORTHOGONAL_TO_ TANGENT, the race car image rotates to match the path while traversing the route. The other option is to set this to NONE, the default. When orientation is set to NONE, the race car will not rotate at all. Obviously, for an object like a race car that has inherent direction, this is probably not desirable. However, if you have a node that does not imply direction, like a Circle, then setting it to NONE would be sufficient.

The last step is to create the presentation showing the map of midtown Manhattan, and adding the race car image and the route.

```
Group {
    translateX: bind (scene.width - image.width)/2
    content: [
        ImageView{
            image: image ¯
        },
        route, racear
    ]
},
```

Using the animation variable, you can control the play of the animation similar to regular types of timelines. Figure 7.8 shows the map of midtown Manhattan, New York City, with a car image on the street. In this animation, the car travels along a route on the map.

Listing 7.5 shows the main code for traversing the map. The full example, Path-Animation, can be downloaded from http://jfxbook.com.

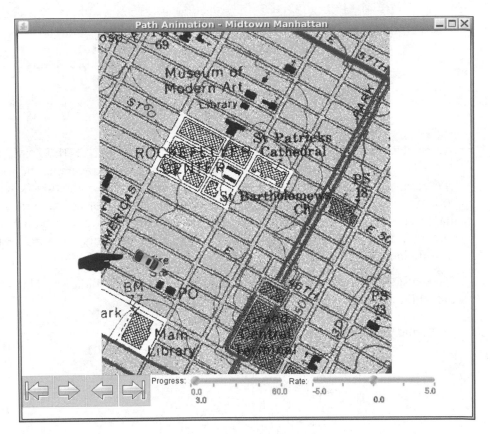

Figure 7.8   Path Animation on Map of Midtown Manhattan

Listing 7.5   Path Animation

```
import javafx.stage.Stage;
import javafx.scene.Scene;
import javafx.scene.Group;
import javafx.scene.layout.*;
import javafx.scene.image.Image;
import javafx.scene.image.ImageView;
import javafx.scene.input.MouseEvent;
import javafx.scene.input.MouseButton;
import javafx.scene.shape.SVGPath;
import javafx.scene.shape.Rectangle;
import javafx.scene.paint.*;
import javafx.animation.transition.*;
import javafx.animation.*;
import javafx.scene.text.Text;
```

```
import jfxbook.shared.PathAnimationControl;
import jfxbook.shared.ProgressSlider;

// The defualt route using SVG path

var routePathStr =
    "M21.5,330.0 L186.5,421.0 235.5,335.0 293.5,368.0 "
    "407.5,167.0 287.5,103.0 181.5,302.0 68.5,244.0 z";
var buildPathStr:String;
var route = bind SVGPath {
    fill:  Color.TRANSPARENT
    stroke: Color.TRANSPARENT
    strokeWidth: 15
    content: routePathStr
};

var racear = ImageView {
    scaleX: 0.5
    scaleY: 0.5
    image: Image{ url: "{__DIR__}images/racecar.gif" }
}

var duration = 60s;

def animation = PathTransition {
        node: racear
        path: bind AnimationPath.createFromPath(route)
        orientation: OrientationType.ORTHOGONAL_TO_TANGENT
        interpolate: Interpolator.LINEAR
        duration: duration
        repeatCount: Timeline.INDEFINITE
};

def image = Image {
    url: "{__DIR__}images/RockefellerCenter.tif"};

var scene: Scene;
var moveto = true;
Stage {
    title: "Path Animation - Midtown Manhattan"
    scene: scene = Scene {
        width: 700
        height: 650
        content: VBox {
            content: [
                Group {
                    translateX: bind
                            (scene.width - image.width)/2
```

continues

```
content: [
    ImageView{
        image: image
        // mouse button lets you mark a
        //route on the map.
        OnMouseClicked:
          function(e:MouseEvent):Void {
            // reset route
            if(e.button ==
                MouseButton.SECONDARY)
            {
                buildPathStr =
                    "{buildPathStr}z";
                routePathStr =
                        buildPathStr;
                moveto = true;
            }else {
        // build up the path with each
        // click. Click at the turns
            // of the route
                if(moveto) {
                    buildPathStr =
                        "M{e.x},{e.y}L";
                    moveto = false;
                }else {
                    buildPathStr =
        "{buildPathStr} {e.x},{e.y}";
                }

            }
        }
    },
    route, racear
]
},
HBox {
    content: [
        PathAnimationControl {
            transition: bind animation
        },
        ProgressSlider {
            label: Text {
                content: "Progress: " },
            width: 150
            minimum: 0
            maximum: bind
                    duration.toSeconds()
            value: bind
                animation.time.toSeconds();
```

```
            action:
                function(value:Number):Void {
                    println("Change: {value}");
                    var inProgress =
                            animation.running and
                                not animation.paused;
                    if( inProgress) {
                        animation.pause();
                    }
                    animation.time =
                        Duration.valueOf(
                                value * 1000);
                    if(inProgress) {
                        animation.play();
                    }
                }
            },
            ProgressSlider {
                label: Text {
                            content: "Rate: " }
                width: 200
                minimum: -5.0
                maximum: 5.0
                value: bind animation.currentRate
                action: function(value:Number) {
                    animation.rate = value;
                }
            }
        ]
    }
    ]
    }
    }
}
```

Total Solar Eclipse Examples

The total solar eclipse provides a good example of animating movement along with visual changes. During a total solar eclipse, the moon moves across the sun causing a period of darkness during daytime. There are also effects on the sun, with a sun burst visible right before and right after totality. Presented here are two examples of basically the same animation. The first one is based totally on JavaFX shapes, whereas the second example uses the graphical objects generated using JavaFX Production Suite we covered in Chapter 2, JavaFX for the Graphic

Designer. From Chapter 2, there were five main graphical objects: BlueSky, DarkSky, Moon, Sun, SunBurst, and Totality. These are used in both animations, but with different implementations.

JavaFX Shapes

This example implements the total eclipse only using JavaFX shapes and effects. The first task is to create custom nodes for each of the main graphical objects: BlueSky, DarkSky, Moon, Sun, SunBurst, and Totality. Each of these objects extends javafx.scene.CustomNode and implements the abstract function create() from CustomNode.

BlueSky and DarkSky are both rectangular shapes. BlueSky has a LinearGradient fill pattern from light skyblue to white. DarkSky has a black fill pattern with random pattern of circles that represent stars. Listing 7.6 shows the implementation for BlueSky.

Listing 7.6   BlueSky

```
public class BlueSky extends CustomNode {
    public var width:Number = 600;
    public var height: Number = 600;
    public override function create(): Node {
        Rectangle {
            width: bind width
            height: bind height
            fill: LinearGradient {
                endY: 1.0
                endX: 0.0
                stops: [
                    Stop {
                        offset: 0.0
                        color: Color.LIGHTSKYBLUE
                    },
                    Stop {
                        offset: 1.0
                        color: Color.WHITE
                    },
                ]
            }
        }
    }
}
```

DarkSky is shown in Listing 7.7.

Listing 7.7　DarkSky

```
public class DarkSky extends CustomNode {
    public var width:Number = 600;
    public var height: Number = 600;
    def random = Random{};
    public override function create(): Node {
        return Group {
            content: bind [
                Rectangle { // Black sky
                    width: width
                    height: height
                    fill: RadialGradient {
                        centerX: 0.5
                        centerY: 0.5
                        stops: [
                            Stop { offset: 0.0
                              color:
                                    Color.rgb(128,128,128) },
                            Stop { offset: 1.0
                              color: Color.rgb(20,20,20) },
                        ]
                    }
                },
                for(i in [0..100]) { // Stars
                    Circle {
                        centerX: random.nextInt(
                            if(width <= 0) 1 else width);
                        centerY: random.nextInt(
                              if(height <= 0) 1 else height);
                        radius: random.nextInt(5);
                        fill: Color.WHITESMOKE
                    }
                }
            ]
        };
    }
}
```

The Sun is composed of three concentric circles. In the center of the Sun is a pure white circle. Next, there is a circle with a RadialGradient using a center color of white transposing to yellow. Both of these circles use a GaussianBlur effect to blend and smooth the color's edges. The most outer circle is a translucent yellow to represent a glare effect around the Sun. Listing 7.8 presents an implementation for the Sun.

Listing 7.8   Sun

```
public class Sun extends CustomNode {
    public var centerX:Number;
    public var centerY:Number;
    public override function create(): Node {
        return Group {
            content: [
                Circle { // Glare circle
                    centerX: bind centerX
                    centerY: bind centerY
                    radius: 70
                    opacity: 0.2
                    fill: Color.YELLOW
                    effect: GaussianBlur { radius: 10}
                },
                Circle { // Main Sun disc
                    centerX: bind centerX
                    centerY: bind centerY
                    radius: 52
                    fill: RadialGradient {
                        radius: 2
                        centerX: 0.5
                        centerY: 0.5
                        stops: [
                            Stop {
                              offset: 0.0
                              color: Color.WHITE
                            },
                            Stop {
                              offset: 0.3
                              color: Color.YELLOW
                            },
                        ]
                    }
                    effect: GaussianBlur { radius: 10}
                },
                Circle { // Sun WHITE Center
                    centerX: bind centerX
                    centerY: bind centerY
                    radius: 15
                    fill: Color.WHITE
                    effect: GaussianBlur { radius: 10 }
                },

            ]
        };
    }
}
```

The Moon is merely a black circle with a GaussianBlur effect to blend and smooth the edges, as implemented in Listing 7.9.

Listing 7.9 Moon

```
public class Moon extends CustomNode {
    public var centerX:Number;
    public var centerY:Number;
    public override function create(): Node {
        Circle {
            centerX: bind centerX
            centerY: bind centerY
            radius: 50
            fill: Color.BLACK
            effect: GaussianBlur { radius: 10 }
        }
    }
}
```

The SunBurst is an ellipse with a white fill, again using a GaussianBlur effect to diffuse the color. This is illustrated in Listing 7.10.

Listing 7.10 SunBurst

```
public class SunBurst extends CustomNode {
    public var centerX:Number;
    public var centerY:Number;
    public override function create(): Node {
        Ellipse {
            centerX: bind centerX
            centerY: bind centerY
            radiusX: 50
            radiusY: 30
            fill: Color.WHITE
            effect: GaussianBlur{ radius: 30 }
            rotate: 45
        }
    }
}
```

Totality is a set of solar flares rotating around the center point of the Sun outside of its main diameter. The SolarFlare is an Arc with a GaussianBlur effect to diffuse the yellow color. Listing 7.11 shows the SolarFlare class.

Listing 7.11   SolarFlare

```
class SolarFlare extends CustomNode {
    public var centerX:Number;
    public var centerY:Number;
    public var angle: Number;
    public var radiusX:Number = 6;
    public var radiusY:Number = 10;
    public override function create(): Node {
        Group {
            rotate: bind angle
            content: [
                Circle {
                    centerX: bind centerX
                    centerY: bind centerY
                    radius: 75
                    stroke: Color.TRANSPARENT
                    fill: Color.TRANSPARENT
                },
                Arc {
                    centerX: bind centerX - radius;
                    centerY: bind centerY;
                    radiusX: bind radiusX
                    radiusY: bind radiusY
                    startAngle: 90
                    length: 180
                    type:  ArcType.OPEN
                    effect: GaussianBlur { radius: 6}
                    stroke: Color.YELLOW
                    fill: Color.TRANSPARENT
                    strokeWidth: 3
                }
            ]
        };
    }
}
```

The next listing, Listing 7.12, shows the Totality class that contains six SolarFlares of various sizes rotated around the core disc of the Sun.

Listing 7.12   Totality

```
public class Totality extends CustomNode {
    public var centerX:Number;
    public var centerY:Number;
    var radius:Number = 52;
```

```
var x1 = bind centerX - radius;
var y1 = bind centerY;

public override function create(): Node {
    return Group {
        content: [
            SolarFlare {
                centerX: bind centerX
                centerY: bind centerY
            },
            SolarFlare {
                centerX: bind centerX
                centerY: bind centerY
                rotate: 50
                radiusX: 10
                radiusY: 5
            },
            SolarFlare {
                centerX: bind centerX
                centerY: bind centerY
                rotate: 94
                radiusX: 15
                radiusY: 5
            },
            SolarFlare {
                centerX: bind centerX
                centerY: bind centerY
                rotate: 185
                radiusX: 15
                radiusY: 5
            },
            SolarFlare {
                centerX: bind centerX
                centerY: bind centerY
                rotate: 225
                radiusX: 10
                radiusY: 3
            },
            SolarFlare {
                centerX: bind centerX
                centerY: bind centerY
                rotate: 275
                radiusX: 5
                radiusY: 3
            },

        ]

    };
}
}
```

To start the animation, the Sun, Moon, and BlueSky are visible with the Moon left and lower from the Sun. The Moon starts moving along a linear path that intersects with the Sun. Figure 7.9 shows the Moon partially covering the Sun. The Moon's movement is done by transitioning the Moon's translateX and translateY instance variables along a linear path.

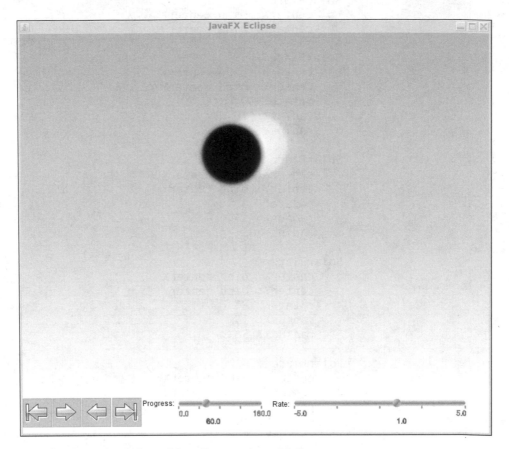

Figure 7.9   Solar Eclipse, Moon Intersecting with Sun

As the Moon nears totality, the DarkSky with stars begins to appear along with a SunBurst at the upper right, the so-called diamond ring effect. This is done by transitioning the opacity for the BlueSky to zero, while transitioning the opacity for the DarkSky and SunBurst to 1.0. This is shown in Figure 7.10.

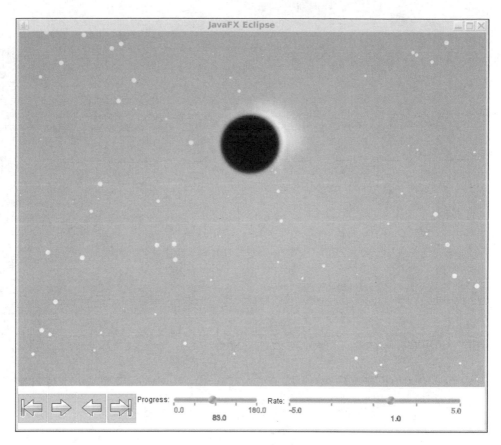

Figure 7.10   Solar Eclipse, Partial with Diamond Ring Effect

At totality, the Moon completely covers the Sun. The SunBurst disappears and Totality becomes totally visible along with the DarkSky. Figure 7.11 displays the animation at Totality.

After totality, the SunBurst moves from the upper right of the Sun to the lower left, and the animation starts to fade out the DarkSky while fading in the BlueSky. Finally, the Sun is in full view and the Moon has moved off the Sun's disc.

The timeline for this is shown in Listing 7.13.

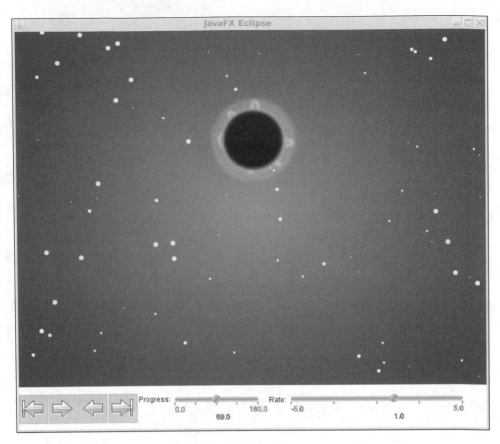

Figure 7.11   Solar Eclipse, Totality with Solar Flares

Listing 7.13   Solar Eclipse Timeline

```
eclipse = Timeline {
    keyFrames: [
        KeyFrame { // initial values
            time: 0s
            values: [
                moon.translateX => -138,
                moon.translateY => 50,
                darkSky.opacity => 0.0,
                blueSky.opacity => 1.0,
                sunBurst.opacity => 0.0,
                sunBurst.translateX => 40.0,
                sunBurst.translateY => -25.0,
                totality.opacity => 0.0
            ]
        },
```

```
KeyFrame { // darkness commences
    time: duration.mul(0.41)
    values: [
        darkSky.opacity => 0.0,
        blueSky.opacity => 1.0,
        sunBurst.opacity => 0.0
    ]

},
KeyFrame { // Upper right SunBurst
    time: duration.mul(0.44)
    values: [
        sunBurst.opacity => 1.0
                    tween Interpolator.EASEIN,
        totality.opacity => 0.0
    ]
},
KeyFrame { // Totality
    time: duration.mul(0.50)
    values: [
        darkSky.opacity => 1.0
                    tween Interpolator.EASEIN,
        blueSky.opacity => 0.0
                    tween Interpolator.EASEOUT,
        sunBurst.opacity => 0.0
                    tween Interpolator.EASEIN,
        sunBurst.translateX => -40
                    tween Interpolator.DISCRETE,
        sunBurst.translateY => 25
                    tween Interpolator.DISCRETE,
        totality.opacity => 1.0
                    tween Interpolator.EASEIN,

    ]
},
KeyFrame { // lower left Sunburst
    time: duration.mul(0.55)
    values: [
        sunBurst.opacity => 1.0
                    tween Interpolator.EASEIN
        totality.opacity => 0.0
                    tween Interpolator.EASEOUT,
    ]
},
KeyFrame { // Daylight returns
    time: duration.mul(0.61)
    values: [
        darkSky.opacity => 0.0
                    tween Interpolator.LINEAR,
```

continues

```
                blueSky.opacity => 1.0
                        tween Interpolator.LINEAR,
                sunBurst.opacity => 0.0
                        tween Interpolator.EASEOUT
            ]
        },
        KeyFrame {
            time: duration
             values: [
                moon.translateX => 138
                        tween Interpolator.LINEAR,
                moon.translateY => -50
                        tween Interpolator.LINEAR
            ]
        }
    ]
};
```

JavaFX Production Suite

Using the output from the JavaFX Production Suite example from Chapter 2, the animation is very similar. However, instead of creating custom nodes for the Sun, Moon, and so on, we use the graphical assets generated from Adobe Illustrator.

First, you need to generate the UI Stub from the Eclipse JavaFX archive file that we produced in Chapter 2. To do this, copy the JavaFX archive file to a NetBeans IDE Project. Then, right-click on the **JavaFX Archive File** and select **Generate UI Stub**. Figure 7.12 shows the menu selection to generate the UI Stub files.

If necessary, edit the UI Stub's location and package, and then press OK to generate the Stub. This is shown in Figure 7.13.

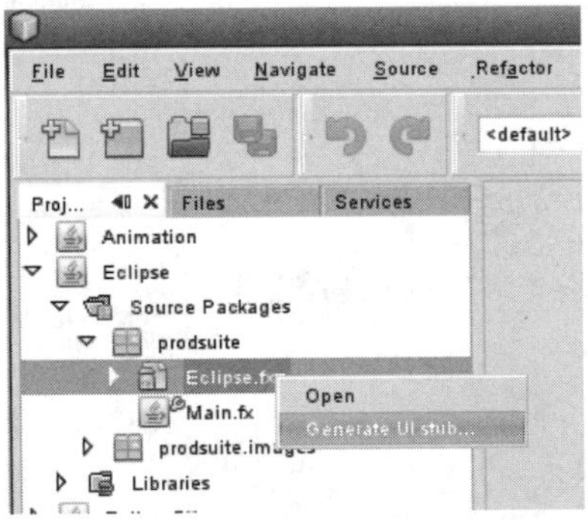

Figure 7.12   Generate UI Stub

Figure 7.13 Generate UI Stub Dialog

The key parts of the UI Stub JavaFX file are

```
public class EclipseUI extends UiStub {

    override public var url = "{__DIR__}Eclipse.fxz";
        public var BlueSky: Node;
    public var DarkSky: Node;
    public var Moon: Node;
    public var Sun: Node;
    public var SunBurst: Node;
    public var Totality: Node;
...
...
```

Notice that there are instance variables created for each of the graphical assets to be used in the animation. To use these assets, merely instantiate an instance of EclipseUI, and then access each of the assets as required. For example, to initialize EclipseUI and then set initial state for each of the graphical assets:

```
var ui = EclipseUI{};

ui.BlueSky.visible=true;
ui.BlueSky.cache = true;

ui.Sun.visible = true;
ui.Sun.cache = true;

ui.DarkSky.visible = true;
ui.DarkSky.cache = true;
ui.Moon.visible = true;
ui.Moon.cache = true;

ui.SunBurst.visible = true;
ui.SunBurst.cache = true;
ui.Totalality.visible = true;
ui.Totalality.cache = true;
```

Notice that the cache instance variable was set to true on each of the assets. This indicates to the JavaFX runtime system that the image produced by the node can be internally kept as a bitmap and may result in a performance improvement when displaying on the screen. This improvement may be quite noticeable when moving or otherwise manipulating objects in an animation. However, any improvement may be dependent on the underlying graphics processing unit (GPU) and its capabilities. You may want to experiment with both settings to see what works best.

The animation is exactly the same as in the JavaFX shape implementation described previously. The only difference is instead of using the object directly, you access the graphical node through the EclipseUI instance. For example:

```
var eclipse: Timeline = Timeline {
    keyFrames: [
        KeyFrame {
            time: 0s
            values: [
                ui.Moon.translateX => -138,
                ui.Moon.translateY => 50,
                ui.DarkSky.opacity => 0.0,
```

Chapter Summary

This chapter discussed the basics of animation in JavaFX. We covered the classes used to define animation and discussed how to use the standard interpolators. We also described how to create a custom interpolator. Next, we walked through an example of path animation by demonstrating a race car travelling the streets of midtown Manhattan in New York City. Lastly, we walked through a complex animation of a total eclipse using both JavaFX shapes and graphical assets produced from Adobe Illustrator using JavaFX Production Suite.

In the next chapter, we cover more "cool" multimedia features, including images, sound, and videos.

8

Include Multimedia

"But theater, because of its nature, both text, images, multimedia effects, has a wider base of communication with an audience. That's why I call it the most social of the various art forms."

—Wole Soyinka

Multimedia

Multimedia is the application of multiple means to present content. Conventionally, the media components include text, interactive controls, special effects, pictures, animation, audio, and video. We have already covered text and interactive controls in Chapter 5, Create User Interfaces; special effects in Chapter 6, Apply Special Effects; and animation in Chapter 7, Add Motion with JavaFX Animation. In this chapter, we will focus on images, sound, and video.

Images

Loading and displaying images in JavaFX is quite simple. First, you create an Image object, `javafx.scene.image.Image`, and then you create an `ImageView`, `javafx.scene.image.ImageView`, to show the image on the display.

Minimally, you can create an `Image` object by just supplying a URL to the location of the image. The URL may be local, beginning with a `file:` protocol, or remote, using an Internet protocol like `http:`. For example, to load an image from the directory of the current script file, in the figures subdirectory, you would use the built-in `__DIR__` variable.

```
var image = Image {
    url: "{__DIR__}figures/myImage.gif"
}
```

If you want to size the `Image`, you can specify the desired `width` and `height`, and also specify whether the aspect ratio of the image should be preserved. The `smooth` variable indicates whether to use a better quality scaling algorithm or a faster one. When `smooth` is set to true, its default value, the scaling will be of higher quality; when set to false, scaling occurs faster, but with lesser quality. This is demonstrated in Listing 8.1.

Listing 8.1   Image Sizing

```
var image = Image {
    url: "http://www.nasa.gov/figures/content/"
        "300763main_image_1258_1600-1200.jpg"

    width: 500
    height: 500
    preserveRatio: true
    smooth: true
}
```

Similar geometry variables, `fitWidth` and `fitHeight`, are also available on the `ImageView`, and these will be discussed a little later in this chapter. This is an alternative way to scale the image.

Because the image may be located on a remote system—maybe it is just large or maybe there are a lot of images to load—it may take some time to load the image. If you do not want to wait for the image to load when you create it, you can set the flag, `backgroundLoading`. When you use this option, you can also specify a `placeholder` image that will be shown while the main image is downloading. Presumably, this `placeholder` image will have already been loaded and will be ready before the primary image is loaded. This is shown in Listing 8.2.

Listing 8.2   Background Loading

```
var image = Image {
    url: "http://www.nasa.gov/figures/content/"
        "300763main_image_1258_1600-1200.jpg"

    backgroundLoading: true
    placeholder: Image {
            url: "{__DIR__}figures/Smiley.gif"
    }
}
```

While the image is loading, the `Image` has a property, `progress`, that holds the percentage progress of the loading operation. This number is expressed as a number from 0.0 to 100.0. You can use this, for example, to bind to a `ProgressBar` node to display the progress.

```
var progressBar= ProgressBar {
    height: 20
    width: bind scene.width
    percent: bind image.progress
}
```

Supported image formats vary by platform; however, on a desktop, the minimum supported formats are listed in Table 8.1 as defined in the `javax.imageio` package.

Table 8.1 Java Desktop Standard Image Formats

Format	Mime Type	File Extension
JPEG	image/jpeg	.jpg, .jpeg
PNG	image/png	.png
BMP	image/bmp	.bmp
WBMP	image/vnd.wap.wbmp	.wbmp
GIF	image/gif	.gif

Developer Tip: With Java 1.6, the `javax.image.ImageIO` class has three methods that list the supported image types on a given platform. `ImageIO.getReaderFormat-Names()` returns the list of supported format names, `ImageIO.getReaderFileSuf-fixes()` returns the registered image file extensions, and `ImageIO.getReaderMIME-Types()` returns the mime types.

If an error is detected during the image loading process, the `error` variable will be set to true. This lets you know that an error has occurred, but it does not let you know why the error happened. From personal experience, the most common error is an invalid `url`, so the runtime system cannot locate the image data.

Developer Warning: One common error is inserting a spurious slash (/) character after the __DIR__ built-in variable. For example, instead of the correct

```
url: "{__DIR__}figures/myImage.gif" // CORRECT
```

you type the spurious slash as in

```
url: "{__DIR__}/figures/myImage.gif" // INCORRECT
```

As a result, the runtime system cannot locate the image file because __DIR__ already ends in a slash (/) character, and you end up with double slashes (//). This issue has been raised on the JavaFX forums, and hopefully a fix will be implemented to handle this automatically, but in the meantime be careful with this.

Now that we have an Image object, to view the image on the display, we need to create a javafx.scene.image.ImageView. An ImageView is a scene graph node that displays an image. Of course, one of its instance variables is image. Using the image object we just created, we create an ImageView.

```
imageView = ImageView {
    image: image = bind image
};
```

This creates a view that takes on the size of the underlying image. If the underlying image is 100×100 pixels, the view will be sized accordingly. If you want to have the image display with another size, you need to use the fitWidth and fitHeight instance variables. Also, if you want to preserve the original aspect ratio for the image, set preserveRatio to true. Just like the smooth variable in the Image object, ImageView has a smooth variable. When smooth is set to true, scaling will favor image quality over performance. On the other hand, when smooth is false, scaling favors performance over quality. An example of doing this is shown in Listing 8.3.

Listing 8.3   ImageView Sizing

```
imageView = ImageView {
    fitWidth: bind scene.width
    fitHeight: bind scene.height - 25
    preserveRatio: true
    smooth: true
    image: image = bind image
};
```

To improve performance, the ImageView can be cached in memory as a bitmap. Do this by setting the variable cache to true. Caching improves performance at the expense of memory. However, on some platforms with graphical processing units (GPU), caching may not provide any benefit to performance at all. We suggest that you try it either way and see if it helps.

Putting this all together in an example, SimpleImage, that is available on the book's Web site, we produce the displays in the figures that follow. In SimpleImage, we used an image from the US National Aeronautics and Space Administration

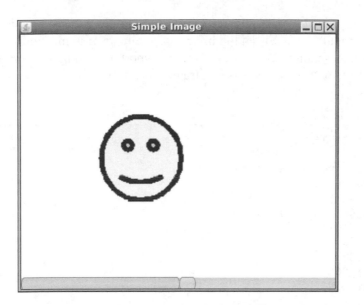

Figure 8.1 Placeholder Display While Loading NASA Image

(NASA) Web site. At first, we see the Smiley face image and the progress bar shows partial progress. Figure 8.1 shows the Smiley Face image and the progress bar while the main image from NASA is loading.

After the NASA image has loaded, the picture is shown and the progress bar shows full completion, as shown in Figure 8.2.

Figure 8.2 NASA Image Display

If you want to only display part of the image, you can create a `viewport`. A viewport is a rectangular area within the image's coordinate system prior to any transformations like scaling. You specify the viewport by using the `javafx .geometry.Rectangle2D` class. This is illustrated in Listing 8.4.

Listing 8.4   Viewport

```
imageView = ImageView {
    fitWidth: bind scene.width
    fitHeight: bind scene.height - 25
    preserveRatio: true
    smooth: true
    image: image = bind image
    viewport: Rectangle2D {
        minX: 200
        minY: 200
        width: 800
        height: 500
    }
};
```

This produces a view of only a portion of the original image, as depicted in Figure 8.3.

Figure 8.3   NASA Image Display Using Viewport

Media—Audio and Video

In JavaFX, there is really no distinction between audio and video. They are both considered playable media, and the same JavaFX classes are used for both types.

In line with this, there is one media class, `javafx.scene.media.Media`, that points to the audio or video location. This class also provides meta-data about the media, like duration, possible width and height resolution, and possible information like artist, title, and so on. The amount of meta-data varies based on the underlying media format.

There is a player, `javafx.scene.media.MediaPlayer`, that controls the play of the media. Do not confuse this with the conventional view of a Media Player application with skins and such that runs on your computer. The `javafx.scene.media.MediaPlayer` is just a class that allows a program to do control actions, like play, pause, resume play, and so on. Your job is to use these classes and the rest of JavaFX to create your own cool Media Player application.

For video, there is a viewer class, `javafx.scene.media.MediaView`. This is a node that you can place in your scene along with other nodes to actually view the video.

To support audio and video playback, JavaFX uses three underlying frameworks. For cross-platform support, including mobile phones, JavaFX uses the On2 VideoVP6 framework from On2 Technologies. For Windows, JavaFX uses the DirectShow framework from Microsoft; for Mac OS, JavaFX uses the Core Video by Apple. Table 8.2 shows the audio/visual formats supported on each platform.

Table 8.2 Supported Media Formats

Format	Windows XP	Windows Vista	MacOS 10.4+	Linux/ Solaris
MPEG-3(.mp3)	X	X	X	X
Flash Video (.flv)	X	X	X	X
Adobe Film Strip .fxm (Sun defined FLV subset)	X	X	X	X
3GPP and 3GPP2			X	
Audio Video Interleave (.avi)	X	X	X	
QuickTime (.mov)			X	

continues

Table 8.2   Supported Media Formats (*Continued*)

Format	Windows XP	Windows Vista	MacOS 10.4+	Linux/ Solaris
MPEG-4 (.mp4)			X	
Waveform Audio Format – WAV (.wav)	X			
Windows Media Video (.wmv)	X			
Advanced Systems Format (.asf)	X			

Table 8.3 shows the Audio codecs supported on each platform.

Table 8.3   Supported Audio Codecs

Codec	Windows XP	Windows Vista	MacOS 10.4+	Linux/ Solaris
MP3	X	X	X	X
MPEG-4 AAC Audio			X	
MPEG-1	X	X		
Windows Media Audio	X	X		
MIDI (.mid)	X	X	X	
Waveform Audio Format	X	X	X	
AIFF			X	

Table 8.4 shows the Video codecs supported on each platform.

Table 8.4   Supported Video Codecs

Codec	Windows XP	Windows Vista	MacOS 10.4+	Linux/ Solaris
On2 VP6	X	X	X	X
Windows Media Video	X	X	X	

Table 8.4 Supported Video Codecs (*Continued*)

Codec	Windows XP	Windows Vista	MacOS 10.4+	Linux/ Solaris
H264	X	X	X	
H.261, H.263			X	
MPEG-1			X	
MPEG-2			X	
MPEG-4			X	
Sorenson Video 2 and 3			X	

To develop a media application, you must first create a javafx.scene.media .Media object with the URL source that points to the location of the audio or video data. The onError function is called if a media error is encountered. These errors might include media that cannot be located or the media format is unsupported on the platform.

```
var media = Media {
    onError: function(e:MediaError) {
        println("got a media error {e}");
    }
    source:
  "http://www.nps.gov/cany/planyourvisit/upload/ClipOne.wmv"

};
```

After the media object is created, you can query it for certain information. The duration specifies the total time for playing the media. The height and width may tell you the resolution of video media unless it cannot be determined, for example if it is a streaming source or is only audio. The variable metadata holds any information about the media, such as title and artist. The actual information varies depending on the media handler.

Next, you need to create a javafx.scene.media.MediaPlayer object. Note that the MediaPlayer has no visual capability, and you need other scene graph nodes for the user to control the play. Listing 8.5 shows how to create a MediaPlayer.

Listing 8.5   MediaPlayer

```
var mediaPlayer:MediaPlayer = MediaPlayer {
    volume: 0.5
    autoPlay: false
    onError: function(e:MediaError) {
        println("got a MediaPlayer error : {e.cause} {e}");
        mediaPlayer.stop();
        mediaPlayer.media = null;

    }
    onEndOfMedia: function() {
        println("reached end of media");
        mediaPlayer.play();
        mediaPlayer.stop();
        mediaPlayer.media = null;
    }
};
```

This merely creates the player; to use it, you have to set the media variable to a Media object that points to a source, then invoke the play(), pause(), *or* stop() functions to control play. There are several instance variables that you may set on the MediaPlayer. If autoPlay is true, playing will start right away. The variables balance, fader, and volume control the left-to-right setting for the audio, the front-to-back audio setting, and the sound volume. The mute variable toggles the sound off or on. The onError and onEndOfMedia functions are invoked when an error occurs or the end of the media is reached. The rate specifies the play speed, 1.0 being normal speed. There are also functions and variables to report status, buffering state, and start, stop, and current time settings.

For audio playback, this is all you need to use audio in your application. However, for video playback, you need a view node, the javafx.scene.media .MediaView. Listing 8.6 shows how to create a MediaView that can display the video.

Listing 8.6   MediaView

```
mv = MediaView {
    translateX: bind (scene.width - mv.layoutBounds.width)/2
    translateY: bind (scene.height -
          mv.layoutBounds.height - bottomBorder)/2
    mediaPlayer: bind mediaPlayer
    preserveRatio: true
    fitWidth: bind scene.width - 4 * borderWidth
    fitHeight: bind scene.height - 4 * borderWidth -
                                        bottomBorder
```

```
onError: function(e:MediaError) {
    println("got a media error {e}");
}
}
```

The MediaView provides a place for the video part of the media to be displayed, similar to what we did for images, and you can set the view's fitWidth and fitHeight, smooth, viewport, and preserveRatio properties. If you do not set these, the window will assume the geometry suggested by the underlying media stream. There are also several properties that can be examined that indicate whether the media view can be rotated or sheared.

The MediaView is a scene graph node that may be placed into the scene graph tree along with other nodes. The example application, Media, on the book's Web site shows a complete player that allows you to view a video from the US National Park Service. When displayed, this application has a viewport in the upper part of the display, showing people rafting down a river. This is shown in Figure 8.4.

Figure 8.4 US National Park Service Video

Let's examine the interaction of the progress bar immediately below the video as shown in Figure 8.5.

Figure 8.5   Video Play and Progress Bar Interaction

This progress bar shows the elapsed percent of the video playback. This is done by binding the media player's current time to the `ProgressBar` as illustrated in Listing 8.7. The percent elapsed time is calculated by dividing the media player's `currentTime` by the total `duration` of the media.

Listing 8.7   MediaPlayer – ProgressBar

```
content: ProgressBar {
    height: 10
    width: bind scene.width
    percent: bind if (mediaPlayer.media != null and
            mediaPlayer.media.duration != null and
            mediaPlayer.media.duration.toMillis() > 0 and
            mediaPlayer.currentTime.toMillis() > 0)
        {
        mediaPlayer.currentTime.toMillis() /
            mediaPlayer.media.duration.toMillis()
        } else {
            0.0
        };
    ...
    ...
```

The left part of the `ProgressBar` has a button that rewinds the media by 10 seconds each time it is pressed. This is an action of the `ProgressBar` called `rewind`. Notice that the player must be paused, the `currentTime` is then set, and play is resumed. Listing 8.8 is an example of how to implement this.

Listing 8.8   MediaPlayer – Rewind

```
rewind: function() {
    mediaPlayer.pause();
    mediaPlayer.rate = 1.0;
    mediaPlayer.currentTime =
                if(mediaPlayer.currentTime.lt(10s)) {
                    0s
```

```
        } else {
            mediaPlayer.currentTime.sub(10s);
        }
    mediaPlayer.play();
}
```

The button to the right of the `ProgessBar` causes the `rate` of play to be increased by 0.5 each time it is pressed. If the play is running at normal speed, the rate is 1.0. After pressing the right button once, the new rate will be 1.5. Pressing it again, the new rate will be 2.0, or 2 times the normal rate. This is done up to a maximum of 3x, when it is then reset to 1.0. Listing 8.9 shows how this may be done. Again, notice that the player must be paused while changing the `rate`.

Listing 8.9   MediaPlayer – Fast Play

```
fastPlay: function() {
    mediaPlayer.pause();
    mediaPlayer.rate = if(mediaPlayer.rate == 3.0)
        1.0 else mediaPlayer.rate + 0.5;
    mediaPlayer.play();
}
```

There is a knob at the head end of the progress part of the progress bar. Progress is noted as a darker color to the left of the knob. The user can drag this knob back and forth to reset the play backward or forward to another position, and play will resume from there. The code that handles this is in Listing 8.10.

Listing 8.10   MediaPlayer – Seek

```
seek: function(per:Number) {
    mediaPlayer.rate = 1.0;
    mediaPlayer.pause();
    mediaPlayer.currentTime =
                mediaPlayer.media.duration.mul(per);
    mediaPlayer.play();
}
```

When the knob is dragged, the `ProgressBar` calculates the new percentage and the seek function multiplies this by the total media duration to set a new `currentTime` for the player.

Now let's examine the bottom controls, as shown in Figure 8.6.

Figure 8.6   Video Play and Player Controls

The left button toggles the play of the media. If the player is stopped or paused, play begins. If the player is running, play is paused. The next button stops the play and resets the media back to the beginning. The third control mutes the sound. These are followed with the volume, balance, and fade controls.

The first three controls are rather simple to implement. For the first one, if the player is stopped or paused, invoke the play function on the media player. Otherwise, invoke the pause function. The next button merely invokes the stop function. The third control just toggles the media player's mute variable. Listing 8.11 contains the code snippet with only the media player interaction shown.

Listing 8.11   Media Control

```
var playing =
    bind mediaControl.player.status == MediaPlayer.PLAYING
    on replace {
        currentPlayShape = if(playing) parallelBars
                                  else rightArrow;
    };

ControlButton {
    id: "play"
    centerShape: bind currentPlayShape
    action: function () {
        if(playing) {
            mediaControl.player.pause();
        }else {
            mediaControl.player.play();
        }
    }
},
ControlButton {
    id: "stop"
    action: function () {
        mediaControl.player.stop();
    }
},
ControlButton {
    id: "mute"
    action: function () {
        mediaControl.player.mute =
                        not mediaControl.player.mute;
```

```
currentMuteShape = if(mediaControl.player.mute) {
        mutedSpeaker;
    } else {
        speaker
    };
}
},
```

The play button changes its internal symbol depending on whether the media player is playing. A triangle is shown if the player is stopped and parallel bars are used when the player is playing. The mute button toggles its symbol based on the player's mute variable.

The volume control binds to the player's volume instance variable and when the user drags the knob, the volume is adjusted from quietest at 0.0 to loudest at 1.0. Similarly, the balance and fader controls adjust their values from -1.0 to 1.0, with 0.0 being equal left and right or front to back settings. Listing 8.12 contains the code snippet for this.

Listing 8.12 Volume Control

```
VolumeControl {
    id: "volume"
    player: bind mediaControl.player
},
Balancer {
    id: "balance"
    player: bind mediaControl.player
    value: bind mediaControl.player.balance
    update: function(n:Number) : Void {
        mediaControl.player.balance = n;
    }
},
Balancer {
    id: "theFader"
    player: bind mediaControl.player
    value: bind mediaControl.player.fader
    update: function(n:Number) : Void {
        mediaControl.player.fader = n;
    }
}
```

This example is focused on showing interaction with the MediaPlayer using a MediaView to see the video portion. You can also use this player with audio files, such as your favorite MP3 song. The only difference is the viewer part will appear black because, of course, an audio media will have nothing to see.

The purpose of this example was to demonstrate the interaction of other UI components and the `MediaPlayer`; as a result, this example is limited. For instance, this example program allows only one hard-coded source URL for the media. A more robust application would load a list of media from a data source or would allow one to enter the URL. Concepts like playlists and sequential play could also be supported.

Chapter Summary

In this chapter, we covered how to include images and sound and video in your applications. For images, we examined the `javafx.scene.image.Image` and `javafx.scene.image.ImageView` classes. For sound and video, we discussed the `Media` and `MediaPlayer` classes in the `javafx.scene.media` package. Lastly, for videos, we showed how to use the `MediaView` class to present the video within a display. We also demonstrated how to use these classes in an application.

We have now covered all the basic components to make a JavaFX application. Next, we will start putting this to use. First, we will examine how to use JavaFX applications on Web pages followed by a discussion of using JavaFX in RESTful applications.

Add JavaFX to Web Pages with Applets

"Civilization advances by extending the number of important operations which we can perform without thinking of them."

—Alfred North Whitehead

JavaFX and Applets

JavaFX makes applet development and deployment easy!! I know what you are thinking: "Applets, aren't they those things we heard about 10 years ago when Java was brand new? Aren't they slow and unreliable?" Well not anymore. Since the release of Java 6 update 10, the entire applet framework has been redone and JavaFX leverages this to make it possible to run any JavaFX application as an applet without code changes. To start with, let's see how easy it is to deploy a JavaFX application as an applet within an HTML page. Next, we will explore a new feature that allows you to drag the applet off the HTML page and onto your desktop. Then we will cover interaction between JavaFX and JavaScript. We will also cover Java Web Start, which is another way to easily install a JavaFX application from an HTML page directly to the desktop.

Deploying a JavaFX Application as an Applet

The first step is to write your JavaFX application. For now, there is nothing out of the ordinary you have to do. Furthermore, you can run and test your JavaFX application just like any other JavaFX application. After you are satisfied that your application is working as desired, you can deploy it to a Web page.

The example we are going to use is the NASA Image Browser application that can be found on the book's Web site. This application fetches the RSS feed of the "images of the day" from the US National Aeronautics and Space Administration (NASA) Web site and builds a thumbnail view of all the images; as you select a thumbnail, a higher resolution image is then fetched and displayed from the NASA Web site. When this JavaFX application is run as a standalone application, it looks like a normal JavaFX application, as shown in Figure 9.1.

To deploy this as an applet in an HTML page, there are three steps:

1. Sign the application JAR file.
2. Create the JNLP (Java Network Launch Protocol) descriptor file.
3. Add JavaScript code to the HTML source.

Figure 9.1 NASA Image Browser – Standalone Application

After this is done and when the HTML page is displayed in the browser, the JavaFX application will start and display within the browser page. Figure 9.2 shows the same application running within an HTML page using the Firefox browser.

There are basically two ways to do these three steps. Use NetBeans IDE for JavaFX or do the steps manually, either from the command line or implement them in an Ant build file.

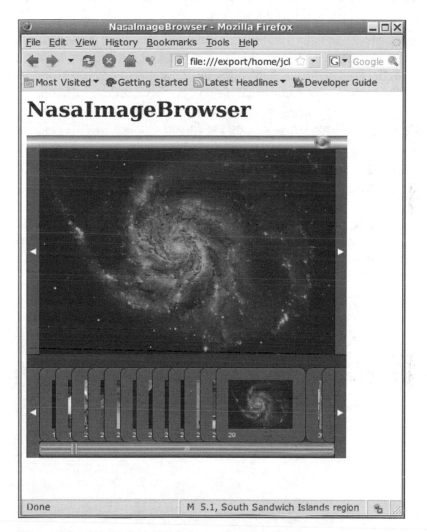

Figure 9.2 NASA Image Browser – Applet in Firefox

NetBeans IDE for JavaFX

The easiest way to do all this is to use NetBeans IDE for JavaFX. When you build the JavaFX project with NetBeans IDE for JavaFX, these steps are done automatically. The JAR is signed, the JNLP file is generated, and a sample HTML page is produced that can be copied into any HTML source file.

There are some parameters to assist in this. Right-click on the **NetBeans Project** and select **Properties**. Then click on **Application**. Figure 9.3 shows the NetBeans properties window for defining applet properties.

The Name field defaults to the Project Name; you can set your company as the Vendor, set the applet's Width and Height, mark it as Draggable, do a Self Signed Jar file, and indicate that you want to support Pack200 Compression. Draggable is a new applet feature that we will discuss a little later in this chapter. Pack200 Compression allows the JAR file to be compressed to a smaller size to minimize download time when starting the applet.

As a part of the applet security model, we need to sign the JAR file in order to have broader permissions to run the application on the user's platform. When the applet is first loaded, the Java Plug-in module will identify the provider of the applet, verify the JAR file has not been tampered with, and ask the user if he grants permission to run the applet on his platform. The JNLP deployment file also has a security section that helps govern security permissions. The NetBeans IDE sets this to "all-permissions." There is more on security later in this chapter.

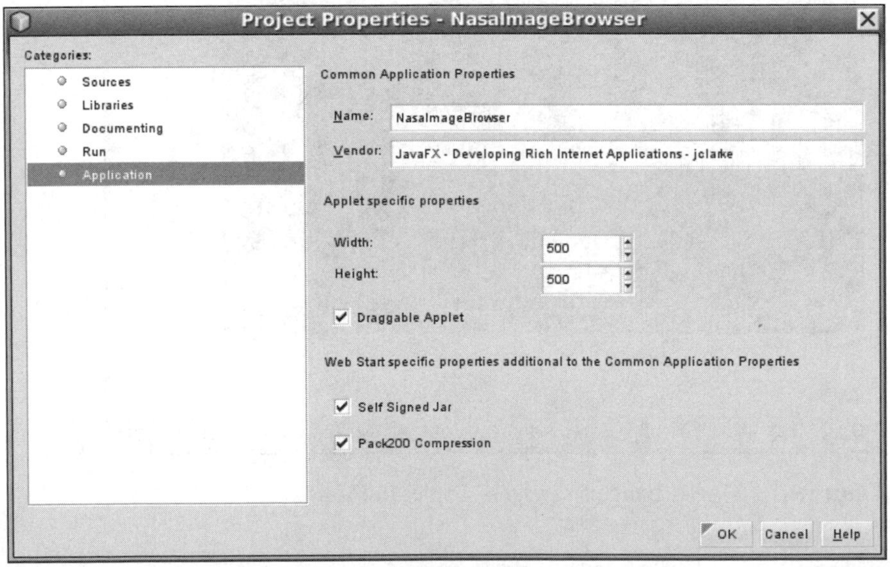

Figure 9.3   Applet Generation Parameters

When the project is built, besides generating the JAR file, two JNLP deployment files will be generated, one used for applet deployment, and the other used for Java Web Start deployment. Java Web Start uses the same protocol as applets, but allows the user the ability to start the application from his desktop without using the browser, even though the application itself is downloaded. These will be explained in detail in the next sections. Besides the JNLP deployment files, a sample HTML file is produced with the appropriate JavaScript code to launch the applet. This file can be used for testing, and the JavaScript launcher code can be copied into any HTML source file.

For our `NasaImageBrowser` application, the following files are generated:

- `NasaImageBrowser.jar`
- `NasaImageBrowser.jar.pack.gz`
- `NasaImageBrowser.html`
- `NasaImageBrowser_browser.jnlp`
- `NasaImageBrowser.jnlp`

Upon opening the `NasaImageBrowser.html` page in a browser, the appropriate JAR's files for the application and JavaFX will be downloaded and cached on the user's machine. Then the application will run in the HTML page as shown in Figure 9.2. One of the enhancements that the new applet framework provides is this local caching mechanism. As long as the version for a JAR file does not change, it does not need to be downloaded each time, thereby improving the user's experience with quicker startup times. Also, if the user does not have the correct version of Java installed on her machine, she is prompted to download the correct Java JRE version.

Manual Generation to Support JavaFX Applets

If you are not using NetBeans IDE for Java, you will need to sign the JAR file manually and create the JNLP deployment and HTML files by hand. Let's look at the signing steps.

Signed JAR

To sign the JAR file, first you need to create a new public/private key pair stored in a new keystore using the Java command `keytool`. For example, you may create a keystore in the current directory, named `myKeystore`, with a store password and a key password of `password`. The store password is the password that protects the integrity of the keystore. The key password protects the private key. The alias `myKey` identifies this new entry in the keystore. The `dname` entry is the X500 Distinguished Name and identifies the entity that is signing the applet.

Typically, when the user attempts to start the JavaFX applet, this name is presented to the user and the user must accept it before the applet will actually start. For more information, consult the Java documentation for the keytool command.

```
keytool -genkey -keystore ./myKeystore -storepass password
                    -alias myKey -keypass password
                    -dname CN=JFXBOOK
```

After the key is generated, you need to create a self-signed certificate, again using the Java keytool command.

```
keytool -selfcert -alias myKey -keystore ./myKeystore
                                    -storepass password
```

Using a Verified Certificate

Using a self-signed certificate is useful for testing, but when your application goes into production, you should sign the JAR files with a valid certificate. A valid certificate can be obtained from a Certificate Authority such as Verisign (http://www.verisign.com/) or Thawte (http://www.thawte.com/). Consult the Java documentation on how to obtain a valid certificate and then how to import that certificate into the keystore. A good source detailing this entire procedure can be found at http://java.sun.com/docs/books/tutorial/security/sigcert/index.html.

Lastly, you need to sign the JAR file with a self-signed or a trusted certificate by using the Java jarsigner command.

```
jarsigner -keystore ./myKeystore -storepass password
                                NasaImageBrowser.jar myKey
```

All these examples assume you are in the same directory as the directory containing the NasaImageBrowser.jar file.

JNLP File

The new applet browser plug-in software leverages the Java Network Launching Protocol (JNLP) first introduced with Java Web Start. Java Web Start allows you to start an Internet Java application outside of the browser. This capability is now being applied to applets themselves, so that applets no longer run within the browser application, but rather run in a background Java process with a window on the browser page. Using JNLP makes dealing with issues like security and runtime settings easier to maintain in a downloadable form.

Ant Tasks

There are two Ant tasks that assist in signing JARs. First, there is the `genkey` task that generates the key. Second, there is the `signjar` task that facilitates signing JAR files. The following is an example build.xml that uses these tasks to sign the `NasaImageBrowser` JAR file.

```xml
<?xml version="1.0" encoding="UTF-8"?>
<project name="NasaImageBrowser" default="default"
        basedir="." >
    <target name="default" >
        <genkey alias="myKey" storepass="password"
            dname="CN=JFXBOOK"
            keystore="./myKeystore" />
        <signjar alias="myKey"
            storepass="password"
            keystore="./myKeystore"
            jar="NasaImageBrowser.jar" />
    </target>
</project>
```

To run a JavaFX applet, it is necessary to create a JNLP XML file that defines the required resources, security settings, and applet configuration properties for deployment. By default, the `javafx()` JavaScript function, defined in the next section, defines this filename for this JNLP deployment file to be the concatenation of the applet name with _browser.jnlp. For the NASA Image Browser application, this is `NasaImageBrowser_browser.jnlp`. This can be changed to point to another name by including a `"jnlp_href"` launch parameter in the JavaScript function, `javafx()`. This is described in the next section, JavaFX Applet Launch JavaScript.

There are four main sections to the JNLP XML, `<information>`, `<security>`, `<resources>`, and `<applet-desc>`. These are shown in Listing 9.1.

Listing 9.1 JNLP XML File

```xml
<?xml version="1.0" encoding="UTF-8"?>
<jnlp spec="1.0+"
href="NasaImageBrowser_browser.jnlp">

    <information>
        <title>NasaImageBrowser</title>
        <vendor>jfxbook</vendor>
        <homepage href="http://www.jfxbook.com"/>
        <description>NasaImageBrowser</description>
```

continues

```
        <offline-allowed/>
        <shortcut>
            <desktop/>
        </shortcut>
    </information>

    <security>
        <all-permissions/>
    </security>

    <resources>
        <j2se version="1.5+"/>
        <property name="jnlp.packEnabled" value="true"/>
        <property name="jnlp.versionEnabled" value="true"/>
        <extension name="JavaFX Runtime"
            href="http://dl.javafx.com/javafx-rt.jnlp"/>
        <jar href="NasaImageBrowser.jar" main="true"/>
    </resources>

    <applet-desc name="NasaImageBrowser"
        main-class="com.sun.javafx.runtime.adapter.Applet"
        width="500" height="500">
        <param name="MainJavaFXScript"
                        value="nasaimagebrowser.Main">
    </applet-desc>

</jnlp>
```

<jnlp> *codebase* **Property:** In the main <jnlp> tag, codebase is an optional property that tells the system to locate any resources defined in the JNLP file. If the codebase property is not specified, the JNLP file inherits the codebase from the HMTL document. The recommendation for the codebase property when a JNLP is used with an applet is either to not specify one in the JNLP file so that the codebase is inherited from the HTML file or to specify an absolute codebase. By not specifying a codebase, the JNLP file is more portable when moving it from one server location to the next. The NetBeans IDE for JavaFX generates an absolute codebase property within the <jnlp> tag, so when placing the files into production, it either has to be changed or removed.

<information>

The <information> element identifies the application and its source. The key element under <information> is <offline-allowed>. If this is set, the applet can be run when the system is off the network. When the system is connected to the network, the applet framework will automatically check for updates. If

`<offline-allowed>` is not specified, the application can only be run when the system is connected back to the applet's source location.

`<security>`

The `<security>` element defines the security permissions the applet is allowed to have. Each applet, by default, is run in a security-restricted environment. If `<all-permissions>` is defined, the applet will have full access to the user's machine. In this case, the JAR files must be digitally signed and the user is asked whether to grant this permission prior to the applet running.

`<resources>`

The `<resources>` element identifies the resources needed for running the applet. This includes specifying which versions of Java are required to run the applet. This section also identifies all the archive files needed by the applet.

`<applet-desc>`

The `<applet-desc>` element defines the properties for the applet. There is some overlap with these settings and the settings set from the HTML page using the JavaScript code defined in the next section. The overlap is resolved as defined in Table 9.1.

Table 9.1 Precedence Rules for <applet> HTML Tag and JNLP Settings

Property	Precedence
`width`	HTML
`height`	HTML
`codebase`	JNLP (If absolute)
`code*`	JNLP
`archive*`	JNLP
`java_arguments*`	JNLP
`java_version*`	JNLP

* When using JNLP applets, applet properties code, `archive`, `java_arguments`, and `java_version` are unnecessary as these are defined in the JNLP file. Applet parameters are merged with the settings defined in the JNLP file. If the same parameters are specified in both, the applet's settings take precedence except for `java_arguments` and `java_version`.

For more information on the JNLP XML and how it applies to applets, go to http://
java.sun.com/javase/6/docs/technotes/guides/jweb/applet/applet_deployment.html#
jnlp_href. For a detailed description on the JNLP XML, go to http://java.sun.com/
javase/6/docs/technotes/guides/javaws/developersguide/syntax.html.

JavaFX Applet Launch JavaScript

To make JavaFX applet deployment easier and portable across browsers, Sun has
developed a JavaScript function for launching JavaFX applets. This JavaScript
function is defined as `javafx(launchParams, appletParams)`. The second parameter, `appletParams`, is optional. To include this JavaScript code into your HTML
page, you must first reference it. The standardized location for this JavaScript
code is http://dl.javafx.com/dtfx.js. An example of using this in an HTML page is

```
<script src="http://dl.javafx.com/dtfx.js"></script>
```

Including this script provides JavaScript functions for automatic checking for the
correct Java version and defines the JavaScript function for loading the appropriate JavaFX runtime archive files.

To use the JavaFX launch function, `javafx()`, in an HTML page, include it
within a JavaScript section as shown in Listing 9.2.

Listing 9.2   JavaScript for Launching JavaFX Applet in a Browser

```
<script>
  javafx(
     {
        archive: "NasaImageBrowser.jar",
        width: 500,
        height: 500,
        code: "nasaimagebrowser.Main",
        name: "NasaImageBrowser"
     }
  );
</script>
```

Listing 9.3 shows using the JavaFX Applet launcher function in an HTML page.
The JavaScript code for the applet is shown in bold and includes two script sections.

Listing 9.3   JavaFX Launcher Script in HTML Page

```
<html>
  <head>
    <title>Nasa Image Browser</title>
  </head>
```

```
<body>
<h1>Nasa Image Browser</h1>
  <script src="http://dl.javafx.com/dtfx.js"></script>
  <script>
    javafx(
        {
         archive: "NasaImageBrowser.jar",
         width: 500,
         height: 500,
         code: "nasaimagebrowser.Main",
         name: "NasaImageBrowser"
        }
    );
  </script>
</body>
```

The second `<script>` tag invokes the `javafx` deployment function defined in the JavaFX deployment script file. This deployment function may have two arguments. The first contains the launch properties for the applet, and the second parameter set contains any parameters available to the application. In this example, only the launch properties are used. By default, this launcher will use a "jnlp_href" of "NasaImageBrowser_browser.jnlp".

Table 9.2 lists the possible launch properties.

Table 9.2 JavaFX Applet Launch Properties

Property	Meaning	Type
archive	One or more archives separated by comma.	String
code	JavaFX class to run.	String
name	Name of the applet.	String
width	Width of the display area.	Number
height	Height of the display area.	Number
codebase	The base URL of the applet; default is the location containing the HTML page.	String
alt	Any text that should be displayed if the applet cannot run.	String
align	Specifies the alignment of the applet. Possible values: left, right, top, texttop, middle, absmiddle, baseline, bottom, absbottom.	String

continues

Table 9.2   JavaFX Applet Launch Properties (*Continued*)

Property	Meaning	Type
vspace	Space above and below the applet.	Number
hspace	Space left and right of the applet.	Number
version	Specifies the JavaFX version to use.	String
jnlp_href	The file containing information that the plug-in should use to launch the applet using Java Web Start.	String
draggable	Indicates whether the applet is allowed to be dragged out of the HTML page to the desktop (true or false).	Boolean

Developer Tip: There is a special launch property, display_html, used for debugging your settings. When this is set to true, instead of launching the applet, the generated HTML code is displayed in the browser. This is useful to determine exactly what is being sent to the browser and to figure out if any settings are wrong.

Listing 9.4 shows an example that adds an applet parameter, isApplet, that will be used by the NasaImageBrowser application to determine whether it has been launched as an applet or as a standalone application. We will see how this is used later in this chapter when we discuss dragging the applet off the browser to the desktop. There is also a launch property to indicate the applet is draggable.

Listing 9.4   Draggable Applet

```
<script src="http://dl.javafx.com/dtfx.js"></script>
<script>
  javafx(
      {
        archive: "NasaImageBrowser.jar",
        width: 500,
        height: 500,
        code: "nasaimagebrowser.Main",
        name: "NasaImageBrowser",
        draggable: true
      },
    {
        isApplet: true
    }
  );
</script>
```

The next section will explore how to take advantage of a new feature that lets you "undock" the applet and move it off the browser onto the desktop. We have just shown that we need to set the launch attribute, draggable, in the preceding example. We also added an applet parameter, isApplet, that will be used by the NASA Image Browser application to determine whether it was started as a stand-alone application or as an applet in a browser.

Undocking from the Browser

You might be asking, "What is this Undocking feature?" Basically, it allows you to click on the application and drag it off the browser to anywhere on your desktop. Figure 9.4 shows the NASA Image Browser after it has been dragged off the Firefox browser. It is now undocked from the browser and will continue to run even if the user exits the browser.

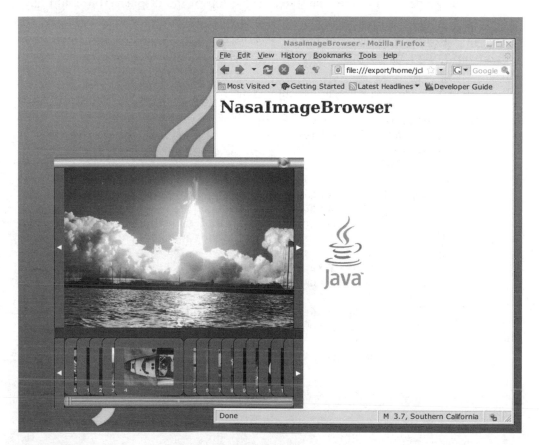

Figure 9.4   Undocked NASA Image Browser Applet

To allow this feature, we have to make some code changes to our application. First, we have to add a `javafx.stage.AppletStageExtension` object to the stage for the viewer. The most important variable in `AppletStageExtension` to enable dragging the applet off the browser is to define a function for `should-DragStart`. When this function is invoked, it returns true if an undocking drag is allowed. In our case, we first check to see if the `"isBrowser"` script variable is true. `"isBrowser"` is set if the Applet Parameter `"isApplet"` is set in the HTML JavaFX launcher function. From JavaFX, you set this using the `javafx.lang.FX` getArgument function.

```
var isBrowser:Boolean =
    (FX.getArgument("isApplet") as String).equals("true");
```

Next, you check to see if the primary mouse button is down. Lastly, because the user can use the mouse in the application to select images to view, you restrict this drag operation to the "bar" area at the top of the display. You could have done this differently by just changing the logic defined in the `shouldDragStart` function. For example, you could have used the secondary mouse button and changed the area to the entire application. This is demonstrated in Listing 9.5.

Listing 9.5   Draggable Applet – JavaFX Code

```
var stage:Stage = Stage {
    title: "NASA Image Viewer"
    width: 1000
    height: 1000
    extensions: [
        AppletStageExtension {
                shouldDragStart: function(e): Boolean {
                    return isBrowser and e.primaryButtonDown
                                        and dragArea.hover;
                }
                onDragStarted: function() {
                    isBrowser = false;
                }
                onAppletRestored: function() {
                    isBrowser = true;
                }
                useDefaultClose: false
        }
    ]
    ...
    ...
```

The useDefaultClose variable indicates whether to use a default close mechanism or whether the close should be under the control of the developer. We have chosen to implement our own close button so we will set this to false. The default is true. When the application is "closed," it actually docks back into the browser page, if the page is still visible.

In our application, we use a ControlButton to close the application. There are two important concepts here. One is that the ControlButton is only visible when the application is not docked to the browser. Figure 9.5 shows the close button.

Figure 9.5   Close Button

Listing 9.6 shows the implementation of the close button.

Listing 9.6   Close Button

```
ControlButton {
    translateY: bind gap/2
    translateX: bind scene.width - 2 * gap
    visible: bind not isBrowser
    width: bind gap-6
    height: bind gap-6
    centerShape: Circle {
        radius: bind (gap-8)/2;
        fill: RadialGradient {
            stops: [
                Stop {
                    offset: 0.0
                    color: Color.WHITE
                },
                Stop {
                    offset: 1.0
```

continues

```
                    color: Color.rgb(100,100,100)
                },
            ]
        }
    }
    action: function() {
        stage.close();
    }
}
```

The second concept is that when the button is clicked, the action calls the stage's `close()` function. The `stage.close()` function then causes the application to be again docked to the browser page, if that page is still visible. Figure 9.6 shows the application redocked. Notice the close button does not show when it is docked.

Figure 9.6   Docked Applet

JavaFX and JavaScript Interaction

Interaction between a JavaFX applet and JavaScript on the HTML page is fairly simple and two-way interaction is supported. From the JavaFX applet, you can invoke arbitrary JavaScript on the Web page. On the other hand, from JavaScript on the Web page, you can get and set variables and invoke functions on the JavaFX applet.

JavaFX to JavaScript

First, let's discuss the JavaFX to JavaScript interaction. The `javafx.stage` `.AppletStageExtension` class that we used in our "undocking" exercise earlier also contains a function, `eval()`, that takes a string argument of JavaScript code. This is executed in the HTML document that hosts the JavaFX applet. If the JavaScript code returns an object, `eval()` returns it. Let's look at an example using the `NASAImageBrowser` applet.

First, let's add a read-only text field to the HTML page, identified as `"numPics"`. This field will hold the total number of pictures that the `NasaImageBrowser` applet currently has. The HTML code is in Listing 9.7.

Listing 9.7   HTML – Input Type "id"

```
<p>Number of pictures:
<input type="text" name="numPics" readonly="readonly"
                  id="numPics" value="0" size="10" >
```

To update this field from the JavaFX code, we bind a variable to the size of the image list. When the image list size is updated, we invoke a JavaScript function that sets the value of the read-only field, `"numPics"`. The JavaFX code is in Listing 9.8.

Listing 9.8   JavaFX Script – Locate JavaScript Item by ID

```
var applet: AppletStageExtension;
public var totalImageCount =
        bind sizeof imageList.images on replace {
    applet.eval("document.getElementById('numPics').value =
            {totalImageCount}");
};
```

The `applet` variable is assigned to the `AppletStageExtension` when we created the stage, as shown in Listing 9.9.

Listing 9.9   JavaFX Script – AppletStageExtension

```
var stage:Stage = Stage {
    title: "NASA Image Viewer"
    width: 1000
    height: 1000
    extensions: [
        applet = AppletStageExtension {
        ...
        ...
```

When the HTML page is first loaded and the JavaFX applet starts, this number rapidly updates as the applet processes the returned XML from the NASA site.

Let's add another HTML input field that displays the current picture index. Besides showing the current picture index as set by the JavaFX applet, this field also allows the user to enter an arbitrary index and then click the Set Current button to send the index to the JavaFX applet. We will be discussing this feature when we talk about JavaScript communicating with JavaFX.

The HTML code is in Listing 9.10.

Listing 9.10   HTML – currentIndex Input Field

```
<p>Current Picture Index:
<input type="text" name="currentIndex"
                   id="currentIndex" value="0" size="10">
```

The JavaFX applet code is in Listing 9.11.

Listing 9.11   JavaFX Script – Access HTML Field currentIndex

```
public var currentIndex: Integer = bind imageList.currentIndex on
replace {
    thumbnailViewer.currentIndex = currentIndex;
    // tell the web page
    applet.eval(
     "document.getElementById('currentIndex').value =
     {currentIndex}");
};
```

Figure 9.7 shows the new HTML page, with the two fields numPics and currentIndex. The JavaFX applet has already updated the Number of Pictures and the Current Picture Index.

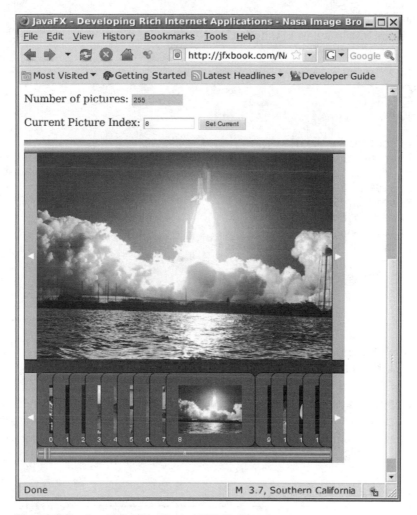

Figure 9.7 JavaFX – JavaScript HTML Page

As you can see, calling JavaScript from JavaFX is fairly simple to implement. Now let's explore the other way, JavaScript to JavaFX.

JavaScript to JavaFX

Calling JavaFX from JavaScript is fairly straightforward, but there are some rules that you need to follow.

First, you need to add an id launch parameter to the javafx launch function. We will use "app" as the id, and this lets us refer to the applet in our JavaScript code as "document.app". If we had chosen a different ID, let's say "myApplet", access to the JavaFX applet would be with that code, as in "document.myApplet". The HTML for this is shown in Listing 9.12.

Listing 9.12   HTML – Define Applet "id"

```
<script>
    javafx(
    {
        codebase: "./dist",
        archive: "NasaImageBrowser.jar",
        draggable: true,
        width: 500,
        height: 500,
        name: "app",
        id: "app",
        title: "Nasa Image Browser - JavaScript - JavaFX"
    }, {
        isApplet: "true"
    } );
</script>
```

Next, we will define a JavaScript function, setIndex(), to set the current index from the currentIndex <input> field that we previously defined in the HTML page. This function calls a script function on the JavaFX applet, passing in the value taken from the currentIndex <input> field. The JavaFX function then takes this value and sets the current index, and the display updates. The public script variables and functions are then accessed using the script keyword "document .app.script". The JavaScript code for this is in Listing 9.13.

Listing 9.13   HTML – JavaScript

```
<script>
function setIndex() {
    document.app.script.setCurrentPic(
            document.Form1.currentIndex.value);
}
</script>
```

The JavaFX code for the setCurrentPic function is in Listing 9.14. Notice that it is necessary to use the javafx.lang.FX.defAction() function. This makes sure that the changes to the JavaFX classes are done on the JavaFX Main processing thread. Without this, you can expect erratic behavior and possibly exceptions.

Listing 9.14   JavaFX – deferAction()

```
// The applet uses this to set the current Image shown
public function setCurrentPic(ndx:Integer) : Void {
    FX.deferAction(function(): Void {
        try {
            imageList.setIndex(ndx);
        } catch(ex: java.lang.Exception) {
            applet.eval("alert('{ex}')");
        }
    });
}
```

You can also set and get any public script variables defined in the JavaFX applet. In the next example, we want to change the fill script variable in the NASAImage-Browser applet to silver. The JavaScript code in Listing 9.15 shows how to do this.

Listing 9.15   HTML-JavaScript Access Public JavaFX Variables

```
<script>
document.app.script.fill =
    document.app.Packages.javafx.scene.paint.Color.SILVER;
....
</script>
```

The Packages per-Applet keyword provides JavaScript access to the JavaFX and Java packages visible to the JavaFX applet. In the preceding example, we accessed the script variable, SILVER, from the javafx.scene.paint.Color class.

You can also use the Packages keyword to instantiate new Java objects in the JavaScript code. Instantiating JavaFX objects within JavaScript is not currently supported. Listing 9.16 shows how to do this.

Listing 9.16   HTML-JavaScript – Instantiate Java Objects

```
var point = new document.app.Packages.java.awt.Point();
point.x = 100;
point.y = 150;
```

The main restriction when accessing JavaFX applets from JavaScript is that you can only directly access the public script variables and functions defined for the JavaFX applet. If you need to access instance variables or functions, you need to create a script level variable or function that lets you get to the instance. For example, the JavaFX code could be structured as shown in Listing 9.17.

Listing 9.17   JavaFX – Accessing Instance Variables via Script Variables

```
public var myInstance: MyApplet;
public class MyApplet {
...
}
function run(args: String[] ) : Void {
    myInstance = MyApplet{};
}
```

JavaScript can then access the instance via the `myInstance` script variable. For example, the JavaScript code could be

```
var theAppletInstance = document.app.myInstance;
```

This JavaScript variable, `AppletInstance`, could then be used to access the instance variables and functions contained in the JavaFX `MyApplet` class.

Java Web Start

Java Web Start is a technology that allows you to start a networked application from an HTML Web page or directly from the desktop. This is an alternative way to distribute your applications without having to go through a specific install process. The first time you launch a Java Web Start application, all the necessary files are downloaded off the network and cached locally on your computer. If there are updates, Java Web Start automatically pulls down the updated files. As a result, you do not have to worry about distributing updates to your customers. When they run the application, the Java Web Start will make sure they have the most up-to-date version.

The applet framework we just covered is based on Java Web Start, so there will be a lot of commonality between the two. The first step is to create your application, test it, then create signed JAR files for the application. These steps are the same as those we covered in the section for JavaFX applets. For creating signed JAR files, see the section under Java Applets, Manual Generation, Signed Jars. Of course, if you build your distribution with NetBeans IDE for JavaFX, the IDE does this automatically for you.

The next step is to create a Java Network Launch Protocol (JNLP) deployment file. This is similar to the way we created a JNLP file for JavaFX Applets that we discussed previously in the Deploying a JavaFX Application as an Applet section of this chapter. However, there is a difference in one area. Instead of having an `<applet-desc>` section under the `<jnlp>` tag, there is an `<application-desc>` section.

The <application-desc> contains a main-class attribute that points to the main JavaFX class, and may have zero or more <argument> elements for passing the equivalent of command-line arguments to the JavaFX application. Listing 9.18 shows an example <application-desc> section.

Listing 9.18 JNLP – <application-desc>

```
<application-desc main-class="nasaimagebrowser.Main">
    <argument>arg1</argument>
</application-desc>
```

Except for swapping out the <applet-desc> section for the <application-desc> section, the JNLP deployment file for applets is identical to the one for applications. Using the NASABrowserImage application, the Java Web Start JNLP file is shown in Listing 9.19.

Listing 9.19 JNLP Deployment File for Java Web Start Application

```
<?xml version="1.0" encoding="UTF-8"?>
<jnlp spec="1.0+" href="NasaImageBrowser_browser.jnlp">
    <information>
        <title>NasaImageBrowser</title>
        <vendor>jclarke</vendor>
        <homepage href="http://www.jfxbook.com"/>
        <description>NasaImageBrowser</description>
        <offline-allowed/>
        <shortcut>
            <desktop/>
        </shortcut>
    </information>

    <security>
        <all-permissions/>
    </security>

    <resources>
        <j2se version="1.5+"/>
        <property name="jnlp.packEnabled" value="true"/>
        <property name="jnlp.versionEnabled" value="true"/>
        <extension name="JavaFX Runtime"
            href="http://dl.javafx.com/javafx-rt.jnlp"/>
        <jar href="NasaImageBrowser.jar" main="true"/>
    </resources>

    <application-desc main-class="nasaimagebrowser.Main"/>
</jnlp>
```

Using Java Web Start, there are three ways to launch the application. First is to embed a link to the JNLP deployment file in a Web page, which could look like this:

```
<a href="dist/NasaImageBrowser.jnlp">Launch with Java Web
Start</a>
```

The second way is to associate the Java Web Start mime type, `application/x-java-jnlp-file`, to the JNLP file type (.jnlp) in your operating system. Then, when the user clicks on the JNLP file, the application will automatically start. This association should have been set up when Java was installed on the platform.

The third way is to create a desktop launcher. If you include the `<shortcut>` hint in the `<information>` section of the JNLP file, the Java Web Start system creates a desktop launcher. Depending on configuration settings for Java Web Start, it probably will ask the user's permission to do this first. For more information on all the capabilities for Java Web Start, go to http://java.sun.com/javase/6/docs/technotes/guides/javaws/index.html.

Chapter Summary

In this chapter, we covered the steps to create a JavaFX applet and Java Web Start JavaFX application. We also covered how to interact with the Web page using the JavaScript to JavaFX bridge. The essence of this is that the JavaFX applet model has been totally rewritten to be based on Java Web Start. This allows applets to now take advantage of the caching mechanisms inherent in Java Web Start, and thus speed up applet startup time. This framework also has built-in automatic version and update support, so the user always has a current and consistent set of libraries to ensure reliability. Also, this new framework removes dependencies on the underlying browser, so now applications can be consistent across different browser types. Many of the shortcomings of the old applet model have been fixed.

JavaFX helps abstract out interactions with the underlying framework, so now applet and Java Web Start deployments are relatively simple and easy. Also, because both frameworks are based on the same underpinnings, the same JavaFX code can run, untouched, as a standalone application, a Java Web Start application, or a JavaFX applet.

In the next chapter, we will explore an architectural pattern for Web Services, called Representational State Transfer, commonly known as REST. This will allow us to take what we have just learned for JavaFX applets and Java Web Start, and employ them in a full Web Services architecture.

Create RESTful Applications

"Rest, the sweet sauce of labor."
—Plutarch

What Is REST?

Service-oriented architecture (SOA) and development is a paradigm where software components are created with concise interfaces, whereby each component performs a discrete set of related functions. Each component, with its well-defined interface and contract for usage, can be described as providing a service to other software components. This is analogous to an accountant who provides a service to a business, even though that service consists of many related functions (i.e., bookkeeping, tax filing, investment management, and so on).

With SOA, there are no technology requirements or restrictions. You can build a service in any language with standards such as CORBA, platform-specific remote procedure calls (RPC), or the more universally accepted XML. Although SOA has been around as a concept for many years, its vague definition makes it difficult to identify or standardize upon. The client/server development model of the early 90s was a simple example of an SOA-based approach to software development.

A Web service is an example of an SOA with a well-defined set of implementation choices. In general, the technology choices are the Simple Object Access Protocol (SOAP) and the Web Service Definition Language (WSDL), both XML-based. WSDL describes the interface (also called the contract), whereas SOAP describes the data that is transferred. Because of the platform-neutral nature of XML, SOAP, and WSDL, Java tends to be a popular choice for Web service implementation due to its OS-neutrality.

Web service systems are an improvement of client/server systems, and other proprietary object models such as CORBA or COM, because they're built to standards and are free of many platform constraints. Additionally, the standards, languages, and protocols typically used to implement Web services helps systems built around them to scale better.

Representational State Transfer (REST)

However, there exists an even less restrictive form of SOA than a Web service. This style of architecture is called *representational state transfer* (REST), as labeled by Dr. Roy Fielding in his doctoral dissertation. REST is a collection of principles that are technology independent, except for the requirement that it be based on HTTP, the protocol of the World Wide Web. In short, a system that conforms to the following set of principles is said to be RESTful:

- All components of the system communicate through interfaces with clearly defined methods and dynamic, mobile, code
- Each component is uniquely identified through a hypermedia link (i.e., URL)
- A client/server architecture is followed (i.e., Web browser and Web server)
- All communication is stateless
- The architecture is tiered, and data can be cached at any layer

These principles map directly to those used in the development of the Web and, according to Dr. Fielding, account for much of the Web's success. The HTTP protocol, its interface of methods (GET, POST, HEAD, and so on), the use of URLs, HTML, and JavaScript, as well as the clear distinction between what is a Web server and a Web browser, all map directly to the first four principles. The final principle, regarding tiers, allows for the common network technology found in most Web site implementations: load balancers, in-memory caches, firewalls, routers, and so on. These devices are acceptable because they don't affect the interfaces between the components; they merely enhance their performance and communication.

The Web is the premier example of a RESTful system, which makes sense since much of the Web's architecture preceded the definition of REST. What the Web makes clear, however, is that complex remote procedure call protocols are not needed to create a successful, scalable, understandable, and reliable distributed software system. Instead, the principles of REST are all that you truly need.

Overall, REST can be described as a technology and platform-independent architecture, where loosely coupled components communicate via interfaces over standard Web protocols. Software, hardware, and data-centric designs are employed to maximize system efficiency, scalability, and network throughput. The underlying principle, although never explicitly mentioned in any REST description, is simplicity.

REST differs from other software architecture in that it marries the concepts common to software architecture (interfaces, components, connectors, patterns, and so on) with those of network architecture (portability, bandwidth management, throughput measurement, protocol latencies, and so on). This combination makes REST ideal for distributed software systems where scalability in terms of both processing power and communication efficiency are critical.

Figure 10.1 illustrates the REST architecture in one comprehensive diagram that combines logical software architecture with physical network elements. For instance, it demonstrates the following REST principles:

- Communication is performed over HTTP.
- Clients contain optional server caches for efficiency.
- Services can employ caches to back-end systems.
- There are no restrictions on the number of clients per service, or the number of services per client.
- Services can call services.

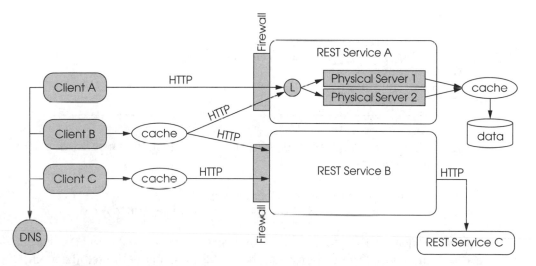

Figure 10.1   Overview of REST Components

- Load-balancing hardware is used for scalability.
- Firewalls can be used for security.

In this diagram, the physical components have been shaded for clarification.

There are some interesting points on data caching that need to be made. First, data must be marked, either implicitly or explicitly, as cacheable or non-cacheable. Second, although specialized caches may be used (custom, in-memory data structures), general-purpose caches, such as Web browser caches, or third-party Web caches (such as Akamai) may also be used.

Building a RESTful System

If you eliminate typical Web service protocols (XML-RPC SOAP, WSDL, and so on), how do you build an SOA-based RESTful system? With REST, you use the same mechanism used to request a Web page: the HTTP query URL. For instance, take a look at the sample SOAP call in Listing 10.1. Here, a request is made for an employee's benefits information from a human resources Web service.

Listing 10.1   Sample SOAP Call

```
<SOAP-ENV:Envelope xmlns:SOAP
 ENV="http://schemas.xmlsoap.org/soap/envelope/">
    <SOAP-ENV:Header>
        some data here…
    </SOAP-ENV:Header>
    <SOAP-ENV:Body>
    <GetBenefits>
        <user>123-45-6789</user>
        <type>full_time_employee</type>
    </GetBenefits>
    </SOAP-ENV:Body>
</SOAP-ENV:Envelope>
```

With REST, you can replace a SOAP call, such as that shown in Listing 10.1, with the following URL:

```
http://humanresources.com/benefits?
            user=<USER_SSID>&type=full_time_employee
```

The HTTP query URL definition is all you need to know and use to make calls to a RESTful service. The response can be HTML, comma-delimited data, XML, JavaScript Object Notation (JSON)—which we'll explore in the next section—or a more sophisticated document type such as a spreadsheet.

REST Response Types: Some feel that the return of anything but hypermedia-based content is not truly RESTful. However, in our opinion, as long as the system stays true to the REST principles for the request and the communication protocol, the response *type* is unimportant.

When you build a Web application with a Java Servlet, for example, it's straightforward to read the data passed through URL query parameters, and to return any text-based response to the caller. The Java Servlet doPost method implementation in Listing 10.2 illustrates this. Here, the parameters used in the HTTP query URL above are read and used to retrieve a user's employee benefits. The results are encoded as human-readable text. Because this is an example of a RESTful service, the request can be initiated—and the response viewed—by a Web browser, or any component in a distributed application.

Listing 10.2 Java Servlet doPost

```
protected void doPost( HttpServletRequest req,
                       HttpServletResponse resp)
   throws ServletException, IOException
{
    ServletOutputStream out = resp.getOutputStream();
    String response;

    String userSSID = req.getParameter("user");
    String userType = req.getParameter("type");
    if ( userType.equals("full_time_employee")) {
        Employee emp = lookupUser(userSSID);
        String medPlan = emp.getMedicalPlan();
        String dntPlan = emp.getDentalPlan();
        String retPlan = emp.getRetirementPlan();
        Response = "User " + emp.getFullName() +
                   " has medical plan: " + medPlan +
                   ", and dental plan: " + dntPlan +
                   ", and retirement plan: " + retPlan;
    }
    else {
        // ...
    }

    // Output the response from the worker
    out.println(response);
}
```

For the remainder of this chapter, we're going to focus on *consuming* RESTful services from a JavaFX application. In particular, we're going to examine just how straightforward it is to request and consume Web service data in both JSON and XML formats. First, let's take a closer look at the details of JSON.

JavaScript Object Notation (JSON)

With the emergence of dynamic Web-based applications based on Asynchronous JavaScript and XML (Ajax) technology, JavaScript Object Notation (JSON) became a popular alternative to XML. This is mainly because JSON tends to be smaller and more readable than XML, making it both more efficient to send over the Internet uncompressed, and more convenient to work with. Although it's closely associated with JavaScript—in fact it's a subset—in practice it's language independent.

There are JSON parsers available for most of the popular languages, including C++, Java, Perl, Python, and now JavaFX. JSON's basic object types, which map very well to both Java and JavaFX types, are

String. A Unicode text string of characters enclosed in double quotes, with backslash escaping.

Number. An integer, real, or floating-point numeric value.

Boolean. A flag that contains a true or false value.

Object. A collection of associated data, represented as key:value pairs, separated by commas, and grouped together with curly braces. For example:

```
"author": {
    "last": "Bruno",
    "first": "Eric",
    "book": "JavaFX: Developing Rich Internet Applications",
    "ISBN": 013701287X,
    "yearPublished": 2009,
    "publisher": "Pearson"
}
```

Array. An ordered pair of comma-separated values grouped together with square braces. For example:

```
"authors": [
    "Clarke",
    "Connors",
    "Bruno"
]
```

The value null is also valid. These types and structures were chosen because modern programming languages support them natively. For instance, Listing 10.3 shows a sample JSON object structure, named Image, as returned from Yahoo! Web Services.

Listing 10.3   Sample JSON Object

```
{
  "Image": {
    "Width":123,
    "Height":145,
    "Title":"Java Duke Guitar",
    "Thumbnail": {
      "Url":
"http:\/\/sk1.yt-thm-a01.yimg.com\/image\/b6ece07210e09816",
      "Height": 20,
      "Width": 25
    },
    "IDs":[ 116, 943, 234, 38793 ]
  }
}
```

This JSON data defines an Object (named Image) that contains two Number fields (named Width and Height), a String field (named Title), another Object (named Thumbnail), and an array (named IDs). The Thumbnail object contains its own String and Number fields, and the IDs array contains a series of Number values.

Let's take a closer look at some Web services that are available publicly for you to use in your applications. The two we'll discuss in this chapter, Yahoo! and GeoNames, both support JSON for many of their services. In the next section, we'll build an application that combines these two Web services to form a mashup JavaFX application.

Yahoo! Web Services

Yahoo! offers a large number of Web service APIs that you can use to create your own applications; you can explore these Web services at http://developer .yahoo.com/everything.html. Although the APIs all support XML as a return type, a good number of them also provide JSON as an alternative (see http:// developer.yahoo.com/common/json.html). By adding the output= parameter onto the request URL, you can specify XML or JSON as the response data type.

For instance, one Yahoo! service allows you to do image searches from your application. To make a request for, say, images from JavaOne with the results in JSON form, you can use the following URL:

```
http://search.yahooapis.com/ImageSearchService/V1/
imageSearch?appid=YahooDemo&query=JavaOne&results=
2&output=json
```

Here, we've specified the `ImageSearchService`, with the text *JavaOne* as the search query, and the output set to *JSON*. Another service that Yahoo! provides is called the *LocalSearchService*, which allows you to search for anything in a particular location. We'll use this service in the sample JavaFX mashup application, discussed in the next section. However, let's first take a quick look at the GeoNames Web service.

GeoNames Web Services

GeoNames provides a number of Web service APIs that return interesting data relevant to specific locations. For instance, there are services that provide weather data, Wikipedia data, earthquake data, and so on, for locations you specify. You can explore the full set of Web service APIs at http://www.geonames.org/export/ws-overview.html. Most of the GeoNames services support both XML and JSON as output.

For instance, you can look up weather by airport code (using an airport close to the location you want the current weather for) with the following URL:

```
http://ws.geonames.org/weatherIcaoJSON?ICAO=KJFK
```

Here, we've requested the JSON weather service specifically, and have provided the airport code JFK with a K as a prefix, per the service contract. Alternatively, you can request weather data for a specific location supplied as longitude and latitude data. We're going to use this form of the weather service in the sample JavaFX mashup application. Let's take a look at how to use JavaFX to call external Web services, and then parse the output.

JavaFX and REST

As of version 1.0, JavaFX includes two classes that allow you to easily build REST clients. These classes are `javafx.async.RemoteTextDocument` and `javafx.data.pull.PullParser`. With `RemoteTextDocument` (see Figure 10.2), you can asyn-

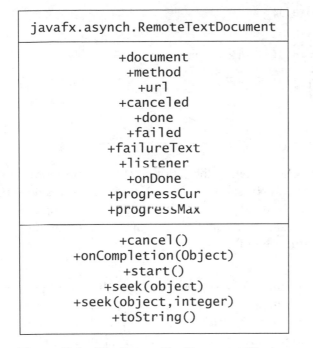

Figure 10.2 The RemoteTextDocument Class

chronously make an HTTP request to a URL that you provide. When the return document has been received, the `onDone` function, which you implement, is called with an indication of success or failure. Next, you can access the returned document through the `RemoteTextDocument.document` member variable. Listing 10.4 shows an example of these steps in action.

Listing 10.4 Using RemoteTextDocument

```
var rtd: RemoteTextDocument = null;
var bis: InputStream = null;
var serverURL = "http://...";
// ...

function requestData() : Void {
    // Request data from remote server
    rtd = RemoteTextDocument {
        url: bind serverURL
        onDone: function(success:Boolean):Void {
            if(success) {
                var doc = rtd.document;
                bis= new ByteArrayInputStream(doc.getBytes());
                parser.parse();
```

continues

```
                    bis.close();
                }
                else {
                    println("failure = {rtd.failureText}");
                }
                rtd = null;
            }
        };
}
```

When the `requestData` function is called, the act of creating a new `RemoteText-Document` instance with a valid URL starts the request process. When a document has been received successfully, the data is read in as a `ByteArrayInputStream` as it would with Java, and this step is complete. At this point, it doesn't matter what the response type is; the job of the `RemoteTextDocument` class is to get the document to you.

However, if the returned document is XML or JSON, you'll need to parse it to make use of it. This is where the `PullParser` class (see Figure 10.3) comes in, which is called in Listing 10.4, highlighted in bold type. There's some more code behind this that you need to provide, such as the code in Listing 10.5. It begins with a custom class, `Location`, since this code illustrates parsing location data as received from Yahoo! Web Services.

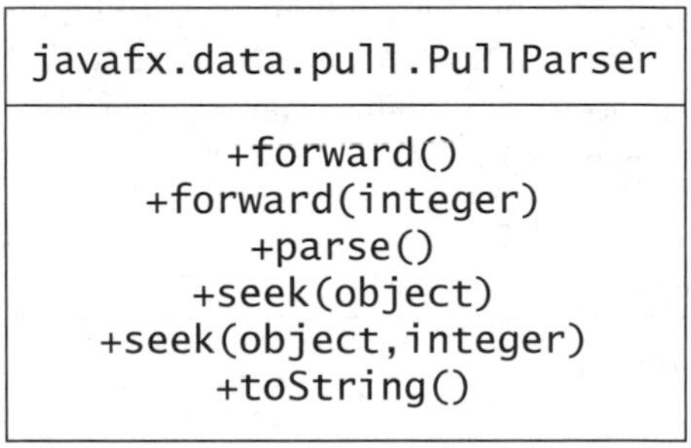

```
┌─────────────────────────────────┐
│ javafx.data.pull.PullParser     │
├─────────────────────────────────┤
│           +forward()            │
│        +forward(integer)        │
│            +parse()             │
│          +seek(object)          │
│       +seek(object,integer)     │
│           +toString()           │
└─────────────────────────────────┘
```

Figure 10.3   The PullParser Class

The real work begins with the object, `parser`, which is an instance of the `Pull-Parser` class. It begins parsing as soon as its `input` object is set and the `parse` method is called. Because it's bound to the `ByteInputStream` object `bis` from Listing 10.4, it has access to the data as soon as the `RemoteTextData` object populates it. It's this bound variable that allows the code in Listing 10.4 (which requests data from a remote server) to cooperate with the code in Listing 10.5 (which parses the received JSON document).

Listing 10.5 Using PullParser

```
class Location {
    public var city: String;
    public var state: String;
    public var lat: String;
    public var long: String;
}
var location: Location = Location{};
// ...

var parser = PullParser {
    documentType: PullParser.JSON;
    input: bind bis
    onEvent: function(event: Event) {
        // parse the JSON data and populate object
        if(event.type == PullParser.END_VALUE) {
            if(event.name == "City") {
                location.city = event.text;
            }
            else if (event.name == "Latitude") {
                location.lat = event.text;
            }
            else if (event.name == "Longitude") {
                location.long = event.text;
            }
            else if (event.name == "State") {
                location.state = event.text;
            }
        }
    }
}
```

As `PullParser` progresses through the document, it fires a series of events (see Table 10.1) that are handled by your code in the onEvent function.

As shown in Listing 10.5, each time a value is completely parsed, the onEvent function compares the name to those that we're interested in. If there's a match, the value is simply stored. In this case, as location specific data is received, the code populates the `Location` object. With further use of object binding (which was discussed in Chapter 4, Synchronize Data Models—Binding and Triggers), it's easy to envision how individual UI elements will be updated to display the location data—such as the city name—as the data is parsed in this code. In fact, the sample JavaFX application we're going to explore in this section does just that. Let's examine the complete sample application now, which shows the current weather conditions for any valid ZIP code entered.

Table 10.1   PullParser Events to Process

Event	Description
ERROR	A syntax error in the XML or JSON document structure
CDATA	A value containing an XML CDATA structure
INTEGER	A JSON integer value
NUMBER	A JSON floating-point value
TEXT	A text value (in XML or JSON)
START_DOCUMENT	The start of an XML or JSON document
END_DOCUMENT	The end of an XML or JSON document
START_ELEMENT	The start of an XML or JSON object
END_ELEMENT	The end of an XML or JSON object
START_VALUE	The start of a JSON object's value
END_VALUE	The end of a JSON object's value
START_ARRAY	The start of a JSON array
END_ARRAY	The end of a JSON array
START_ARRAY_ELEMENT	The start of a JSON array element
END_ARRAY_ELEMENT	The end of a JSON array element
FALSE	A JSON true Boolean value
TRUE	A JSON false Boolean value
NULL	A JSON null value

The JavaFX Weather Widget

As an example of how to make use of RESTful services from a JavaFX application, we're going to build a simple weather widget (shown in Figure 10.4). The widget accepts a ZIP code as input, and in turn displays detailed current weather conditions for the applicable region. This includes cloud conditions, wind speed and direction, temperature, humidity, and air pressure at sea level.

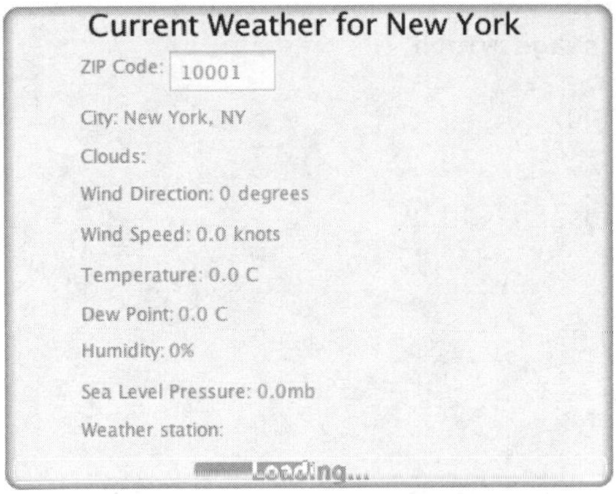

Figure 10.4   The JavaFX Weather Widget

The widget's GUI is a JavaFX scene that contains a group of three main components: title text, a progress bar, and a vertical box that contains the individual
weather text components. Some of the code for this is shown in Listing 10.6. The
progress bar remains hidden until a request is made to a REST service, at which
point it's made visible and is activated. When all of the requested data is
received, it's hidden again.

Listing 10.6   The Weather Widget Scene Structure

```
var app: VBox;
// ...

var scene: Scene = Scene {
  content: Group  {
    content: bind [
      // Widget title text
      Text {
        content: bind "Current Weather for {location.city}"
        font: Font { size: 20 }
        textOrigin: TextOrigin.TOP
        translateX:
            bind (stage.width-titleText.layoutBounds.width)
                    / 2.0 + titleText.layoutBounds.minX
        y: 5
      }

      // Progress bar
      bar = IndeterminateProgressBar {
              translateY: bind stage.height - 20;
```

continues

```
                  visible: false
                  width: bind stage.width
                  height: 15
                  text: "Loading..."
            },

        // Weather data fields
        app=VBox {
          translateX: 50
          translateY: 30
          spacing: 10
          content: [
            HBox { content: [
              Text {
                translateY:
                        bind input.boundsInLocal.height/2;
                content: "ZIP Code:"
              },
              input = TextBox {
                columns: 6
                value: bind zipCode with inverse
                selectOnFocus: true
                action: function(): Void {
                  requestCoordinatesAndWeather();
                }
              }]
            },
            HBox { content: [
              Text {
                textOrigin: TextOrigin.TOP
                content: "City:"
              },
              Text {
                textOrigin: TextOrigin.TOP
                content:
                    bind "{location.city}, {location.state}"
                fill: Color.BLUE
              }]
            },
            // ...
          ]
        }
      // ...
}
```

Each weather text field, which actually consists of two JavaFX Text fields—a
label and value both arranged horizontally—are bound to variables that are

updated with the latest weather data received from the GeoNames weather service. We'll examine the data structure and request process later in the chapter. The entire weather request sequence is started when you enter a valid ZIP code and press the Return key. The weather widget can be considered a mashup application, as it uses data from both Yahoo! and GeoNames. Let's take a closer look at this process now.

A Mashup Application

The weather widget first requests location data from Yahoo! Web Services with the ZIP code provided, then it makes a request to the GeoNames weather service with the returned location data. This four-step process is illustrated in Figure 10.5.

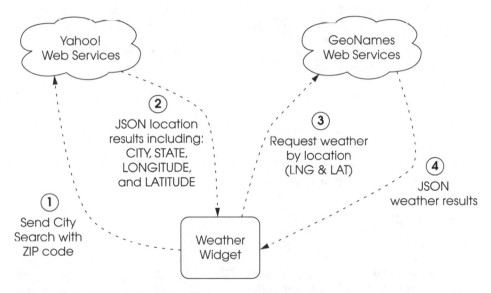

Figure 10.5   The Mashup Data Flow

As data is received, and the bound data structure values are updated, the widget's GUI is automatically updated to reflect the new data.

Using Yahoo! Web Services

Because the GeoNames service requires location data in terms of longitude and latitude to return local weather conditions, we use Yahoo!'s city search feature to get this data. The request is made, including the ZIP code entered, with the following URL in the JavaFX code:

```
var locationURL = bind
    "http://local.yahooapis.com/"
    "LocalSearchService/V3/localSearch?"
    "appid=YahooDemo&query=city&zip={zipCode}&"
    "results=1&output=json";
```

Being bound to the zipCode field, which is entered by the user, the string is updated automatically with its value when changed. This request returns location data for the ZIP code, as well as local search results that are limited to one result as specified in the URL. The only data we're interested in, however, are the fields of the Location class, shown in Listing 10.7.

Listing 10.7   The Location Data Structure

```
class Location {
    public var city: String;
    public var state: String;
    public var lat: String;
    public var long: String;
}
```

These fields are updated when the JSON names that match are located within the JSON text, as read by the PullParser class, locationParser (see Listing 10.8). Although many other fields and values are encountered while parsing the location data, only the four Location class values are stored.

Listing 10.8   The Location JSON Data Parser

```
var locationInput: InputStream;
var locationParser = PullParser {
    documentType: PullParser.JSON;
    input: bind locationInput
    onEvent: function(event: Event) {
        // parse the JSON Yahoo data and
        //populate the location object
        if(event.type == PullParser.END_VALUE) {
            //println("{event}");
            if(event.name == "City") {
                location.city = event.text;
            }else if (event.name == "Latitude") {
                location.lat = event.text;
            }else if (event.name == "Longitude") {
                location.long = event.text;
            }else if (event.name == "State") {
                location.state = event.text;
            }
```

```
        }
      }
}
```

Being that the `PullParser`'s member variable, `input`, is bound to the `location-Input` variable, this code is invoked whenever the input stream is updated and the `parse` method is called. This occurs when the user enters a ZIP code and presses Return, as processed in the `action` function highlighted in bold typeface in Listing 10.6. After the location data is processed, the results are used in the request to the GeoNames service to receive the current weather conditions. Let's take a look at this process now.

Using GeoNames Web Services

As mentioned earlier, the GeoNames service returns the current weather conditions by either a supplied airport code or location (longitude and latitude). For the weather widget, we want to make the request by location. The location data is used with the following JavaFX URL string to form the request:

```
var coordURL = bind "http://ws.geonames.org/
findNearByWeatherJSON?lat={location.lat}&lng={location.long}";
```

Being bound to both the `Location.lat` and `Location.lng` variables, the text is automatically updated with these values when they're changed. The request returns detailed weather conditions that are stored in the fields of the `Weather` class, shown in Listing 10.9.

Listing 10.9 The Weather Data Structure

```
class Weather {
    public var station: String;
    public var clouds: String;
    public var windDirection: Integer;
    public var windSpeed: Number;
    public var temperature: Number;
    public var dewPoint: Number;
    public var humidity: Integer;
    public var seaLevelPressure: Number;
    public var observation: String;
}
```

These fields are updated when the JSON names that match are located within the JSON text, as read by the `PullParser` class, `weatherParser` (see Listing 10.10).

Note that because some fields differ in their value types (i.e., `String`, `Number`, and `Integer`), Java classes such as `Double` and `Integer` are used to get the proper values from the JSON text.

Listing 10.10   The Weather JSON Data Parser

```
var weatherInput: InputStream;
var weatherParser = PullParser {
  documentType: PullParser.JSON;
  input: bind weatherInput
  onEvent: function(event: Event) {
    // Parse the JSON Weather data and
    // populate the Weather object
    if(event.type == PullParser.END_VALUE) {
      if(event.name == "clouds") {
          weather.clouds = event.text;
      }else if (event.name == "stationName") {
          weather.station = event.text;
      }else if (event.name == "windDirection") {
          weather.windDirection = event.integerValue;
      }else if (event.name == "windSpeed") {
          weather.windSpeed = Double.valueOf(event.text);
      }else if (event.name == "temperature") {
          weather.temperature = Double.valueOf(event.text);
      }else if (event.name == "dewPoint") {
          weather.dewPoint = Double.valueOf(event.text);
      }else if (event.name == "humidity") {
          weather.humidity = event.integerValue;
      }else if (event.name == "seaLevelPressure") {
          weather.seaLevelPressure = event.numberValue;
      } else if (event.name == "observation") {
          weather.observation = event.text;
      }
    }
  }
}
```

As with the request to Yahoo! for the location data, since `weatherParser`'s member variable, `input`, is bound to the `weatherInput` variable, this code is invoked when the input stream is updated and `parse` is called. This is triggered when the location data is completely received. When all of the weather data is received, and the `Weather` class' member variables have been set, the JavaFX `Text` components that are bound to them are automatically updated. This completes the weather widget's request, update, and display processes. When compared to implementing the same functionality with plain Java code, the power of JavaFX object binding greatly simplifies the entire process.

JavaFX and XML

The weather widget application is a simple example of how to process JSON Web services, but what about XML? Consuming XML-based REST services is completely supported, and the code only changes slightly. The two main differences are

- Document type: Set to `PullParser.XML` (instead of `PullParser.JSON`).
- Use of `javafx.data.xml.QName`: XML node names arrive via this object, with namespace information, referenced from the `Event` object.

For instance, the code to parse the Yahoo! location data in XML form is shown in Listing 10.11. The two differences listed in the preceding are highlighted in the code in bold type.

Listing 10.11 Parsing XML

```
var locationInput: InputStream;
var locationParser = PullParser {
    documentType: PullParser.XML;
    input: bind locationInput
    onEvent: function(event: Event) {
        // parse the XML Yahoo data and
        // populate the location object
        if (event.type == PullParser.END_ELEMENT) {
            if(event.qname.name == "City") {
                location.city = event.text;
            }else if (event.qname.name == "Latitude") {
                location.lat = event.text;
            }else if (event.qname.name == "Longitude") {
                location.long = event.text;
            }else if (event.qname.name == "State") {
                location.state = event.text;
            }
        }
    }
}
```

The `QName` class is part of the `javafx.data.xml` package that also contains the `XMLConstants` class. This class contains the following standard XML constant strings:

XMLNS_ATTRIBUTE. Example: "xmlns"

XMLNS_ATTRIBUTE_NS_URI. Example: "http://www.w3.org/2000/xmlns/"

XML_NS_PREFIX. Example: "xml"

XML_NS_URL. Example: "http://www.w3.org/XML/1998/namespace"

XML_VERSION. Example: "1.0"

The remainder of the application code remains the same as the JSON version, presented earlier in this chapter. This makes parsing XML and JSON documents quite straightforward, with very little work to switch between the two.

Chapter Summary

This chapter illustrated how the JavaFX classes, RemoteTextDocument and PullParser, combined with the power of object binding make JavaFX applications ideal REST clients. In this chapter, we explored the creating of a widget that displays current weather conditions from the combination of JSON (or XML) data received from Yahoo! and GeoNames Web services. Thanks to the power of JavaFX, simple data structures bound to JavaFX GUI components and updated by classes provided by the JavaFX framework are all that's required to create a working Web 2.0 mashup.

11

JavaFX and Java
Technology

*"In art there are only fast or slow developments.
Essentially it is a matter of evolution, not revolution."*

—Bela Bartok

A real advantage of JavaFX is that the entire platform is extended by the full power and capabilities of the Java platform. This allows existing Java frameworks and custom libraries to fully participate in a JavaFX application.

At its core, JavaFX classes are compiled into Java bytecode, so JavaFX, at the runtime level, is tightly integrated with the Java platform. However, the JavaFX language is a declarative language with an object-oriented flavor, whereas Java is an object-oriented imperative language. The main difference is that in JavaFX you tell the system what needs to be done and the runtime determines how to do it; in Java, you explicitly program what is to be done. When crossing the JavaFX/Java boundary, you must keep this difference in mind.

Basically, the JavaFX runtime is always in the background, so you need to be careful how you interact with JavaFX from Java. Nonetheless, it is still possible to leverage Java classes from JavaFX, and with a little effort, you can leverage JavaFX scripts within your Java code. This chapter describes some of the basic rules that must be obeyed when crossing the JavaFX/Java boundary.

The first part of this chapter discusses the rules for using Java objects and classes within JavaFX and you should be familiar with this to write JavaFX scripts. However, the last two sections, Java Scripting and JavaFX Reflection, discuss accessing JavaFX from Java. This is more important to people doing intense development with Java and JavaFX and by its nature requires a more in-depth knowledge of Java. If you are not interested in accessing JavaFX from Java, you may skip these last two sections.

Classes

As we mentioned in Chapter 3, JavaFX Primer, JavaFX classes can extend multiple Java interfaces, but can only extend at most one Java class, and that Java class must have a default (no args) constructor.

```
public class MyJavaFXClass extends java.awt.Point {
```

When extending a Java class, all the accessible methods and attributes of that class are available to the JavaFX class. *However, none of the Java class attributes or functions may participate in JavaFX binding.* Remember from Chapter 3 that JavaFX Script is a declarative language with object orientation and is a forgiving environment. Even if you try to bind to a Java object's attribute, the runtime system will silently ignore the updates. To illustrate this

```
 class FooBar1 extends java.awt.Point {
     public var fxPointX = bind x;
}

var f = FooBar1{};
println("f.x = {f.x} f.fxPointX = {f.fxPointX}");
f.x = 100;
println("f.x = {f.x} f.fxPointX = {f.fxPointX}");
```

When this is run, f.x is updated, but f.fxPointX is not updated, and there is no error or warning message.

```
f.x = 0 f.fxPointX = 0
f.x = 100 f.fxPointX = 0
```

The main message here is you can extend Java classes, but the attributes and methods from those classes have no inherent connection to some of the advanced binding and trigger features found in JavaFX. For more detailed information on binding and triggers, check out Chapter 4, Synchronize Data Models—Binding and Triggers.

JavaBeans: Please note that JavaFX triggers and JavaBeans have no built-in connection. If you update a bean property, it will not automatically update a bound JavaFX variable. The inverse is true too: if you update a JavaFX variable, it does not automatically update a JavaBean property. In Chapter 12, JavaFX Code Recipes, we present a way to do this, using Java property change listeners and JavaFX on replace triggers.

When extending Java interfaces or Java abstract classes, the JavaFX class must implement all the abstract methods contained within the interface or abstract class or be declared abstract itself. These function signatures must be able to map to the Java methods being implemented. For example, when extending the java.awt.event.ActionListener interface, the Java method

```
public void actionPerformed(ActionEvent);
```

needs to be converted to a JavaFX function:

```
public override function
            actionPerformed(e: ActionEvent) : Void { }
```

The override keyword is required, as this instructs the system that this method overrides a method defined in the super class. The full example is

```
class MyActionListener extends
                    java.awt.event.ActionListener {
    public override function
        actionPerformed(e:java.awt.event.ActionEvent) :
                                                    Void {
        // do something
    }
}
```

Java Objects

You can instantiate Java objects from JavaFX using one of two methods. First, if the Java object has a default (no args) constructor, you can use the JavaFX object literal syntax. However, you cannot initialize any of the Java object's attributes this way.

Developer Warning: The JavaFX compiler and runtime will allow you to enter initializers for Java object attributes, but the compiler and runtime will just silently ignore them. For example:

```
var dim = java.awt.Dimension {
    width: 500
    height: 600
};
println(dim);
prints:  java.awt.Dimension[width=0,height=0]
```

To create a JavaFX instance from a Java object, use the object literal syntax with open and close curly braces. For example, the following script will print the date 24 hours from now.

```
var millis = java.lang.System.currentTimeMillis() +
                                24 * 60 * 60 * 1000;
var date = java.util.Date { };
date.setTime(millis);
println(date);
```

Although you cannot initialize the Java object attributes, it is possible to define abstract function implementations within an object literal. The first example shows how to override the methods in a Java interface with JavaFX functions. For example, the Comparator interface's Java functions are

```
public int compare(Object o1, Object o2);

public boolean equals(Object obj);
```

In JavaFX, these can be implemented within the object literal syntax:

```
var comp = java.util.Comparator {

    override function compare(o1:Object, o2:Object) :
                                                Integer {
        if(o1 instanceof java.lang.Comparable and
            o2 instanceof java.lang.Comparable) {
          (o1 as java.lang.Comparable).compareTo(
            o2 as java.lang.Comparable);
        }else { -1; }
    }

    override function equals(obj:Object) : Boolean {
        this == obj;
    }
};
```

This next example shows how to override a method in a Java class. This overrides the Java method:

```
public String toString() {}
```

The object literal declaration for this is

```
var rand = java.util.Random {
    override function toString(): String {
        return "[{nextDouble()}]";
    }
};
println(rand);
```

When declaring Java methods in JavaFX, the JavaFX syntax must be used, and the parameters declared using the mapped JavaFX type. For example, the Java method

```
public double getWidth()
```

is represented in JavaFX as

```
public override function getWidth() : Double
```

Likewise, the Java method

```
public void setSize(double width, double height)
```

is represented as a JavaFX function:

```
public override function setSize(width:Double, height:Double)
: Void
```

The second way to instantiate a Java object from JavaFX is to use the new operator similar to the way it is used in Java, passing any required constructor arguments. Here is another way to create a Date object that contains the time 24 hours from now. The variable, millis, is passed to the constructor for Date.

```
var millis = java.lang.System.currentTimeMillis() +
                                24 * 60 * 60 * 1000;
var date = new java.util.Date ( millis );
println(date);
```

Notice the parentheses rather than the curly braces. Arguments are converted according to the rules outlined in the next section, Function Parameter and Return Mapping. Also, when using the new operator, it is not possible to override any of the Java object's methods. Of course, if the Java class is an interface or abstract class, it cannot be instantiated this way. It needs a subclass to implement the abstract methods.

Function Parameter and Return Mapping

JavaFX has ten basic types: `Number`, `Double`, `Float`, `Long`, `Integer`, `Short`, `Byte`, `Character`, `Boolean`, and `String`. The preferred types for normal use are `Number`, `Integer`, `Boolean`, and `String`. Unless you have a specific need for the other types, stick with the preferred types. All these types are represented by corresponding Java classes and therefore have access to the corresponding Java methods available to them. For example, the following illustrates use of the `Character` class method, `isWhiteSpace()`, and the `Integer` class `compareTo()` method.

```
var aCharacter:Character = 0x20;
println(aCharacter.isWhitespace(aCharacter));

var aInteger:Integer = 1000;
println(aInteger.compareTo(25));
```

Table 11.1 maps the JavaFX type to its corresponding Java type.

Table 11.1 JavaFX Types – Classes

JavaFX Type	Java Class
Double	java.lang.Double
Number	java.lang.Number
Float	java.lang.Float
Long	java.lang.Long
Integer	java.lang.Integer
Short	java.lang.Short
Byte	java.lang.Byte
Character	java.lang.Character
Boolean	java.lang.Boolean
String	java.lang.String

JavaFX literals are also JavaFX objects, so it is possible to access their class's respective methods directly from the literal. For example, the number literal 3.14 can be converted to an integer by calling its `intValue()` method inherited from `java.lang.Number.`

```
var i:Integer = 3.14.intValue();
println(i);
```

Likewise, the integer literal 4 can be used to get its bit count by invoking the `bitCount()` method inherited from `java.lang.Integer.`

```
println(4.bitCount(1));
println("Now is the time".substring(0,3));
```

When the basic JavaFX types are passed as parameters to Java methods or a Java type is being assigned to one of the JavaFX basic types, an attempt is made to convert between the two. The following eight tables, Tables 11.2 through 11.9, illustrate the conversion rules for each of the JavaFX basic types, including sequences. The first column is the JavaFX type, the second column is the Java type, the third column is the rule when the JavaFX type is passed as a parameter to a Java method call. The last column is the rule when a Java type is being assigned to a JavaFX type, either directly or as a result of a return type from a function or Java method.

For parameter conversion, if an automatic conversion is not supported, an alternative is presented in the Parameter Conversion column. Usually, the type needs to be converted to the Java Type using one of the `xxxValue()` methods on the JavaFX object. For example, if the JavaFX type is a `Number`, when trying to convert to the Java `java.lang.Double` class in the Java method parameter, you need to invoke the `doubleValue()` function on the JavaFX `Number` class. This listing illustrates this.

```
var aNumber = 3.14;
aJavaObject.callDoubleMethod(aNumber.doubleValue());
```

In the Assignment column, the message, "possible loss of precision" means the compiler will issue a warning message that the conversion will lose some accuracy. If you want to avoid this warning message, the return type should be narrowed to the JavaFX type. For example, when converting a Java double to a JavaFX Long, use the `longValue()` function on the returned type. For example:

```
var aLong : Long =
javaObject.callJavaMethodReturn_double().longValue();
```

Table 11.2   JavaFX – Java Type Conversion Mappings – Number/Float

JavaFX Type	Java Type	Parameter Conversion	Assignment
Number/Float	`double`	YES	YES
	`java.lang.Double`	n.doubleValue()	YES
	`float`	YES	YES
	`java.lang.Float`	YES	YES
	`long`	YES	YES
	`java.lang.Long`	n.longValue()	YES
	`int`	YES	YES
	`java.lang.Integer`	n.intValue()	YES
	`short`	YES	YES
	`java.lang.Short`	n.shortValue()	YES
	`byte`	YES	YES
	`java.lang.Byte`	n.byteValue()	YES
	`char`	NO	YES
	`java.lang.Character`	NO	YES

Table 11.3   JavaFX – Java Type Conversion Mappings – Double

JavaFX Type	Java Type	Parameter Conversion	Assignment
Double	`double`	YES	YES
	`java.lang.Double`	YES	YES
	`float`	YES	YES
	`java.lang.Float`	d.floatValue()	YES
	`long`	YES	YES

continues

Table 11.3   JavaFX – Java Type Conversion Mappings – Double (*Continued*)

JavaFX Type	Java Type	Parameter Conversion	Assignment
Double	java.lang.Long	d.longValue()	YES
	int	YES	YES
	java.lang.Integer	d.intValue()	YES
	short	YES	YES
	java.lang.Short	d.shortValue()	YES
	byte	YES	YES
	java.lang.Byte	d.byteValue()	YES
	char	NO	YES
	java.lang.Character	NO	YES

Table 11.4   JavaFX – Java Type Conversion Mappings – Long

JavaFX Type	Java Type	Parameter Conversion	Assignment
Long	double	YES	Possible loss of precision
	java.lang.Double	l.doubleValue()	Possible loss of precision
	float	YES	Possible loss of precision
	java.lang.Float	l.floatValue()	Possible loss of precision
	long	YES	YES
	java.lang.Long	YES	YES
	int	YES	YES
	java.lang.Integer	l.intValue()	YES

continues

Table 11.4   JavaFX – Java Type Conversion Mappings – Long (*Continued*)

JavaFX Type	Java Type	Parameter Conversion	Assignment
Long	short	YES	YES
	java.lang.Short	l.shortValue()	YES
	byte	YES	YES
	java.lang.Byte	l.byteValue()	YES
	char	NO	YES
	java.lang.Character	NO	YES

Table 11.5   JavaFX – Java Type Conversion Mappings – Integer

JavaFX Type	Java Type	Parameter Conversion	Assignment
Integer	double	YES	Possible loss of precision
	java.lang.Double	i.doubleValue()	Possible loss of precision
	float	YES	Possible loss of precision
	java.lang.Float	i.floatValue()	Possible loss of precision
	long	YES	YES
	java.lang.Long	i.longValue()	YES
	int	YES	YES
	java.lang.Integer	YES	YES
	short	YES	YES
	java.lang.Short	i.shortValue()	YES
	byte	YES	YES

Table 11.5 JavaFX – Java Type Conversion Mappings – Integer (*Continued*)

JavaFX Type	Java Type	Parameter Conversion	Assignment
Integer	java.lang.Byte	i.byteValue()	YES
	char	NO	YES
	java.lang.Character	NO	YES

Table 11.6 JavaFX – Java Type Conversion Mappings – Short

JavaFX Type	Java Type	Parameter Conversion	Assignment
Short	double	YES	Possible loss of precision
	java.lang.Double	s.doubleValue()	Possible loss of precision
	float	YES	Possible loss of precision
	java.lang.Float	s.floatValue()	Possible loss of precision
	long	YES	YES
	java.lang.Long	s.longValue()	YES
	int	YES	YES
	java.lang.Integer	s.intValue()	YES
	short	YES	YES
	java.lang.Short	YES	YES
	byte	YES	YES
	java.lang.Byte	s.byteValue()	YES
	char	NO	Possible loss of precision
	java.lang.Character	NO	NO

Table 11.7 JavaFX – Java Type Conversion Mappings – Byte

JavaFX Type	Java Type	Parameter Conversion	Assignment
Byte	double	YES	Possible loss of precision
	java.lang.Double	b.doubleValue()	Possible loss of precision
	float	YES	Possible loss of precision
	java.lang.Float	b.floatValue()	Possible loss of precision
	long	YES	YES
	java.lang.Long	b.longValue()	YES
	int	YES	YES
	java.lang.Integer	b.intValue()	YES
	short	YES	YES
	java.lang.Short	b.shortValue()	YES
	byte	YES	YES
	java.lang.Byte	YES	YES
	char	NO	Possible loss of precision
	java.lang.Character	NO	NO

Table 11.8 JavaFX – Java Type Conversion Mappings – Character

JavaFX Type	Java Type	Parameter Conversion	Assignment
Character	double	YES	Possible loss of precision
	java.lang.Double	NO	NO

Table 11.8 JavaFX – Java Type Conversion Mappings – Character (*Continued*)

JavaFX Type	Java Type	Parameter Conversion	Assignment
Character	float	YES	Possible loss of precision
	java.lang.Float	NO	NO
	long	YES	Possible loss of precision
	java.lang.Long	NO	NO
	int	YES	Possible loss of precision
	java.lang.Integer	NO	NO
	short	NO	Possible loss of precision
	java.lang.Short	NO	NO
	byte	NO	Possible loss of precision
	java.lang.Byte	NO	NO
	char	YES	YES
	java.lang.Character	YES	YES

Table 11.9 JavaFX – Java Type Conversion Mappings – Boolean, String Sequence

JavaFX Type	Java Type	Parameter Conversion	Assignment
Boolean	boolean	YES	YES
	java.lang.Boolean	YES	YES
String	java.lang.String	YES	YES
Sequence	type[]	YES	YES

Sequences are converted to an array of the Java type—for example, the `String` sequence

```
var authors = [ "Clarke", "Connors", "Bruno" ];
```

is passed as a Java `String[]` array because `authors` is a sequence of `String`. Likewise, the integer sequence

```
var numbers = [ 2, 4, 6, 8, 10 ];
```

can be applied to Java type, `int []` or `Integer[]`. However, there is no automatic conversion from a sequence of integer to other types, like `double[]`, `float[]`, `long[]`, and so on. To convert from one number type to the other, use a for loop to convert to the desired type, and then use that result. For example, the `numbers` integer sequence is converted to a sequence of type `Double` using a `for` loop, as shown in the following example.

```
// returns Seq of Integer
var numbers = aJavaObject.callIntegerArray();
// convert to Sequence of Double
var dumbers = for(i in numbers) i.doubleValue();
anotherJavaObject.callDoubleArray(dumbers);
```

All other JavaFX object types not listed in the Tables 11.2 through 11.9 are passed, unchanged, to and from the Java methods. For example, if you pass a `javafx.geometry.Point2D` object to a Java method, it will still be a `javafx.geometry.Point2D` object within the Java method. If the Java method returns a Java object, like `java.util.HashMap`, it will still be a `java.util.HashMap` in JavaFX.

Developers Warning: If you are passing a JavaFX object to Java that is not automatically converted to a Java type as outlined in the preceding, it is important that the Java code not manipulate it without using the JavaFX Reflection API.

Never manipulate a JavaFX object in any thread other than the main JavaFX thread. Manipulating JavaFX objects outside of the main processing thread *is not safe*. A way to make sure JavaFX object changes are executed on the main JavaFX thread is presented at the end of this chapter.

When passing JavaFX objects to Java methods, interactions to those objects should be made via the `javafx.reflect` package or via a JavaFX function. Direct manipulation of the JavaFX variables within a JavaFX object must be done via the JavaFX reflection framework. Another instance when the JavaFX reflection framework is required is when the Java code needs to create a JavaFX object. The `javafx.reflect` package is actually written directly in Java and is safe to use from Java code assuming you are in the main JavaFX thread. The package `javafx.reflect` is covered in more detail later in this chapter.

Java Scripting

If you want to run JavaFX script source from your Java program, you need to use the Java Scripting API. The Java Scripting API, JSR-223, is a standard framework for running a script from Java code. Any scripting language can be used as long as it is JSR-223 compliant. Some examples of these supported languages are JavaScript, Groovy, Python, Ruby, and of course JavaFX script.

Basic Scripting Evaluation

The simplest way to accomplish this is to use the `javafx.util.FXEvaluator` class. This class is actually a Java class and can be safely used in a Java program. `FXEvaluator` has a static method `Object eval(String script)` that takes a JavaFX script as a string and returns the JavaFX object created within that script, if any. To run your application when using scripting, you must include the JavaFX compiler JAR, `javafxc.jar`, in your classpath.

Let's start with a simple Hello World example:

```
import javafx.util.FXEvaluator;


public class Main {
    public static void main(String[] args) {
        Object fxObj = FXEvaluator.eval(
                        "println('hello world');");
        System.out.println("JavaFX Object = " + fxObj);
    }
}
```

When run, this program produces the following output:

```
hello world
JavaFX Object = null
```

The script is just `"println('hello world');"` and this merely prints to the console. Because `println` does not return anything, the returned object is null. So, let's modify it a bit:

```
Object fxObj = FXEvaluator.eval(
        "println('hello world'); 'hello world';");
System.out.println("JavaFX Object = " + fxObj);
if(fxObj != null) {
    System.out.println("JavaFX Class = " +
                                    fxObj.getClass());
}
```

This now produces

```
hello world
JavaFX Object = hello world
JavaFX Class = class java.lang.String
```

Now let's do something a bit more complicated, as depicted in Listing 11.1.

Listing 11.1 Java Scripting for JavaFX

```
import javafx.util.FXEvaluator;

public class Complex {
    public static void main(String[] args) {
        String script =
            "public class Student {" +
            "       public var name:String;" +
            "       public var age:Integer;" +
            "}" +
            " function run(args: String[]):Void { " +
            "       Student { name: 'Jim' age: 29 };" +
            "}";
        Object fxObj = FXEvaluator.eval(script);
        System.out.println("JavaFX Object = " + fxObj);
        if(fxObj != null) {
            System.out.println("JavaFX Class = " +
                                    fxObj.getClass());
        }
    }
}
```

This produces a returned object for Student:

```
JavaFX Object = ___FX_SCRIPT___$Student@c8769b
JavaFX Class = class ___FX_SCRIPT___$Student
```

FXEvaluator is a way to simply execute a JavaFX script and get a resulting object back. However, instead of hard coding "jim", age 29, in the script, what if you want to pass in arguments to the script? FXEvaluator does not provide a means for this. To add this kind of functionality, you need to directly work with the Java Scripting API.

Java Scripting API with Global Bindings

To add bindings to a script, first, get the JavaFX script engine by creating a ScriptEngineManager and using it to get the JavaFX script engine by either name, getEngineByName(), or extension getEngineByExtension(). In either case, the argument can be "javafx" or "fx". This needs to be cast to a JavaFXScripEngine.

Next, any global bindings may be bound to the script using the engine.put() methods. In this example, we are adding name and age global bindings. The script has been modified to use these global bindings when the Student class is instantiated and is shown in Listing 11.2.

Listing 11.2   Java Scripting for JavaFX – Global Bindings

```
import javax.script.ScriptEngine;
import javax.script.ScriptEngineManager;
import javax.script.ScriptException;

import com.sun.javafx.api.JavaFXScriptEngine;

public class FXScripting {

    public static void main(String[] args) {
        String script =
        "public class Student {\n" +
        "        public var name:String;\n" +
        "        public var age:Integer;\n" +
        "}\n" +
        " function run(args: String[]):Void { \n" +
        "        var m = Student { name: name as String
                        age: age as Integer};\n" +
        "        println('Name = {m.name}, " +
                    "age = {m.age}');\n" +
        "        m;\n"+
        "}";

        ScriptEngineManager manager =
                            new ScriptEngineManager();
        ScriptEngine scrEng =
                    manager.getEngineByExtension("javafx");
        JavaFXScriptEngine engine =
                            (JavaFXScriptEngine)scrEng;
```

continues

```
        if (engine == null) {
            System.out.println(
                            "no scripting engine available");
        }else {
            engine.put("name", "Eric");
            engine.put("age", 25);
            Object fxObj = null;
            try {
                fxObj = engine.eval(script);
            } catch (ScriptException ex) {
                ex.printStackTrace();
            }
            System.out.println("JavaFX Object = " + fxObj);
            if(fxObj != null) {
                System.out.println("JavaFX Class = "+
                                        fxObj.getClass());
            }
        }
    }
}
```

The result of running this program produces the Student with the values for name and age of "Eric" and 25, respectively.

```
Name = Eric, age = 25
JavaFX Object = ___FX_SCRIPT___$Student@1083717
JavaFX Class = class ___FX_SCRIPT___$Student
```

Java Scripting API with Compilation

Let's say we want to reuse the Student object and invoke methods on it. You do this by first compiling the object, setting the bindings, then creating an instance of the object. After we have the object instance, we can invoke methods on the Student object.

First, let's modify the script to add an instance function, getName(), as shown in Listing 11.3.

Listing 11.3   Java Code – Sample JavaFX Script for Java Scripting API

```
String script =
    "public class Student {\n" +
    "    public var name:String;\n" +
    "    public var age:Integer;\n" +
    "    public function getName():String { \n" +
```

```
"            this.name;\n" +
"       }\n" +
"}\n"+
"function run( args:String[] ):Void {\n" +
"      Student { name: name as String \n" +
"                age: age as Integer};\n" +
"}\n";
```

Notice that since we will be using `Bindings` (`SimpleBindings`) rather than the `engine.put()` methods for adding bindings, we need to cast `name` to `String` and `age` to `Integer` within the script.

Next, the Java code compiles the JavaFX script string into a `CompiledScript` object. Then we get the `Student` object by calling `eval()` with the bindings on the `CompiledScript`. Lastly, we use the resulting `Student` object to invoke the `getName()` function. This is shown in Listing 11.4.

Listing 11.4 Java Code – Java Scripting API Invoking JavaFX Function

```
CompiledScript compiled = engine.compile(script);
Bindings bindings = new SimpleBindings();
bindings.put("name", "Eric");
bindings.put("age", 25);
Object fxObject = compiled.eval(bindings);
Object result = engine.invokeMethod(fxObject,
                                    "getName");
System.out.println("Result = " + result);
```

This prints out to the console:

```
Result = Eric
```

The ScriptEngine method, `invokeMethod`, can also be used to call functions with arguments and provides a flexible way to manipulate the state of a JavaFX object. However, it is not possible to directly manipulate JavaFX instance variables through the Java Scripting API framework.

Java Scripting API with Error Handling

If you played around with the previous examples, you may have noticed that some JavaFX compilation errors print out to the console, and some do not. To overcome this, you need to add a diagnostic handler to collect the errors and then show them if a `ScriptException` is encountered. The `javax.tools.Diagnostic-Collector` class provides a means to do this.

First, create an instance of `DiagnosticCollector`, then pass this to either the `compile()` or `eval()` methods on the `JavaFXScriptEngine` instance.

```
DiagnosticCollector diags =
                    new DiagnosticCollector();
try {
  CompiledScript compiled =
                  engine.compile(script, diags);
  ...
```

Now, when a `ScriptException` is thrown, detailed error messages are contained in the `DiagnosticCollector` object. Listing 11.5 shows how to list all the error messages.

Listing 11.5   Java Code – Java Scripting API Error Handling

```
} catch (ScriptException ex) {
  List<Diagnostic> errorList =
                  diags.getDiagnostics();
  Iterator<Diagnostic> iter =
                  errorList.iterator();
  while (iter.hasNext()) {
    Diagnostic d = iter.next();
    System.out.println(
        d.getKind().toString() + ": Line:" +
        d.getLineNumber() + " Col:" +
        d.getColumnNumber() + "\n'" +
        d.getMessage(null) + "'");
  }
}
```

To illustrate this, if we take the `Student` script and change the `getName()` function to return the erroneous instance variable `nameBogus`. Without diagnostic handling, we get the following fairly useless error message from `ScriptException`.

```
javax.script.ScriptException: compilation failed
    at com.sun.tools.javafx.script.JavaFXScriptEngineImpl.
        parse(JavaFXScriptEngineImpl.java:260)
    at com.sun.tools.javafx.script.JavaFXScriptEngineImpl.
        compile(JavaFXScriptEngineImpl.java:119)
    at com.sun.tools.javafx.script.JavaFXScriptEngineImpl.
        compile(JavaFXScriptEngineImpl.java:110)
    at FXCompile.main(FXCompile.java:45)
```

However, with diagnostic handling, we get the far more informative message:

```
ERROR: Line:5 Col:13
'cannot find symbol
symbol  : variable nameBogus
location: class ___FX_SCRIPT___.Student'
```

Java Scripting for JavaFX provides a powerful tool for running JavaFX Script from Java code. It allows you to evaluate scripts and get returned objects so that later you can invoke functions on them. It is limited in that you cannot directly manipulate instance variables. However, if used in conjunction with the JavaFX Reflection API, even this limitation can be overcome.

JavaFX Reflection

The JavaFX `Reflection` package, `javafx.reflect`, allows complete access to JavaFX objects from both Java and JavaFX code. The classes in `javafx.reflect` are actually Java classes and can safely be used from Java programs. Nonetheless, you need to have the appropriate JavaFX SDK libraries in your classpath.

The first task to use the JavaFX `Reflection` is to find an object's class. You do this by getting the `javafx.reflect.FXContext`, then using that to find the class reference. We are using `javafx.reflect.FXLocal.Context` that implements **FXContext,** because this class allows us to additionally *mirror* JavaFX objects, whereas `FXContext` only allows *mirroring* of the JavaFX basic types. Mirroring provides a proxy (a level of indirection) so that the same API could potentially work with remote objects in a separate JVM. However, for now, the only implementation is on a local VM, hence the `FXLocal` implementation.

FXContext and the other `javafx.reflect.FXxxxxx` classes, like `javafx.reflect` `.FXClassType` and `javafx.reflect.FXValue,` are abstract APIs, whereas `FXLocal.Context` and other `FXLocal.Xxxxxx` classes, like `javafx.reflect` `.FXLocal.ClassType` and `javafx.reflect.FXLocal.Value`, are concrete implementations of the JavaFX Reflection API. These `FXLocal` classes sit on top of Java reflection, and thus require the *mirrored* values and types to be in the same VM.

```
FXLocal.Context context = FXLocal.getContext();
FXClassType classRef =
    context.findClass("javafx.geometry.Point2D");
```

After you obtain the `classRef`, you can either create an instance of the class or use an existing object of that type to manipulate the object's state. To create a new instance, call `newInstance()` on the `classRef`.

```
FXLocal.ObjectValue obj =
                    (ObjectValue)classRef.newInstance();
```

Or, if you need to initialize some of the objects instance variables:

```
FXLocal.ObjectValue obj =
                    (ObjectValue) classRef.allocate();
obj.initVar("x", context.mirrorOf(-1.0));
obj.initVar("y", context.mirrorOf(-1.0));
obj.initialize();
```

After the object instance is created, you can get instance variables via the FXClassType getVariable() methods and access the class functions via the get-Function() methods. To set the x and y instance variables in javafx.geometry .Point2D, you must first get the FXVarMember for the x and y instance variables, and then set their respective values:

```
FXVarMember xVar = classRef.getVariable("x");
FXVarMember yVar = classRef.getVariable("y");
xVar.setValue(obj, context.mirrorOf(25.0));
yVar.setValue(obj, context.mirrorOf(50.0));
```

The context.mirrorOf() function wrappers the value with a proxy that uses the local VM to handle the reflection.

If you have a Java method parameter that is a JavaFX object, you convert that to a FXLocal.ObjectValue using context.mirrorOf as shown in Listing 11.6.

Listing 11.6   JavaFX Reflection

```
public static void manipulate(
                        javafx.geometry.Point2D point) {
    FXLocal.Context context = FXLocal.getContext();
    FXClassType classRef =
        context.findClass(point.getClass().getName());
    FXObjectValue obj = context.mirrorOf(point);
    FXVarMember xVar = classRef.getVariable("x");
    FXVarMember yVar = classRef.getVariable("y");
    xVar.setValue(obj, context.mirrorOf(55.0));
    yVar.setValue(obj, context.mirrorOf(777.0));
```

To invoke functions, get the FXFunctionMember object for the function, then invoke it using the instance obj as shown in Listing 11.7.

Listing 11.7 JavaFX Reflection – Function Invocation

```
// call Point2D.toString():String;
FXFunctionMember func =
          classRef.getFunction("toString");
FXValue val = func.invoke(obj);
System.out.println(val.getValueString());
```

JavaFX and Java Threads

JavaFX is *not* thread safe and all JavaFX manipulation should be run on the JavaFX processing thread. To ensure that interactions from Java code to JavaFX objects are safe, you need to run the Java code that manipulates JavaFX objects on the main JavaFX thread. If JavaFX is invoking the Java method, you probably are already on the main processing thread. However, for other conditions, like remote procedure callbacks, this may not be true. In the next chapter, JavaFX Code Recipes, we present an example of how to do this using the Java Message Service (JMS) API.

If you are not on the main processing thread, with JavaFX 1.2, you need to use the `com.sun.javafx.runtime.Entry.deferAction()` method. However, the way to do this is expected to change in future releases to use a public API. Still, the new way will be similarly designed to use a `Runnable`. For example:

```
import com.sun.javafx.runtime.Entry;

Entry.deferAction(new Runnable() {
    public void run() {
        manipulateJavaFX();
    }
});

private void manipulateJavaFX() {
    ...
}
```

If you are a Swing programmer, this is similar to using the `SwingUtilities` `.invokeLater()` method. However, the JavaFX main thread is not necessarily the EventDispatchThread that is used in Swing. This is especially true for devices that do not use Swing, like JavaFX mobile and JavaFX TV. Therefore, use the `Entry` `.deferAction()` method for moving tasks onto the JavaFX main thread and do *not* use the `SwingUtilities` methods.

For parameterized functions, locate the function using the function name and parameter types. When invoking this kind of function, pass in the object as the first argument followed by the parameter objects wrapped in mirrors. This is shown in Listing 11.8.

Listing 11.8   JavaFX Reflection – Function Invocation with Parameters

```
// call Point2D.distance(x:Number, y:Number): Number;
FXFunctionMember func = classRef.getFunction(
                "distance",
                context.getNumberType(),
                context.getNumberType());
FXValue val = func.invoke(obj,
                context.mirrorOf(3.0),
                context.mirrorOf(3.0));
System.out.println(val.getValueString());
```

Because the JavaFX Reflection API is written in Java, you can easily use the same classes from within a JavaFX script. Just change the format to JavaFX. Listing 11.9 shows an example of using the JavaFX Reflection API from JavaFX.

Listing 11.9   JavaFX Reflection – from JavaFX

```
def context:FXLocal.Context = FXLocal.getContext();
def classRef = context.findClass(
                        point.getClass().getName()));
var obj = context.mirrorOf(point);
var xVar = classRef.getVariable("x");
xVar.setValue(obj, context.mirrorOf(55.0));
```

Chapter Summary

It is easy to incorporate Java classes into JavaFX script. However, it helps to understand some of the basic rules for doing this. This chapter has provided you with the basics for interacting between the two environments. First, we discussed the inclusion of Java object within JavaFX script, then we discussed the Java Script API for JavaFX, and lastly we covered the JavaFX Reflection API.

Now you have the basics. In the next chapter, we cover JavaFX code recipes. After that, we are going to bring it all together in a JavaFX Sudoku application. Even the Sudoku application uses Java by incorporating an open source Java library from SourceForge to generate and solve the Sudoku puzzle.

12

JavaFX Code Recipes

"As everybody knows, there is only one infallible recipe for the perfect omelette: your own."

—Elizabeth David

JavaFX code recipes are simple pieces of code that show how to tackle a unique coding problem. There are probably a million such recipes, we have chosen a few to detail in this chapter that are somewhat unique to the JavaFX environment.

The first section, JavaFX and JavaBeans, shows a way to bridge the JavaFX and JavaBeans frameworks. Next, the section on Server Call Back details how to deal with asynchronous call backs from a server. The Node Effects—Fader and Magnifier section demonstrates how to use generic classes for two common effects. Wizard shows how to implement the Wizard pattern for breaking a complex process into smaller tasks. Progress Bar and Slider lay out how to implement two common components. Finally, Matrix details how to implement a two-dimensional array in JavaFX.

On the book's Web site at http://jfxbook.com, you can find the full listing for all these recipes.

JavaFX and JavaBeans

JavaBeans technology is a component architecture with the Java platform that supports component reuse. It has been around since the early days of Java, and most of the Java GUI components are built using it. One of the primary concepts behind JavaBeans is the concept of properties, or named attributes. JavaBean components have a set of properties accessed through get and set methods called getters and setters. Another core feature is events. Events provide a standardized mechanism for a JavaBean to notify an interested object that its state has changed.

Though there is no built-in link between JavaFX and JavaBean components, it is easy to write some glue code to bridge these two. To demonstrate this, we will implement a number spinner in JavaFX based on the Java Swing class JSpinner. A number spinner lets the user select an integer by sequencing through the numbers one at a time in either direction, but using mouse clicks. This is shown in Figure 12.1.

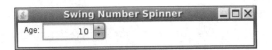

Figure 12.1   Swing Number Spinner

To implement the SpinnerNumber class, we must first create a custom Swing component, by extending the javafx.ext.swing.SwingComponent class.

```
public class SwingNumberSpinner extends SwingComponent {
```

Next, we need to implement the createJComponent() method from SwingComponent. This is where we instantiate the javax.swing.JSpinner object. The default constructor for JSpinner automatically installs an integer data model, javax.swing.SpinnerNumberModel, to support the JSpinner.

```
protected override function createJComponent(): JComponent {
    new JSpinner();
}
```

For this particular example, the properties that we are really interested in are found in the SpinnerNumberModel. These are the maximum and minimum value for the spinner, the step size that tells the spinner how much to step when the user selects up or down, and of course the value of the number. In JavaFX, we will create instance variables for each of these.

```
public var value:Integer;
public var minimum:Integer;
public var maximum:Integer;
public var stepSize:Integer;
```

This provides the basic JavaFX code, but these instance values are still not connected at all to the JSpinner object. To start connecting these instance variables to JavaBeans properties, you assign a default value from the SpinnerModel and then when the instance variable changes, you set that value in the JSpinner object. Here is how value is now set.

```
public var value:Integer =
    getModel().getNumber().intValue() on replace {
        getModel().setValue(value);
};
```

There are a couple of things to point out with this. First, getModel() is a convenience function that just gets the SpinnerNumberModel object from the JSpinner.

```
function getModel() : SpinnerNumberModel {
    getJSpinner().getModel() as SpinnerNumberModel;
}
```

Second, it is necessary to narrow the model's getNumber() result. The getNumber() method returns a java.lang.Number and this needs to be coerced to an integer by calling its intValue() method. The rest of the variables work similarly; however, the variables minimum and maximum have a little twist.

In the SpinnerNumberModel, the minimum and maximum properties return an object that may be null. When they are null, there is no minimum or maximum integer, in effect they are infinite. The issue with this is that currently, Number and Integer in JavaFX cannot be null, so we have to deal with this. There are several options for handling this. One is to create a flag, one for each of the two instance variables, to indicate that they are infinite. The other is to convert the null to a very low minimum or a very high maximum, respectively. We decided to do the latter. For the minimum variable, we created the getMinimum() function as shown in the following listing.

```
function getMinimum() :  Integer {
    if(getModel().getMinimum() == null) {
        java.lang.Integer.MIN_VALUE;
    }else {
        (getModel().getMinimum() as java.lang.Number).
                                            intValue();
    }
}
```

If the SpinnerNumberModel minimum property is null, this function returns java.lang.Integer.MIN_VALUE. Next, we modify the minimum instance variable to be initialized using this function.

```
    public var minimum:Integer = getMinimum() on replace {

        getModel().setMinimum(minimum);
    };
```

The maximum variable is handled in a similar way with the getMaximum() returning java.lang.Integer.MAX_VALUE if the SpinnerNumberModel maximum property is null.

Now, all the JavaFX instance variables are connected to the JavaBean properties, but only in one direction. Whenever the JavaFX instance variable changes, the corresponding property in the JavaBean class will also be updated. For example, if the JavaFX variable, value, is set to 50, the SpinnerNumberModel value property will also be set to 50 and the JSpinner's view will accordingly be updated to show 50. To finish the connection, though, we need to know when the JSpinner changes its properties. These kinds of changes can originate from the user typing in a number in the JSpinner's entry box or using the up or down buttons to sequence through the numbers.

To connect changes originating from the JavaBean, we need to install event listeners on the JavaBean object. The type of event listener to install varies depending on what the JavaBean object supports. Many of the Java GUI classes support the java.beans.PropertyChangeListener interface to notify other objects of change to one of its properties. However, in this example, we are more interested in the properties contained in the SpinnerNumberModel object that is installed in the JSpinner component. JSpinner supports the javax.swing.event.ChangeListener interface that handles ChangeEvents. Change events are fired when the source object wants to notify interested listeners that some state has changed within the object. We need to register a ChangeListener on the JSpinner object so that our JavaFX object is notified that the JSpinner has changed its state.

To do this, we need to add code to the init block for the JavaFX SwingNumberSpinner class.

```
    init {
        var sp = getJSpinner();
        sp.addChangeListener( ChangeListener {
          override function stateChanged(e:ChangeEvent)
                                                    : Void {
              if(not inChange) {
                  value = getModel().getNumber().
                                                intValue();
                  minimum = getMinimum();
                  maximum = getMaximum();
                  stepSize = getModel().getStepSize().
                                                intValue();
```

```
            }
        }
    } );
}
```

Now whenever the JSpinner changes state, we are notified, and then we can update the instance variables in JavaFX SwingNumberSpinner. Unfortunately, the ChangeEvent does not tell us which value changed, so we have to update them all. However, the JavaFX runtime knows if the value is actually changing so any triggers or bind actions will only occur if there is a real change in value.

You may have noticed that we slipped in a Boolean variable, inChange, in the preceding example. This is necessary, because if the change initiates from the JavaFX code by changing one of the instance variables, the corresponding JSpinner property will also be updated. This will cause the JSpinner object to fire a change event, which in turn tries to change the instance variable. So we end up in an unending loop. To avoid this, we introduce the Boolean variable, inChange. When the change originates with a change to the JavaFX variable, inChange is set to true so that the state changed handler will not then update the same instance variable. The following listing shows how this is done with the JavaFX instance variables.

```
var inChange = false;

public var value:Integer =
    getModel().getNumber().intValue() on replace {
    try {
        inChange = true;
        getModel().setValue(value);
    } finally {
        inChange = false;
    }
};
```

Now we have full bidirectional coordination from the JavaFX object to the Java-Beans component. Whenever the JavaFX object's state changes, the JavaBeans object will immediately be updated to stay in synch. On the other side, whenever the JavaBeans object changes state, the JavaFX object state will likewise be updated.

Server Call Back

Servers can asynchronously send messages to a JavaFX application using a variety of frameworks such as Message Oriented Middleware (MOM). To receive asynchronous messages, the first step is to register some form of call back address with the server. Then, whenever the server decides that a message should be sent, it is sent to this call back location using an agreed upon protocol. Different frameworks may use different message formats and protocols and varying transport, but conceptually they work the same.

Typically, when the client receives an asynchronous message, the receiver framework is running in its own thread and dispatches messages either from that thread or via a thread from a thread pool. If you recall, JavaFX runs in its own main thread and all updates to JavaFX objects must occur on that main thread. This requires that the message be pushed onto the main JavaFX thread before any JavaFX objects are modified. The main objective of this code recipe is to show how to receive an asynchronous message from the server, and then move it into the JavaFX main thread for processing.

To illustrate this, we will use an example based on the Java Messaging Service (JMS) API. In this example, the server process publishes to a JMS Topic; the JavaFX client subscribes to the JMS Topic and receives the messages. This is the classical Pub/Sub paradigm.

For our simple example, the server, written in Java, periodically updates the time. This kind of service is useful if the client application needs to synchronize its notion of time with the server platform. Every second, the server sends a JSON message to the JMS topic named "clock". The message includes the milliseconds obtained from the Java call, `System.currentTimeMillis()`. The following is an example of this JSON message.

```
{ "clock": "1232822581540" }
```

The client receives this message and displays the time represented by the clock millisecond value in a JavaFX Text object as shown in Figure 12.2. This is updated roughly every second.

Figure 12.2   JavaFX Call Back – Clock

To implement this in the JavaFX client, first create a Java class, called Subscriber. This class connects to the JMS broker, subscribes to the "clock" topic, then starts listening for messages. The Subscriber class implements the javax.jms.MessageListener interface and registers itself with the JMS client framework to be notified whenever a new message arrives. The MessageListener defines a method that Subscriber must implement, public void onMessage(Message msg). When a message is received by the JMS client, it in turn calls the onMessage() method in Subscriber.

ClockUpdater is a JavaFX class and it also extends javax.jms.MessageListener and implements its own onMessage() function. The reason we cannot use this directly with the JMS client framework is that the JMS client framework would call this function using one of its threads, not the main JavaFX thread. Modifying JavaFX objects on any other thread than the main JavaFX thread is not supported and likely will cause a serious exception.

When the JMS client calls the Java Subscriber.onMessage() method, it will not be on the JavaFX main thread. We need to move the message over to the JavaFX main thread, and then push that message over to the JavaFX object. To do this, we need to use the com.sun.javafx.runtime.Entry.deferAction() method to invoke the JavaFX function on the main JavaFX thread.

The constructor for Subscriber takes two arguments: the first identifies the JMS topic, and the second is the JavaFX class to notify when a message is detected from JMS. Because the JavaFX class extends the Java interface MessageListener, we can refer to this class directly. This is shown as Java code in Listing 12.1.

Listing 12.1 Subscriber.java

```
...
...
    private MessageListener fxListener;

    public Subscriber(String topicName,
        MessageListener fxListener) throws JMSException {

        this.fxListener = fxListener;
...
...
```

When the JMS client calls the Subscriber.onMessage(Message msg) Java method, we then use the Entry.deferAction() method to call the JavaFX onMessage(msg:Message) function from the JavaFX main thread. Notice that we need to change the message parameter to the Java onMessage() method to final. This is so that it can be visible when the deferAction Runnable is invoked. Listing 12.2 shows the Java onMessage(Message msg) implementation.

Listing 12.2   Subscriber.java – onMessage()

```java
public void onMessage(final Message msg) {
    try {
        // must run this on the JavaFX Main thread
        // If you don't you will eventually get
        // exceptions in the JavaFX code.
        Entry.deferAction( new Runnable() {
            @Override
            public void run() {
                fxListener.onMessage(msg);
            }
        } );

    } catch (Exception ex) {
        Logger.getLogger(Subscriber.class.getName()).
            log(Level.SEVERE, null, ex);
    }
}
```

On the JavaFX side in `ClockUpdater.fx`, the implementation is normal JavaFX. The message is checked to make sure it is a `javax.jms.TextMessage`, and then the JSON string is set and parsed. Listing 12.3 shows how this is done.

Listing 12.3   ClockUpdater.fx

```java
public class ClockUpdater extends MessageListener {
    public var millis: Number;
    ...
    ...
    // this is called from the Java class Subscriber
    public override function onMessage(msg: Message):Void {
        if(msg instanceof TextMessage) {
            var jsonStr = (msg as TextMessage).getText();
            var input =
              new ByteArrayInputStream(jsonStr.getBytes());
            try {
                parser.input = input;
                parser.parse();
            } finally {
                input.close();
            }
        }
    }
}
```

This JavaFX code then gets the JSON string from the TextMessage object and parses it using a javafx.data.pull.PullParser. For detailed information on using the PullParser class, consult Chapter 10, Create RESTful Applications. Listing 12.4 shows the simple implementation to process the clock JSON message.

Listing 12.4 JSON Clock Message

```
public var millis: Number;

var parser = PullParser {
    documentType: PullParser.JSON
    onEvent: function(e: Event) : Void {
        if(e.type == PullParser.END_VALUE and
                               e.name == "clock") {
            var milliStr = e.text;
            millis = java.lang.Long.valueOf(milliStr);
        }
    }
};
```

The instance variable, millis, needs to be a Number rather than an Integer, because the actual value of the System time is larger than an Integer can hold. Another way to declare millis is with a Long.

Node Effects—Fader and Magnifier

A common effect is for a node to fade in to out as a transition between views. A transition effect allows a smoother change from one view to another. Another common effect is to magnify a node when the mouse hovers over it. The following code recipes show a way to implement these effects using reusable classes.

Fader

The Fader class supports the visual fade in or out of a node. If *fade in* is desired, when a node is shown, it will transition from invisible to visible over a period of time. If *fade out* is chosen, it will change from visible to invisible. There is also a setting for scaling while these transitions occur. Using scaling, the node can grow from small to normal size as it transitions to visible. On the reverse side, while fading out, the node can shrink from its normal size.

The Fade type can be IN, OUT, or BOTH, and these are defined in the Java enumeration FadeType. If the fade type is IN, when the node is shown, its opacity changes from zero, or invisible, to 1.0, totally visible. Also, its scaling transitions from a minimum to a maximum scale, with the default set to 0.0 and 1.0, respectively. It the fade type is OUT, when the node is changing to not shown, the node's opacity and scaling will reverse direction, with opacity changing to 0.0 and scaling to the minimum. Of course, the BOTH type does this when the node is changing from not shown to shown and again when the node is changing from shown to not shown. The duration of the transition is set using an instance variable, duration. Listing 12.5 shows the JavaFX code for these attributes in the Fader class.

Listing 12.5   Fader.fx

```
public class Fader extends CustomNode {
    // holds the node that will be faded.
    public var node:Node;

    public var type = FadeType.IN on replace {
        if(type != null)
            fade();
    };

    public var duration:Duration = 2s;
    public var startScale: Number = 0.0;
    public var endScale: Number = 1.0;
```

To control the transitions, we added an instance variable, show. When show is set to true, the node is made visible, and then the transition starts. When show changes to false, the reverse transition is started, and the node's visible variable is set to false. The actual fade transitions are controlled with a Timeline that is started in the function fade(). This is demonstrated in Listing 12.6.

Listing 12.6   Fader.fx – show()

```
public var interpolator = Interpolator.LINEAR;
var scale = 0.0;

public var show: Boolean on replace {
    if(show) {
        visible = true;
        fade();
    }else if(visible) {
        if ( type == FadeType.OUT or
```

```
                    type == FadeType.BOTH ) {
            fade();
        } else {
            visible = false;
        }
    }
}
```

You may be wondering why we did not just use the `visible` variable and add a trigger to it to commence the animations. Normally, a node becomes visible when the `visible` instance variable is set to true and invisible when it is set to false. We could have done an override on the `visible` variable and added an on replace trigger to start the fade animation, similar to Listing 12.7.

Listing 12.7 Fader.fx – visible

```
public override var visible on replace {
    if(visible) {
        fade();
    } else if ( type == FadeType.OUT or
                    type == FadeType.BOTH ) {
        fade(); // WILL NOT SHOW BECAUSE
                // NODE IS ALREADY MADE INVISIBLE
    }
}
```

This does work when the `visible` variable is set to true. However, when the `visible` variable is set to false, the JavaFX framework immediately sets the node to invisible, so any subsequent animations do not have any visual effect. Because of this, we introduced the `show` instance variable. When show is set to true, visible is set to true and the fade animation starts. When show is set to false, the fade animation starts and the end result of the animation is to set the node's `visible` variable to false.

The strategy is to use one `Timeline`. For fade in, the `Timeline` progresses forward and the `opacity` transitions from transparent (0.0) to fully opaque (1.0), while the `scale` transitions to endScale. For fade out, the `Timeline` plays in reverse from the end to the beginning, so that `opacity` transitions to transparent (0.0), and the `scale` transitions back to startScale. In this reverse direction, when the timeline reaches the beginning or 0 instant, then the `visible` variable is set to false. The timeline is shown in Listing 12.8.

Listing 12.8   Fader.fx – timeline

```
var timeline = Timeline {
    keyFrames: [
        KeyFrame {
            time: 0s
            values: [
                opacity => 0,
                scale => startScale,
            ]
            action: function() {
                if(not show) { visible = false; }
            }
        },
        KeyFrame {
            time: duration
            values: [
                opacity => 1.0 tween interpolator,
                scale => endScale tween interpolator,
            ]
        },
    ]
};
```

The fade function merely controls the playing of the timeline based on the options chosen. If the fade type is either IN or BOTH and show is set to true, then the timeline will play forward from the start. On the other hand, if the fade type is OUT or BOTH and show is set to false, the timeline will play in reverse from the end. Listing 12.9 illustrates how to control the fade animation.

Listing 12.9   Fader.fx – fade

```
function fade() {
    if(show and (type == FadeType.IN or
                        type == FadeType.BOTH )) {
        timeline.rate = 1.0; // play forward
        // start from beginning
        timeline.playFromStart();
    }else if( not show and ( type == FadeType.OUT or
                        type == FadeType.BOTH ) ) {
        timeline.rate = -1.0; // play in reverse
        timeline.time = duration; // start at end
        timeline.play();
    }
}
```

The actual `CustomNode` is a `Group` that holds the node with a `Scale` transformation that is bound to the `scale` instance variable that changes in the timeline. This is shown in Listing 12.10.

Listing 12.10   Fader.fx – create()

```
public override function create(): Node {
    return Group {
        transforms: Scale {
            x: bind scale
            y: bind scale
        }
        content: bind node
    ];
```

An example of using this class is in the following listing. Listing 12.11 is an excerpt of the sample application that is available on the book's Web site.

Listing 12.11   Fader Usage

```
var node = Group {...};
    Stage {
     title: "Fader"
     width: 500
     height: 500
     scene: scene = Scene {
        content:  fader = Fader {
                // center on scene
                translateX: bind (scene.width -
                    fader.layoutBounds.width)/2.0
                translateY: bind (scene.height -
                    fader.layoutBounds.height)/2.0
                show: false
                type: FadeType.BOTH
                node: bind node
            }
        }
    }
}
```

Figure 12.3 shows the `Group` node as it is growing and becoming more visible on to the scene. Figure 12.4 shows the node fully visible and at its normal size. By depressing the Hide button, the process reverses and the node shrinks and becomes invisible. After the node is again hidden, the button name changes to Show so that you can repeat the process.

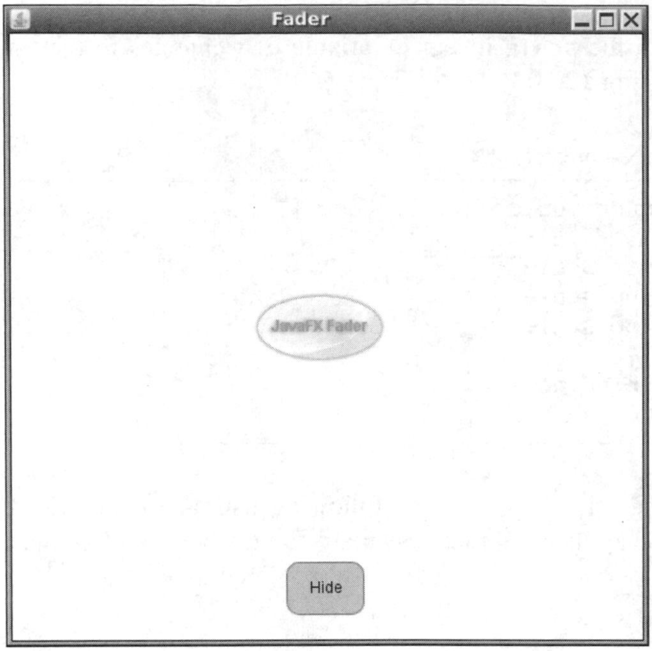

Figure 12.3   Fader – Initial Fade In

Figure 12.4   Fader – Fully Shown

Magnify

The Magnify class allows the node to grow when the mouse hovers over it. When the mouse is moved off the node, it returns to its normal size. This class is similar to the Fader class in that an animation plays when the mouse moves over the node, and plays in reverse when the mouse moves off the node.

This is done by adding an on replace trigger to the hover instance variable inherited from javafx.scene.Node. The following code in Listing 12.12 demonstrates this.

Listing 12.12 Magnify – hover

```
override var hover on replace {
    if(hover) {
        timeline.rate = 1.0; // play forward
        timeline.playFromStart(); // from the beginning
    }else {
        timeline.rate = -1.0; // play backward
        timeline.time = duration; // from the end
        timeline.play();
    }
}
```

The timeline modifies the scale from its start setting to its end setting, 1x and 1.5x, respectively, by default. The default is to use a linear interpolator. Listing 12.13 shows how this is done.

Listing 12.13 Magnify – timeline

```
var scale = 1.0;
var timeline = Timeline {
    keyFrames: [
        KeyFrame {
            time: 0s
            values: [
                scale => startScale,
            ]
        },
        KeyFrame {
            time: duration
            values: [
                scale => endScale tween interpolator,
            ]
        },
    ]
};
```

The CustomNode uses the same structure as used in Fader. The node is included in a Group that has a Scale transform that is bound to the scale instance variable that is used in the timeline. Listing 12.14 depicts how this is accomplished.

Listing 12.14   Magnify – create()

```
public override function create(): Node {
    var group: Group;
    return group = Group {
        transforms: Scale {
            x: bind scale
            y: bind scale
        }
        content: bind node
    };
}
```

To use this class in a stage, just instantiate it with a node and include it in the scene's contents. Listing 12.15 shows a way to do this.

Listing 12.15   Magnify – Usage

```
var scene: Scene;
var magnify: Node;
Stage {
    title: "Magnify"
    width: 500
    height: 500
    scene: scene = Scene {
        content:  magnify = Magnify {
            // Center in scene
            translateX: bind (scene.width -
                magnify.layoutBounds.width)/2.0
            translateY: bind (scene.height -
                magnify.layoutBounds.height)/2.0
            node: node
        }
    }
}
```

When this is run, the node is centered in the scene at normal size. This is shown in Figure 12.5.

When the mouse is moved over the node, it grows to 1.5 times its normal size. This is demonstrated in Figure 12.6.

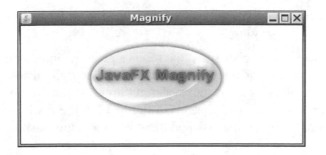

Figure 12.5   Magnifier – Normal Size

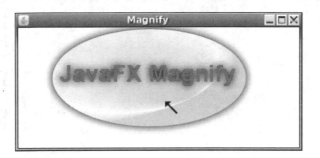

Figure 12.6   Magnifier – Mouse Hover – Magnified

When the mouse is moved off the node, it returns to normal size.

Wizard Framework

When a user needs to process a lot of information, breaking this process into a series of discrete steps allows the whole process to be simplified. In essence, this allows the user to see a clear path to the end goal, while making each subtask smaller and more comprehensible. Typically, wizards are used for assignments that are long or complicated or in cases where the process is novel to the user. Examples of when wizards should be used include first-time customer registration or order processing for the casual user.

A simple wizard pattern is just a series of sequential displays presented to the user, so that the user can complete each task. Users are often presented with buttons to move to the next task or move backward to the previous task. A Cancel button is provided so that the user can cancel the entire operation. After all the tasks are completed, the computer program can do the necessary processes for completing the operation. A more complex wizard could move on to alternative tasks depending on how the user responds to previous tasks. Usually, the user is kept abreast of the progress through the entire process, showing which tasks have been completed and which are pending.

Figure 12.7 shows a typical wizard display. At the top is a progress indicator; the current task is highlighted and the remaining tasks appear to the right in sequential order. In the middle of the display is the user input area. At the bottom are areas for three buttons: Back, Next, and Cancel. In Figure12.7, the Back button is not shown as the wizard is on the first task and there is no previous task.

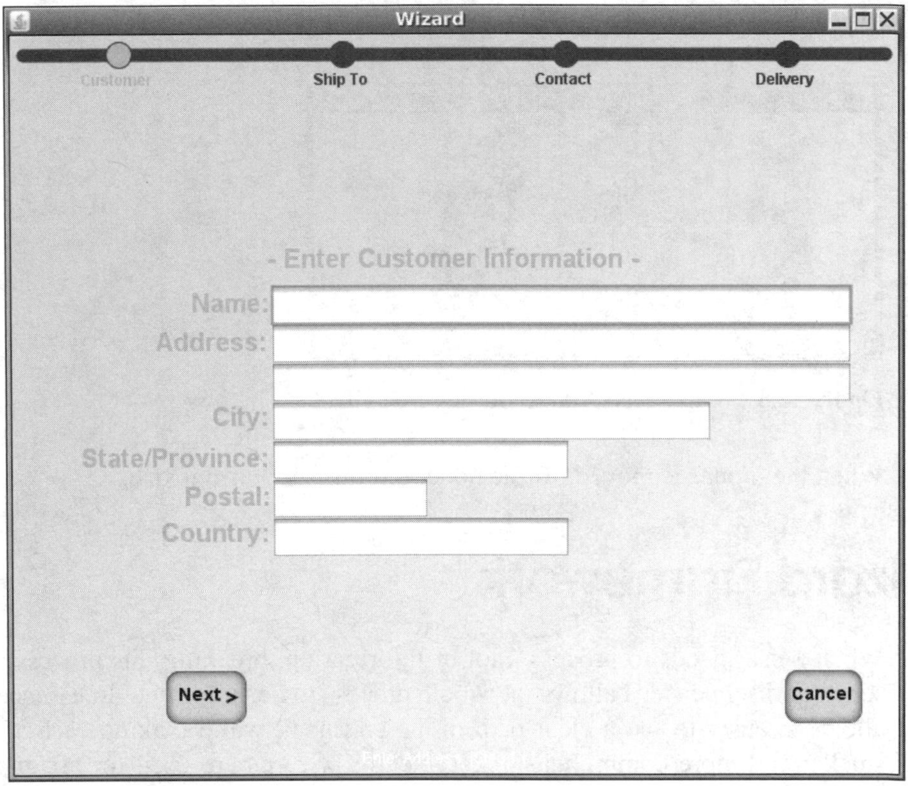

Figure 12.7   Wizard – First Task

To implement the wizard pattern in JavaFX, we have created a `Wizard` class that controls the display of all the tasks defined for the wizard. This class uses the `WizardItem` class that defines the individual displays used by each task. The `Wizard` class contains an instance variable, `currentItem`, that defines the displayed item represented by a `WizardItem` object. The instance variable, `tasks`, is a sequence of the task names that are displayed in the progress indicator at the top of the window. Each `WizardItem` contains an instance variable, `taskId`, that indexes into the wizard `tasks` sequence and maps the `WizardItem` to a task name. When the user finishes all the tasks, the `WizardItem`'s instance variable, `complete`, function is invoked. If the user selects the Cancel button, the `Wizard-Item`'s instance variable, `cancel`, function is called. An example of creating a wizard is shown in Listing 12.16.

Listing 12.16 Wizard Object Literal

```
Wizard {
    currentItem: root
    tasks: ["Customer", "Ship To", "Contact", "Delivery"]

    cancel: function() {
        ...
    }
    complete: function() {
        ...
    }
}
```

Notice that the `currentItem` is set to the starting `WizardItem` named `root` in this example. Each `WizardItem` contains a node that holds a generic `javafx.scene.Node` object that is displayed in the middle of the Wizard window when the `WizardItem` is selected. Each `WizardItem` also contains a `taskId` integer variable that maps the item to a task defined in the wizard. When the `WizardItem` is selected, this causes the appropriate node on the progress indicator to be highlighted. In addition, the `WizardItem` may contain a `message` that will be displayed above the wizard buttons.

The `WizardItem` has an instance variable, `next`, that holds a function for determining the next wizard item when the user selects the Next button. In conjunction with this, the variable `nextItems` holds a sequence of the possible next `WizardItems`. In a simple case, this will only contain one `WizardItem`. In a complex case, this may contain multiple items and represent alternative paths that may be chosen based on user input. By default, `next` is set to a function that returns the first item from the `nextItems` sequence. This covers the simple case of one item sequentially after another. If there are alternative paths or if special processing is required before advancing to the next item, a custom `next` function may be defined to determine the next `WizardItem`.

An example `WizardItem` object literal is shown in Listing 12.17. In this example, the node is a `CustomerAddressControl` that extends `javafx.scene.control.Control`. This item maps to the first task in Wizard, "Customer" by using the taskId of 0. The next function copies data from the current item's node to the next item's node, then returns the first "next" item.

Listing 12.17   WizardItem Object Literal

```
var root:WizardItem = WizardItem {
    node: CustomerAddressControl{}
    message: "Enter Address   [Step 1 of 4]"
    taskId: 0
    wizard: bind wizard
    next: function(): WizardItem {
        var ca = root.node as CustomerAddressControl;
        var ship = root.nextItems[0].node as ShipToControl;
        if(ship.shipToAddress.name == "" ) {
            ship.shipToAddress.name =
                ca.customerAddress.name;
            ship.shipToAddress.addressLine1 =
                ca.customerAddress.addressLine1;
            ...
        }
        root.nextItems[0];
    }
    nextItems: WizardItem {
        wizardParent: bind root
        ....
    }
}
```

The individual wizard items are linked using the nextItems sequence. As WizardItems are added to the nextItems sequence, each of their wizardParent variables are set to the containing WizardItem. By setting the parent, this allows the user to select the Back button to make the wizardParent the current item, in effect moving backward in the task chain.

In the sequential example depicted in Figure 12.7, the WizardItem task tree is laid out so that the user first enters the customer address, followed by the shipping address, then the contact information, and finally the shipping date. The root's nextItems contains the WizardItem for customer address. The customer address's nextItems contains the WizardItem for the ship to address task, and so on. This is depicted logically in the following pseudo code listing.

```
root:"CustomerAddress" ==> nextItems[0]
    "Ship To Address" ==> nextItems[0]
        "Contact Information" ==> nextItems[0]
            "Shipping Date"
```

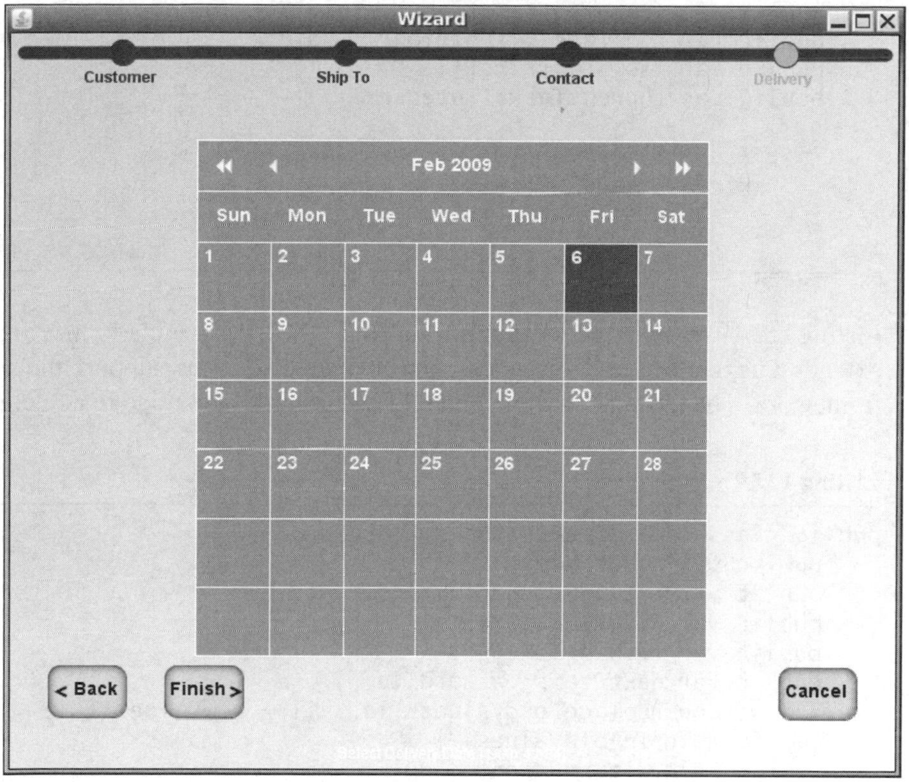

Figure 12.8 Wizard – Last Task

When there are no more `nextItems`, the Next button name changes to Finish. When the user selects the Finish button, the wizard's `complete` variable's function is called. Figure 12.8 shows the display when the last item has been reached.

Listing 12.18 shows the definition for the `Wizard` class. Because this is a Control, the `WizardSkin` class defines the presentation, and can utilize CSS style sheets to change the display attributes like `text-fill` and `font`. JavaFX's use of style sheets and custom controls are discussed in depth in Chapter 5, Create User Interfaces.

Listing 12.18   Wizard Control

```
public class Wizard extends Control {
    public var currentItem: WizardItem on replace {
        currentTask= currentItem.taskId;
    };
```

continues

```
        public var cancel : function(): Void;
        public var complete : function(): Void;
        public var tasks: String[];
        public var currentTask: Integer;

        init {
            skin = WizardSkin {};
        }
}
```

Listing 12.19 shows the definition for the WizardItem class. WizardItem extends CustomNode and provides control functionality to support the wizard framework. The WizardItem itself merely encapsulates the node in a Group.

Listing 12.19   WizardItem

```
public class WizardItem extends CustomNode {
    public var node: Node;
    public var wizardParent: WizardItem;
    public var wizard:Wizard;
    public var taskId:Integer;
    public var nextItems: WizardItem[]
            on replace oldValues [lo..hi] = newValues {
        for(old in oldValues) {
            old.wizardParent = null;
        }
        for(item in newValues) {
            item.wizardParent = this;
        }
    }
    public var next: function(): WizardItem = function() {
        nextItems[0];
    };
    public var message: String;

    public override function create(): Node {
        return Group {
            content: bind node
        };
    }
}
```

Progress Bar

A progress bar is fairly simple to implement. There are two classes, the Progress-Bar that is a control and the ProgressBarSkin that is the ProgressBar's skin class. ProgressBar contains a percent variable that holds the fraction representing the percent complete and an optional message variable that is centered in the display. If this message is not defined, the actual percent will be displayed as a percentage. Listing 12.20 shows the ProgressBar class.

Listing 12.20   ProgressBar

```
public class ProgressBar extends Control {
    public var percent: Number;
    public var message:String;
    package var useMessage:Boolean = bind (message != "");
    protected override var skin = ProgressBarSkin{};
}
```

ProgressBarSkin defines a rectangle for the entire background area, and another rectangle that grows in width based on the percent complete. This second rectangle graphically depicts the percent complete. Each of these two rectangles has its own fill color.

What is interesting about this implementation is that the message is displayed in a different color when the progress bar is over it. If you look carefully at Figure 12.9, you will notice the letters P, r, o, g are painted in a different color from the remaining characters that fall outside of the progress bar.

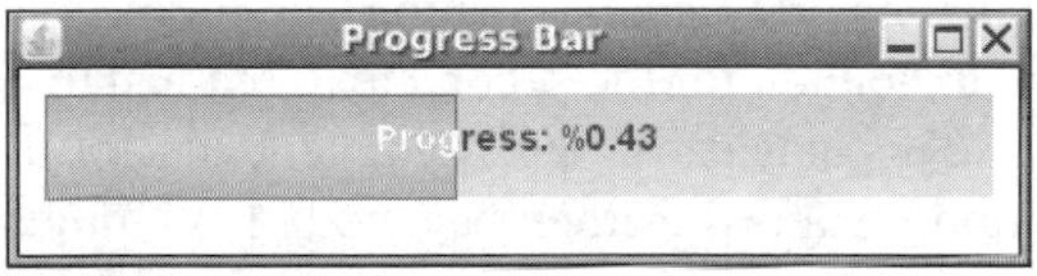

Figure 12.9   Progress Bar

To accomplish this, the ProgressBarSkin class uses two text shapes for the same string and font located in identical positions centered in the ProgressBar space on top of each other. The first Text object uses one color, whereas the second Text class uses another color. By using the progress rectangle as a clipping region, we can control when and what part of this second text is displayed. Listing 12.21 shows how this is done.

Listing 12.21   ProgressBarSkin – Text Elements

```
text = Text {
    translateX: bind (progressBar.width -
        text.layoutBounds.width)/2.0 - text.layoutBounds.minX
    translateY: bind (progressBar.height -
        text.layoutBounds.height)/2.0- text.layoutBounds.minY
    content: bind msg
    font: bind font
    textOrigin: TextOrigin.TOP
    fill: bind textFill
},
Text {
    x: bind (progressBar.width -
        text.layoutBounds.width)/2.0 - text.layoutBounds.minX
    y: bind (progressBar.height -
        text.layoutBounds.height)/2.0- text.layoutBounds.minY
    content: bind msg
    font: bind font
    textOrigin: TextOrigin.TOP
    fill: bind textHighlightFill
    clip: bind progressRect
},
```

There are a couple of things to note here. First, the second Text object needs to be located using its x and y variables rather than using its translateX and translateY variables. This is because the clipping region is based on the geometry of the progressRect before the transformations take effect. If we had used translateX and translateY, the clipping action would actually be shifted to the left and the text would show in the alternate color too soon.

The other issue is that in calculating the center position for the second text object, we could not use the layoutBounds for the second text, but had to use the layout bounds from the first text. This is because the layoutBounds for the second text change as the clip region changes. Remember, both Text objects are identical except for color, so the first Text's dimensions stay constant and still represent the dimensions of the second Text object.

The last important point to this is the second text must appear on top of the first text. This is dictated by the order that the Texts are added to the overall Group's content sequence. Nodes added at the end of the content sequence will paint on top of nodes added earlier into the Group's content sequence. Normally, the second text would obscure the first text, but because we are using a clipping region on the second Text object, the first node is not obscured until the progress rectangle crosses over it.

Slider

A slider is a visual component that has a knob that can be moved to change a value between a minimum and a maximum. The user drags the knob to a new value or just clicks on any point on the slider bar to immediately move the knob to this position and set the value accordingly.

We implement this slider as a control with a corresponding skin. The main Slider class contains variables to hold the value, along with minimum and maximum values. There are also two Boolean variables, showLabels and showTicks, to control whether to show the minimum, current value, and maximum labels, and whether to show the tick lines. Lastly, there is a variable, snapTo, that determines the rounding precision for the value. When the value is dragged or otherwise set clicking on the slider bar, the value will be rounded to this precision. The Slider class is shown in Listing 12.22.

Listing 12.22   Slider – Control

```
public class Slider extends Control {
    public var value: Number;
    public var minimum: Number = 0;
    public var maximum: Number = 100;
    public var showTicks: Boolean;
    public var showLabels: Boolean;
    public var snapTo: Number = 0.0;

    init {
        skin = SliderSkin{};
    }
}
```

The SliderSkin class contains a rounded rectangle for the slider bar, a rectangle for the knob, some lines for the tick marks, and some Text objects for the labels. What is most interesting is how the drag operation works.

To make the drag work on the knob rectangle, you need to add functions for mouse pressed, released, and dragged events. First, when the mouse is pressed, we need to save the current horizontal location of the knob into the saveX variable as a starting reference point for the drag. Another variable, controlX, defines the current horizontal location of the knob, this is changed based on the value instance variable as a percentage of the value to the total value range.

```
var controlX: Number =
    bind (slider.value-slider.minimum)/
        range * slider.width;
...
...
    onMousePressed: function(e: MouseEvent) : Void {
        saveX = controlX;
    }
```

As the mouse is dragged and finally released, we calculate the percentage of the mouse horizontal position to the total width of the Slider and use that percentage to adjust the value. The mouse event dragX variable actually represents a delta since the drag started, so we must add this to the saved location for the knob to get a new location for the knob. We do not change the knob location directly because the knob's location, held in the controlX variable, is bound to the slider's value. Instead, we merely set the value based on the percentage of the total slider width. This, in turn, results in the knob moving to the new location. Notice, we have to limit the percentage derived from the mouse position to between 0.0 and 1.0, inclusive. This is because the mouse may be dragged beyond the boundaries of the Slider.

```
onMouseReleased: function(e: MouseEvent) : Void {
    if(inDrag) {
        var newX = saveX + e.dragX;
        var per = newX / slider.width;
        per = if(per < 0) 0.0 else
                if (per > 1.0) 1.0 else per;
        slider.value = calcValue(per);
        inDrag = false;
    }
}
onMouseDragged: function(e: MouseEvent) : Void {
    inDrag = true;
    var newX = saveX + e.dragX;
    var per = newX / slider.width;
    per = if(per < 0) 0.0 else
                if (per > 1.0) 1.0 else per;
    slider.value = calcValue(per);
}
```

The private function, calcValue(), takes the width percentage and applies it to the value range to determine the new slider value. This function also rounds the actual value based on the Slider's snapTo variable. For example, if snapTo is 1.0, the value will be rounded to the nearest whole number. If snapTo is 0.5, the resulting value is rounded to the nearest half. For instance, a value of 50.37 becomes 50.5, whereas 50.21 becomes 50.0. Listing 12.23 shows how this is done.

Listing 12.23   SliderSkin – calcValue()

```
function calcValue(per:Number) : Number {
    var val = per * range + slider.minimum;
    if(slider.snapTo != 0.0) {
        val += slider.snapTo/2.0;
        var rem =
            Math.IEEEremainder(val, slider.snapTo);
        val = val-rem;
    }
    val;
}
```

An example of using a slider is in Listing 12.24. The value is bound to a local variable called lvalue. This must be bound with inverse as a change to lvalue will be reflected on the slider, and if the user changes the slider value, this will in turn be reflected in lvalue. Failure to use the with inverse bind will result in an exception.

Listing 12.24   Slider Usage

```
var scene:Scene;
var lvalue:Number = 50 on replace {
    println(value);
};
Stage {
    title: "Slider"
    width: 300
    height: 80
    scene: scene = Scene {
        content: Slider {
            translateY: 10
            translateX: 10
            height: 50
            snapTo: 0.5
            value: bind lvalue with inverse
            width: bind scene.width-20
        }
    }
}
```

Figure 12.10 shows what the Slider looks like. Also, remember that because Slider is a control, you can use cascading style sheets to control its appearance. This includes the colors, knob size, and fonts. For more information on using cascading style sheets, see Chapter 5.

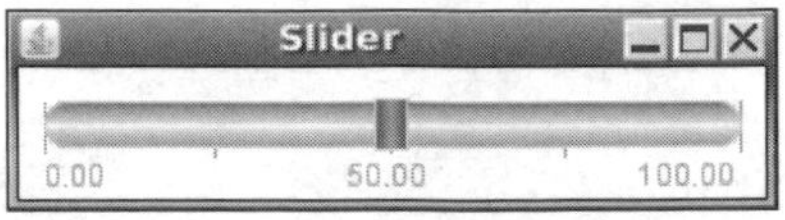

Figure 12.10   Slider

Matrix

In JavaFX, sequences are one dimensional and you cannot create a sequence of a sequence. There is no notion of a two-dimensional array, like `Object[][]`. Even if you attempt to create a matrix by assigning another sequence to one item, the original sequence actually inserts the assigned sequence into itself. To get around this, we have created a matrix class that uses a JavaFX sequence as a backing store, but allows manipulation of the individual items using a row, column approach.

The `Matrix` class contains a variable, `sequence`, that holds the backing sequence. In addition, the `columns` variable holds the number of columns, whereas `rows` holds the number or rows in the matrix. Notice that `rows` is read only and is calculated based on the number of `columns` and the size of the `sequence`. Matrix is defined as illustrated in Listing 12.25.

Listing 12.25   Matrix

```
public class Matrix {
    /** number of columns in Matrix */
    public var columns: Integer = 1;

    /** backing sequence for Matrix */
    public var sequence: Object[];

    /** number of rows in Matrix */
    public-read var rows: Integer = bind
        if(sizeof sequence mod columns > 0)
            sizeof sequence / columns + 1
        else
            sizeof sequence / columns;
```

There are also `get` and `set` functions that use the row, column addressing scheme to manipulate cell contents. These use the function `getIndex()` to calculate the offset into the backing sequence by multiplying the row by the number of columns and adding the column parameter to this.

```
/** set the value of a cell in the Matrix */
public function set(row:Integer, col:Integer,
                            value: Object ):Void{
    sequence[getIndex(row,col)] = value;
}


/** get the value of a cell from the Matrix */
public function get(row:Integer, col:Integer) : Object {
    sequence[getIndex(row,col)];
}
```

There are three functions that retrieve sets of values out of the Matrix. The function getRow() returns a sequence of all the values in a row, whereas getColumn() returns all the values in a given column. The function subMatrix() retrieves a rectangular subset from the matrix based on starting row and column and ending row and column. It returns a new Matrix. These functions are implemented in Listing 12.26.

Listing 12.26   Matrix – getRow(), getColumn(), subMatrix()

```
/** get a row from the matrix */
public function getRow(row:Integer):Object[] {
    var ndx = getIndex(row, 0);
    sequence[ndx..<ndx+columns];
}


/** get a column from the matrix */
public function getColumn(col:Integer): Object[] {
    var ndx = getIndex(0, col);
    for(i in [ndx..<sizeof sequence step columns]) {
        sequence[i];
    }
}


/** get a sub matrix from this matrix */
public function subMatrix(startRow: Integer,
        startColumn: Integer,
        endRow:Integer,
        endColumn:Integer): Matrix {
    var ncols = endColumn - startColumn + 1;
    var ndx = getIndex(startRow, startColumn);
    var sub = for(row in [startRow..endRow]) {
        var ndx1 = ndx;
        ndx += columns;
        sequence[ndx1..<ndx1+ncols];
    };
```

continues

```
Matrix {
    columns: ncols
    sequence: sub
};
}
```

An example of using a `Matrix` is shown in the following listing. This uses a 9×9 matrix similar to the Sudoku pattern. The `getRow(3)` and `getColumn(5)` functions return a sequence of Integers, whereas the `subMatrix(3,3, 5,5)` function returns a new 3×3 matrix.

```
var sudoku = Matrix {
    columns: 9
    sequence: [
        1,2,3,1,2,3,1,2,3,
        4,5,6,4,5,6,4,5,6,
        7,8,9,7,8,9,7,8,9,
        1,2,3,1,2,3,1,2,3,
        4,5,6,4,5,6,4,5,6,
        7,8,9,7,8,9,7,8,9,
        1,2,3,1,2,3,1,2,3,
        4,5,6,4,5,6,4,5,6,
        7,8,9,7,8,9,7,8,9,
    ]
}

var row = sudoku.getRow(3);
var col = sudoku.getColumn(5);
var box = sudoku.subMatrix(3,3, 5,5);
```

Chapter Summary

These are just a few code recipes that may help you develop your applications in JavaFX. There are probably many more, but we wanted to cover a few classes that contained interesting aspects. We hope these recipes help you to better understand some of the finer points that we have experienced while preparing this book.

We have covered all of the basic concepts of JavaFX including the JavaFX language, features, and framework classes. Now it is time to put all this together in an application. We have elected to do a Sudoku game. This application demonstrates most of the concepts we have discussed in this book and we feel it will help you to see how it all comes together.

13

Sudoku Application

"The attempt to combine wisdom and power has only rarely been successful and then only for a short while."

—Albert Einstein

Until now, most of the concepts discussed throughout the course of this book were either described abstractly or, for the sake of simplicity, demonstrated with small blocks of code or trivial programs. For this final chapter, we'll apply what we've learned to create something with a bit more substance. Our sample application utilizes and combines many more of the techniques and mechanisms elaborated upon, more closely resembling how JavaFX might be employed in the real world.

The application we've chosen to implement is the game of Sudoku. As Sudoku has gained considerable worldwide popularity recently, it is likely to have been encountered by many reading this book. To the uninitiated, you'll find that Sudoku is easy to learn, and furthermore easy to become addicted to playing. From a JavaFX perspective, Sudoku represents a reasonable example of how the logic required for the rules of the game and the presentation of that game can be nicely delineated.

For those unfamiliar with the game, a standard Sudoku board has nine rows and nine columns of spaces. The board is also grouped into nine boxes or regions. To solve a Sudoku puzzle, the numbers 1 through 9 must appear in each row, column, and box—but only once—and not in any particular order. New Sudoku puzzles start out with a certain number of spaces already filled in. In general, the fewer the number of pre-defined spaces, the more difficult the puzzle. The job of the person playing the game is to use logic to fill in the rest of the spaces.

How to Access the JavaFX Sudoku Application

The Sudoku application is available online and can be accessed by pointing your browser to the following URL:

```
http://jfxbook.com/Sudoku/
```

Upon reaching this page, you have the option of running Java FX Sudoku in one of two ways:

- **As a standalone application**. This option utilizes Java Web Start technology to start the JavaFX Sudoku application as a separate process, independent from the browser.
- **As an applet**. This option allows you to run JavaFX Sudoku inside the browser as a traditional applet. Depending upon your system configuration (operating system, Java Runtime Environment, browser, etc.), you may be able to take advantage of the *draggable applet* feature, in effect giving you the ability to undock the applet from the browser.

The Interface

Figure 13.1 depicts and describes the onscreen interface of the Sudoku program. Logically, the interface can be divided into three areas:

- The top section of the interface serves as a window frame. If you drag your mouse within this area, you'll be able to reposition the Sudoku application on the screen. If you are running Sudoku as an applet within a browser, dragging your mouse in this area will enable you to undock the applet from the browser if your overall environment supports the draggable applet feature.
- The middle section, which encompasses a majority of the interface, contains the Sudoku board. By hovering your mouse over a space on the board, you can modify its contents by either clicking the mouse to enter in a new number or by typing a number from 1 to 9. If you want to clear a space, you can type either 0 or <space>. When a new puzzle is generated, a certain number of spaces will be filled in for you to aid in solving the puzzle. These spaces cannot be modified.

- The bottom section of the interface contains menu buttons needed to interact with the application. They include buttons to create a new game, instruct the user as to how to play, set the level of difficulty of the puzzle, reset the game to its original state, solve the puzzle, and quit the game.

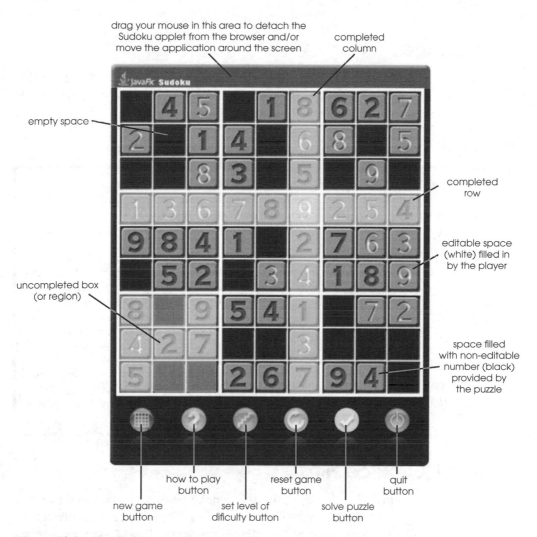

Figure 13.1 The Sudoku Application Interface

Source for the Sudoku Application

The source code for JavaFX Sudoku can also be found at http://jfxbook.com/ Sudoku/. Developed with the NetBeans Integrated Development Environment, the source comes bundled with project metadata to facilitate seamless integration into NetBeans.

Packages

Table 13.1 lists and briefly describes the packages that make up the JavaFX Sudoku application. It incorporates both JavaFX and Java source, plus images that are used as part of the overall presentation.

Table 13.1   Packages in the Sudoku Application

Package	Description
sudoku.*	All JavaFX source files reside under this package. For a description of each of the files contained within, consult Table 13.2.
sudoku.images.*	As part of the overall presentation, the Sudoku application is responsible for displaying a large number of images at any point in time during execution. All images are located in this directory and include things like icons, backgrounds, numbers, and spaces.
net.sourceforge.playsudoku.*	This package is public domain software from source-forge.net and is written in Java. It is used to generate and solve new Sudoku puzzles. It demonstrates software reuse and the easy integration of Java components into a JavaFX application.

JavaFX Source Files

The JavaFX source files that comprise the sudoku package (referenced in Table 13.1) are, in general, divided into two types of files. Those directly involved with the application interface have public classes that extend the CustomNode class and are suffixed with Node (e.g., Board**Node**.fx, IconButton**Node**.fx). Source files without the Node suffix do not extend the CustomNode class and are involved more with the logic behind running the Sudoku application. Table 13.2 lists and describes the sudoku package files.

Table 13.2 JavaFX Source Files in the sudoku Package

JavaFX Source File	Description
Board.fx	This class contains a logical representation of a Sudoku board, including the code necessary to play the game.
BoardNode.fx	This class is primarily responsible for the layout of the Sudoku interface.
Space.fx	A Sudoku Board is comprised of 81 Spaces. Among other instance variables, each Space instance has a number instance variable, whose value is used to interpret the state of the Space.
SpaceNode.fx	For each Space instance, there is a related SpaceNode instance responsible for receiving user input for a space and displaying the contents of that space on the board.
HowToPlayNode.fx	Component representing a pop-up window that appears when the How to Play icon button is pressed.
SliderNode.fx	Slider component that appears when the user clicks on the Skill Level icon button. By repositioning the slider, the user can either increase or decrease the difficulty of the next puzzle to be generated.
ChooseNumberNode.fx	Component that appears over an editable space on the board when the mouse is clicked, giving the user a choice of which number to insert into that space.
IconButtonNode.fx	Component representing the icons appearing near the bottom of the Sudoku interface. These icons are animated such that when a mouse hovers over them they increase in size.
CloseButtonNode.fx	Common component used in both SliderNode and HowToPlayNode classes.
Grouping.fx	This class is created primarily due to the fact that JavaFX currently does not support multi-dimensional sequences. A Board, in addition to containing a sequence of 81 (9×9) Spaces, also includes nine Groupings representing the nine rows, columns, and regions that make up a board.
Main.fx	Responsible for starting up the Sudoku application. This file also contains code to support the dragable applet feature.

The Overall Design

Briefly mentioned earlier, the application has been architected such that the overall game logic and the user interface have been cleanly separated in a relatively straightforward fashion. As a rule of thumb, source files suffixed with Node are presentation or interface files, whereas those without the Node moniker are dedicated to providing the logic necessary to play the Sudoku game.

The Logic

The game logic for the Sudoku application is primarily supplied by two JavaFX classes: Board and Space. The Board class represents a Sudoku board. It has code to interpret the rules of the game and is ultimately responsible for starting a new game, determining if an individual move is valid, maintaining the state of the game, and providing a solution to the puzzle.

The Board class includes a sequence of 81 Spaces representing the 9×9 grid of spaces that make up a standard Sudoku puzzle. At initialization, the Board class identifies which row, column, and region (or box) each of the 81 Spaces belong to and groups them accordingly. Each Space has instance variables that identify its row/column/region, and most importantly, a number variable holding the value that is currently assigned to this space. The value of number is used to interpret the current state of the Space. Externally, Sudoku spaces can only have a numeric value ranging from 1–9, or be blank. Internally, the number value for a Space instance has a larger range. Table 13.3 explains the possible values that can be assigned to a Space's number instance variable, and how they affect what is ultimately displayed to the user.

Table 13.3   Range of Internal Values a number Instance Variable Can Be Assigned and How They Are Ultimately Displayed Externally

'number' value	Description	Appearance
0	Indicates that the space is editable and is currently blank.	The space will be blank.
1–9	Indicates that the space is editable, and that during play the user has entered a valid number into the space represented by the value.	The space will be filled in with a white number represented by the value.

Table 13.3 Range of Internal Values a number Instance Variable Can Be Assigned and How They Are Ultimately Displayed Externally (*Continued*)

'number' value	Description	Appearance
11–19	Indicates that the space contains a number that cannot be modified because it was provided by the puzzle generator as a hint.	The space will be filled in with a black emboldened number that is computed by performing a 'mod 10' on the value.
21–29	Indicates that the space is editable, and that during play the user has entered a number into the space. In addition, the space's number value currently has the same value as (conflicts with) one or more spaces in its row/column/box.	The space will be filled in with a red number that is computed by performing a 'mod 10' on the value.
31–39	Indicates that the space contains a number that cannot be modified because it was provided by the puzzle generator as a hint. Furthermore, the space's number value currently has the same value as (conflicts with) one or more spaces in its row/column/box, because the user has entered at least one conflicting number elsewhere.	The space will be filled in with a red emboldened number that is computed by performing a 'mod10' on the value.
<0, 10, 20, 30, >39	Undefined. A space should never be assigned any of these values.	n/a

The Interface

The Board and Space classes have interface counterparts, named BoardNode and SpaceNode respectively, which handle the task of presenting the Sudoku game to the user. The BoardNode class is responsible for the overall layout of the application; for each Space, there is a corresponding SpaceNode, which manages the input and display of that space on the puzzle. When the BoardNode instance is initialized, it includes an instance variable called board, which is a reference to the Board instance. Likewise, each SpaceNode instance contains an instance variable called space, which points to its Space counterpart. Figure 13.2 shows the relationship between Board/Space and BoardNode/SpaceNode.

With these classes in place, you might be asking the question, how is the internal state of the Spaces picked up by the corresponding SpaceNodes and displayed on the interface? The short answer is through *binding*. Let's run through how this takes place.

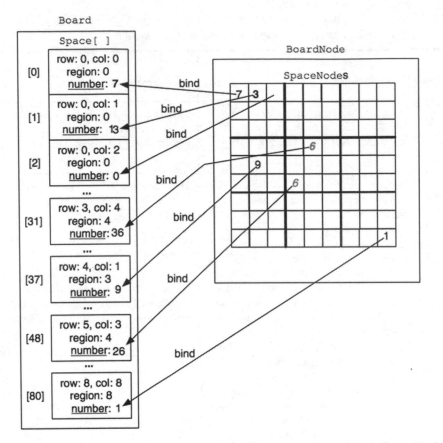

Figure 13.2   Relationship Between Board/Spaces and BoardNode/SpaceNodes

At startup, a series of URLs (filenames) are statically loaded into a String sequence called imageFiles. The initialization of imageFiles looks like this:

```
var imageFiles = [
// 0-9 represents editable spaces, 0 being a blank space
    "{__DIR__}images/blank.png",
    "{__DIR__}images/1-white.png",
    "{__DIR__}images/2-white.png",

    ...
    "{__DIR__}images/9-white.png",
// 10: Should never get here
    "{__DIR__}images/blank.png",
// 11-19 represents non-editable (bold) spaces
    "{__DIR__}images/1-bold.png",
    "{__DIR__}images/2-bold.png",

    ...
    "{__DIR__}images/9-bold.png",
```

```
// 20: Should never get here
    "{__DIR__}images/blank.png",
// 21-29 represents editable spaces in conflict
    "{__DIR__}images/1-red.png",
    "{__DIR__}images/2-red.png",
    ...
    "{__DIR__}images/9-red.png",
// 30: Should never get here
    "{__DIR__}images/blank.png",
// 31-39 represents non-editable spaces in conflict
    "{__DIR__}images/1-red-bold.png",
    "{__DIR__}images/2-red-bold.png",
    ...
    "{__DIR__}images/9-red-bold.png"
];
```

As you may have surmised, the image files coincide with the layout of a Space's number instance variable as described in Table 13.3. For example, imageFiles[0] contains the URL "{__DIR__}images/blank.png"—a blank space—whereas imageFiles[19] points to "{__DIR__}images/9-bold.png"—an image of the number 9 in bold, representing a non-editable space. The imageFiles sequence, however, only contains strings that refer to URLs. What we actually need here is a sequence of type Image to serve as an Image cache. This is achieved by using imageFiles with the following code:

```
// Cached copies of Number Images
var images = for(url in imageFiles) {
    Image {
        url: url
        backgroundLoading: true
    }
}
```

Next, each SpaceNode defines two instance variables, one called spaceImage, which holds the current image displayed for each instance, and number, which contains the value of the corresponding Space's number instance variable. Using a combination of binding and triggers, we can achieve the effect of updating a SpaceNode's current image whenever its corresponding Space has a change in its number variable. This is accomplished with the following code:

```
protected var spaceImage:Image;

public var number:Integer = bind space.number on replace {
    spaceImage = images[number];
};
```

The definition of the preceding `number` variable performs two things:

1. It binds `number` to `space.number`. Whenever the value of `space.number` changes, `number` will automatically change accordingly.

2. The `number` variable uses a trigger to force an update to the value of `space-Image` whenever `number` changes too. In this case, `spaceImage` points to a sequence (a cache) of `Images` indexed by the value of `number`.

Finally, each `SpaceNode` defines an instance of `ImageView`, which is ultimately how the image is displayed. It looks something like this:

```
ImageView {
    ...
    image: bind spaceImage
    ...
}
```

Now, the image for a `SpaceNode` will dynamically change whenever `space.number` changes. Here's the chain of events:

- The user enters a number into an editable space.

- The `space.number` instance variable is assigned a new value.

- The corresponding `SpaceNode` has a `number` instance variable that is bound to `space.number`. Whenever `space.number` changes, so does this `number` variable.

- There is a trigger associated with the `number` instance variable such that whenever it is modified, it causes the `spaceImage` variable to be recalculated. In this case, `spaceImage` uses `number` as an index into a sequence of cached `Images`.

- Each `SpaceNode` instantiates `ImageView`. Its `image` instance variable is bound to `spaceImage`. Whenever `spaceImage` changes, the `image` will change too.

This all comes about because of the capabilities of binding and triggers.

Interfacing with Java Components

So far, we've covered the logic and presentation of our Sudoku application, and how these two worlds relate to one another. The components comprising this portion of our application were written in JavaFX and represent the main effort in creating JavaFX Sudoku. There is a third element, however, which needs to be implemented to complete the Sudoku game. It revolves around the ability to randomly create new Sudoku puzzles and to provide solutions for them.

In conjunction with the popularity of Sudoku, many have put forth algorithms for creating and solving Sudoku puzzles. With this in mind, we had the option of either reinventing the wheel or leveraging the work that's been done already in puzzle generation. In all honesty, there's no real advantage to writing a Sudoku puzzle generator in JavaFX. It could have just as easily and effectively been written in any of the myriad of available high-level programming languages. So why not find what's out there, and see how easily it could be integrated into our application? Code reuse and, in particular, integration with Java, arguably the largest development community on the planet, are key design characteristics of JavaFX.

Sourceforge.net is a well-known centralized repository for open source software projects. At that location, we found a Sudoku application located under the following URL:

```
http://sourceforge.net/projects/playsudoku/
```

This project is a complete program written in Java, including a Swing-based user interface. Our interest was solely in its capability to create new Sudoku puzzles, so we took a subset of the source code, specifically the classes found under the net.sourceforge.playsudoku package, and integrated them into our application.

The integration effort was straightforward and involved two primary tasks:

1. Figuring out what methods need to be called to generate a new Sudoku puzzle.
2. Determining if the data structures used by the Java application can be directly used with JavaFX.

We'll handle the second task first and use our solution there as part of the overall process needed to generate a new puzzle.

Delving into the net.sourceforge.playsudoku package, you'll find that the contents of the puzzle are maintained in a multi-dimensional array called grid. The Java declaration for this array is found in the SudokuGrid.java file and looks like this:

```
private int[][] grid;
```

Unfortunately, JavaFX currently has no support for multi-dimensional arrays. So, the first order of business is to convert grid into something JavaFX understands. Listing 13.1 shows an additional Java method, called returnGridSequence(), that was added to the SudokuGrid.java source file. The purpose of this method is to convert the two-dimensional grid array into a one-dimensional array of type int. This then maps directly to a JavaFX Integer[] sequence.

Listing 13.1   Java Method to Convert a Two-Dimensional Array into a One-Dimensional JavaFX Sequence

```
/*
 * Method to move generated Sudoku game to JavaFX.
 * Internally, the Sudoku grid generated by this
 * program is represented as a 2-dimensional array
 * in Java.  JavaFX 1.1 has no notion of
 * multi-dimensional sequences (arrays), so flatten
 * the grid out to a one-dimensional array of size
 * 81 of type int.  This should map to a JavaFX
 * sequence of type Integer.
 */
public int[] returnGridSequence() {
    int[] gridSequence = new int[81];
    int index = 0;
    for(int i = 0; i < 9; i++) {
        for(int j = 0; j < 9; j++) {
            gridSequence[index++] = grid[i][j];
        }
    }
    return gridSequence;
}
```

Using this method, we can now tackle the first task, constructing the necessary JavaFX code to generate a new JavaFX puzzle using the net.sourceforge .playsudoku package. Listing 13.2 shows the complete newPuzzle() function, which is contained within the Board.fx source file. Let's first take a look at a few of the parts of this function to see what's going on. The first lines of newPuzzle() call the necessary Java methods inside net.sourceforge.playsudoku to generate a new puzzle:

```
/*
 * Call SudokuGenerator Java code to generate new puzzle.
 */
var sudokuGenerator : SudokuGenerator =
    new SudokuGenerator();
sudokuGenerator.generatePuzzle(numHints,
    GV.NumDistributuon.random );
var sudokuGrid : SudokuGrid = sudokuGenerator.getGrid();
```

Next comes the call to the `returnGridSequence()` function, which converts the grid into a JavaFX Integer sequence:

```
/*
 * convert results to a format suitable for JavaFX
 */
var puzzle : Integer[] = sudokuGrid.returnGridSequence();
```

The rest of the function contains code necessary to translate the contents of each cell. Inside `grid`, the way in which state is stored is fairly similar to the way it's done with JavaFX Sudoku. Instead of using number values that are multiples of 10, the author(s) used bitmasks to store multiple values in each cell. Listing 13.2 shows the `newPuzzle()` function.

Listing 13.2   The newPuzzle() Function

```
/*
 * Use the SudokuGenerator code found at
 * sourceforge.net to create a new Puzzle.  Written
 * in Java, the SudokuGenerator requires a small
 * amount of translation code to move the data
 * structure over to a suitable JavaFX form.
 * The sudokuGrid.returnGridSequence() method performs
 * that task.
 *
 * Arguments:
 *    numHints:  Determines the Number of initial spaces
 *               (hints) that will be displayed at
 *               startup.  The larger this number is,
 *               the easier the puzzle is to solve.
 */
public function newPuzzle(numHints : Integer) : Void {
    /*
     * Call SudokuGenerator Java code to generate
     * a new puzzle.
     */
    var sudokuGenerator : SudokuGenerator =
        new SudokuGenerator();
    sudokuGenerator.generatePuzzle(numHints,
        GV.NumDistributuon.random );
    var sudokuGrid : SudokuGrid =
        sudokuGenerator.getGrid();
    /*
     * convert results to a format suitable for JavaFX
     */
    var puzzle : Integer[] =
        sudokuGrid.returnGridSequence();
```

continues

```
    if (sizeof puzzle != sizeof spaces) {
        throw new Exception(
            "SudokuGenerator puzzle incompatible");
    }
    /*
     * Populate our spaces with the Integer sequence
     * returned by the
     * sudokuGrid.returnGridSequence() glue.
     */
    clearPuzzle();
    for (i in [0..<sizeof puzzle]) {
        if ((spaces[i].row !=
            sudokuGrid.getX(puzzle[i])) or
            (spaces[i].column !=
            sudokuGrid.getY(puzzle[i]))) {
            throw new Exception(
            "Bad data returned by SudokuGenerator");
        }
        spaces[i].setSolvedNumber(
            sudokuGrid.getGridVal(puzzle[i]));
        if (sudokuGrid.isDefault(puzzle[i])) {
            spaces[i].setNumberUnEditable(
                sudokuGrid.getGridVal(puzzle[i]));
        }
        else {
            spaces[i].setNumberEditable(0);
        }
    }
}
```

Chapter Summary

We've spent some time dissecting our sample Sudoku application including describing the user interface, the organization of the source, the overall architecture, and the interaction with components written elsewhere in Java. Feel free to take a look at the source and utilize it in any fashion you wish.

Index

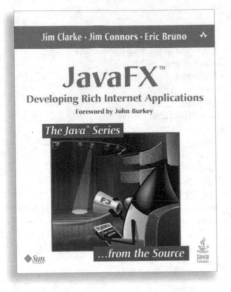

FREE Online Edition

Your purchase of *JavaFX™: Developing Rich Internet Applications* includes access to a free online edition for 45 days through the Safari Books Online subscription service. Nearly every Addison-Wesley Professional book is available online through Safari Books Online, along with more than 5,000 other technical books and videos from publishers such as Cisco Press, Exam Cram, IBM Press, O'Reilly, Prentice Hall, Que, and Sams.

SAFARI BOOKS ONLINE allows you to search for a specific answer, cut and paste code, download chapters, and stay current with emerging technologies.

Activate your FREE Online Edition at
www.informit.com/safarifree

> **STEP 1:** Enter the coupon code: VXDKWWA.

> **STEP 2:** New Safari users, complete the brief registration form.
> Safari subscribers, just log in.

If you have difficulty registering on Safari or accessing the online edition, please e-mail customer-service@safaribooksonline.com